PROPERTY LAW

AUSTRALIA
LBC Information Services
Sydney

CANADA AND THE USA
Carswell
Toronto

NEW ZEALAND
Brooker's
Auckland

SINGAPORE AND MALAYSIA
Thomson Information (S.E. Asia)
Singapore

GREENS CONCISE SCOTS LAW

PROPERTY LAW

Second Edition

By

Peter Robson
Professor of Social Welfare Law
at Strathclyde University

and

Andrew McCowan
Former Senior Lecturer in Law
at Paisley University

EDINBURGH
W. GREEN/Sweet & Maxwell
1998

First published 1991
Reprinted 1996
Second edition 1998

Published in 1998 by W. Green & Son Limited
21 Alva Street
Edinburgh EH2 4PS

Typeset by Hewer Text Ltd
Edinburgh

Printed in Great Britain by Redwood Books Ltd
Kennet Way, Trowbridge, Wiltshire

No natural forests were destroyed to make this product;
only farmed timber was used and replanted

A CIP catalogue record of this book is available from the British Library

ISBN 0 414 01229 1

© 1998
Peter Robson and Andrew McCowan

TACAS VIUR

PREFACE TO SECOND EDITION

Since the first edition of this work much has happened. Kenny Miller's duties as Vice-Dean of the Strathclyde Business School have forced him to step aside and Andrew McCowan has replaced him in the preparation of this edition. We are grateful to Kenny for assigning his copyright. We would like to thank all the people who have helped us to produce this edition and in particular special mention should be made of Linda Baines, Colin Jones, Wim Jansen, and Colin Ramsdale. We hope that we have managed to improve the text and are grateful to those who have given us the benefit of their comments on the first edition. We would also hope that Monkwearmouth will occupy a special place in our hearts in the future.

Peter Robson
Andrew McCowan
October 1998

PREFACE TO FIRST EDITION

This book is intended as an introduction to the Scots law of property. It seeks to outline the basic principles, to explain them and where possible to provide a context for their application. The aim is to produce a clear and concise statement of the law as it applies to property rights generally. Thus the book not only covers those legal concepts which have been regarded traditionally as being part of property law but also deals with the recent statutory developments which both extend and restrict property rights. It examines the common law rules which define property, which regulate ownership rights in moveable property and which create the basic framework of land law in Scotland and also considers the common law and statutory rules pertaining to leases, the statutory regulation of housing and the rights of spouses and cohabitees in matrimonial homes.

The work is aimed principally at law students and is intended to meet the need for a basic textbook which covers the broad principles of Scottish property law. However, the authors have become aware over the years that other groups of students also require access to basic information on the wide scope of Scots property law. Thus the book is also aimed at students attending housing courses or studying land economy at the Scottish universities, polytechnics and colleges. It should also be of value to anyone in Scotland who is seeking membership of the Institute of Housing.

Peter Nicholson at Greens on his many visits to Strathclyde, encouraged us to write this book. Thanks Peter. We are also most grateful to Kenneth Norrie who read the complete book in manuscript and who made numerous helpful suggestions for improvement, most of which have been adopted in the final text. Special thanks are due to Jane Hutton, Denise Greenless, Cathy Smith, Catherine Whitters, Ruth Anderson, Liz McCallum, Irene Williamson, Elaine Smith, Jean Clark and Helen Pratt.

We would also like to put on record our gratitude to our colleagues at this Law School whose patience with Rolf Harris and the Everly Brothers shows no sign of wearying. Thanks must also go to Rosemary Campbell, the Editorial Manager at Greens, who did an excellent job making sure that our manuscript saw light of day as a book. We are grateful to Ian Bryce who is responsible for the Tables of Cases and Statutes and the Index. We would like to thank our wives, Margaret and Andrina whose interest in our work remains constant. Finally, thanks too for Love Street and Roker. Sadly the cover could not cope with these or Parkhead. We have compromised in Hampden and Dens.

We have tried to state the law as at May 31, 1991. Any errors or omissions remain those of the other authors.

Kenny Miller and Peter Robson
Glasgow
July 1991

CONTENTS

TABLE OF CASES

Para.

Table of Cases

Table of Cases

TABLE OF STATUTES

TABLE OF STATUTORY INSTRUMENTS

CHAPTER 1

THE NATURE OF OWNERSHIP OF PROPERTY

1. INTRODUCTION

This chapter is intended to consider some of the basic questions in 1.01 property which will recur throughout much of this book. One critical issue which must be confronted is to explore what is meant in law by "property". As far as common parlance is concerned, the word property can be used either to mean a person's ownership of some thing or, alternatively, to refer to a thing which is actually capable of ownership. Our first task is to discover whether the law acknowledges this particular distinction. It is then necessary to consider what rights are given in law to those who possess property. In this regard, we shall also consider the forms of property ownership which are recognised in Scots law.[1]

2. THE MEANING OF PROPERTY

Just as in everyday use, so too in the legal context, the word 1.02 "property" is capable of use in a number of different senses. More specifically, the law recognises the concept of property both in the sense that is synonymous with ownership and as describing those things which are capable of creating a right of ownership.

(1) PROPERTY AS OWNERSHIP

The first sense in which the word property is used in Scots law is 1.03 consistent with the notion of ownership, *i.e.* to talk of someone's property is to imply that he owns the thing. This ownership can be

---

[1] For reasons of space we discuss what Charles Reich described as new property rights only in relation to housing in Chap. 12—"The New Property" (1964) 73 Yale L.J. 733. For income support see A. Ogus and E. Barendt, *The Law of Social Security* (4th ed., Butterworths, 1995).

Property Law

absolute in the sense of ownership of a house based on the recording of a valid title in the Land Register of Scotland or in the General Register of Sasines. Alternatively it may be limited as, for example, in the case of the restricted rights of ownership enjoyed by a liferenter who obtains the benefits of the income accruing from a thing but has no rights to the capital. However, as we shall discover, even absolute rights of ownership such as those acquired through registration may be subject to qualification. For example, one's right of property may be qualified by the existence of a "servitude" over one's land in favour of a neighbour, or by a lease in favour of a tenant.

(2) PROPERTY AS THE THING OWNED

1.04 The word property is also used to denote the subjects of ownership, *i.e.* the things over which a right of property is enjoyed. In this case Scots law makes a number of divisions, generally based on the divisions which Roman law applies to the word *res*. This can be defined as anything that is the subject of a right and would apply to anything that could form part of a person's property. In Roman law the original division of things was between those things which were the subjects of divine law and those which were not.[2] The former were the property of no person, whereas the latter were usually the property of someone.

A more elaborate division was made by the Emperor Justinian.[3] He divided property into things that could and things that could not be the object of ownership. There were four types of *res* which could not be the object of ownership:

> *res communes*—for example, the air or the sea, which were by the law of nature common to all mankind;
> *res publicae*—for example, public roads and all rivers and parks: since these things were dedicated to public use they could not fall into the ownership of an individual;
> *res universitatis*—for example, baths or theatres which were held by a municipality for the use of people in general; and
> *res nullius*—things that did not have an owner, such as wild animals or unoccupied land.

1.05 This type of division has generally been followed in Scots law. Thus, just as in Roman law, there are certain things which are

---

[2] Gaius, *Inst.* ii. 2.
[3] See generally Just., *Inst.* ii. 1 *et seq.*

incapable of private ownership such as the sea, air or water flowing in a stream (although the latter two can be appropriated to the ownership of someone—for example, by using air to pump up tyres or by obtaining water for drinking purposes). There are also certain things which are reserved for the use of the public as part of the *regalia*, the category of rights traditionally pertaining to the Crown. The *regalia majora* consist of those rights which are vested in the Crown as custodian of the public interest and which cannot be alienated to any subject. The *regalia minora* are rights which are held by the Crown as absolute proprietor, but which can be conveyed to subjects. Examples of the *regalia* include the Crown's rights in the sea and the seabed within territorial waters,[4] the foreshore, navigable rivers, ferries, ports and harbours and roads. In addition certain basic minerals such as gold, coal, gas and oil have in the past been deemed sufficiently important to belong to the community.[5] Treasure and all other ownerless or lost property belongs to the Crown, probably on the basis of the rule *quod nullius est fit domini regis* (literally, anything without an owner becomes the property of the Crown).[6] Equally, as we shall discover, wild animals have no owners until such time as they are appropriated and taken into the possession of the person who becomes their owner. Apart from the above almost everything else is capable of private ownership under Scots law, except where statute declares otherwise.

It should be noted that the things which the law considers capable of ownership are not limited to concrete, tangible things but include intangible, metaphysical things such as the right to be repaid a debt and rights arising from contract. Such rights are considered items of incorporeal property and are discussed in Chapter 2.

(3) RIGHTS IMPLIED BY PROPERTY

The term property can also be used in law to denote the unlimited 1.06 right to the use, enjoyment and disposal of a thing. This would be unlimited in the sense that there are no restraints placed on the thing by the operation of the law or under the terms of any contract.[7] As Lord Halsbury L.C. stated in *Glasgow Corporation v. McEwan*[8]:

---

[4] *Shetland Salmon Farmers Association v. Crown Estate Commissioners*, 1991 S.L.T. 166.
[5] These issues are discussed in more detail in Chap. 7.
[6] *Lord Advocate v. University of Aberdeen*, 1963 S.C. 533; 1963 S.L.T. 361.
[7] Erskine, *Inst.*, II, ii, 1.
[8] (1899) 2 f. (H.L.) 25.

"A person who is entitled to exclude anyone else, and who is himself entitled to enjoy and possess a thing must be in any ordinary sense of the term, the proprietor."

However, the proprietor, as well as having rights of exclusion, enjoyment and possession in relation to the thing, must also have a right to dispose of it. If this right is missing then the proprietor does not have complete rights of ownership. As we shall see, it is not unusual in Scots law for the right of possession and the right of disposal to be separated (as, for example, in the case of landlord and tenant). Where a person does possess the sum of all the rights over the thing (or *res* from Roman law) he is said to have the *dominium*. In certain circumstances property may, however, be owned jointly or in common with others and this places further restrictions on the rights of the owner (see below in this chapter).

(4) Forms of Property Ownership

1.07 There are various ways in which property can be owned. The most straightforward is simple undivided ownership. This arises where one person has complete rights of exclusion, enjoyment, possession and disposal of property (although the nature of this type of ownership will not be altered by the temporary surrender of possession to a tenant). More complex forms of ownership have been developed in Scots law, particularly where the *res* is to be owned by a number of different people. However this is an area where some of the legal concepts are undeveloped and confused.[9] Where property is owned by two or more trustees or partners, this is generally done through the mechanism known as joint property. In addition there are relationships where property is owned by two or more people but where they have the right to insist on the dissolution of the relationship and with it the related property rights. This is known as common property. Although both joint and common property usually exist in relation to heritable property, moveables may also be owned in either of these ways.[10] Finally, certain special property rights exist as a result of the common interest which individuals have to preserve

---

[9] See K. G. C. Reid, "Common Property: Clarification and confusion", 1985 S.L.T. (News) 57; "Common Interest" (1983) 28 J.L.S.S. 428; "The Law of Tenement" (1983) 28 J.L.S.S. 472; "The Law of the Tenement" (1990) 35 J.L.S.S. 368. Much of the confusion should now have been eradicated by Professor Reid's own analysis of this area in the *Stair Memorial Encyclopaedia of the Laws of Scotland* (Law Society of Scotland/Butterworths, 1993), Vol. 18, para. 17 *et seq.* (Hereafter, *Stair Memorial Encyclopaedia*.)

[10] See generally Chaps. 3 and 4.

the structure or amenity of their property. This is best illustrated by the rules governing the maintenance of various parts of tenement buildings.

(a) Simple Property

There are two major considerations affecting the simple ownership 1.08 of property. One is whether the property owner has legal capacity to deal with the property. For example, in the case of children under the age of 16, whilst title to land may be taken in their names they have no active capacity and any dealings in the property must be carried out by the person entitled to act as the child's legal representative within the meaning of Part I of the Children (Scotland) Act 1995.[11] There may also be limitations placed on the enjoyment of the property stemming from legal or conventional restrictions.[12]

(b) Joint Property

Two rules are central to the concept of joint property: 1.09

   (i) the owners of the property have no separate estates, but only one estate vested in them *pro indiviso*, not merely in respect of possession, but also in respect of the right of property; and

   (ii) the right of one owner transfers on that person's death or resignation to the other/s, and cannot be alienated or disposed of either to another living person or on death.

This form of property is generally thought to be restricted to ownership by trustees, club members or partners.[13]

(c) Common Property

Common property is distinct from joint property. Here, although 1.10 the property is again possessed undivided, the property does not pass on to the other owners on the death of one proprietor but rather there exist separate property rights in the property. Two rules are central to common property:

   (i) each proprietor has a title to his own share which he may sell or transfer by his own act; and

   (ii) on the death of one of the owners his share will pass under

---

[11] Age of Legal Capacity (Scotland) Act 1991, s. 5.
[12] See generally Chaps. 3, 4 and 8 below.
[13] See Lord President Cooper in *Magistrates of Banff v. Ruthvin Castle Ltd*, 1944 S.L.T. 373 at 388. *Cf.* the decision of the Second Division in *Murray v. Johnstone* (1896) 23 R. 981 as far as clubs are concerned.

his will or be distributed according to the rules of intestate succession.

Thus, although the property is possessed undivided, each separate owner has his own separate title to some portion of the undivided whole, which he is at liberty to sell and which he can leave in his will or which will otherwise be distributed on death in accordance with the rules of intestate succession. This form of ownership was common prior to 1964 when the phenomenon of "heirs portioner" still existed. An heir portioner existed where there was no male—all the females of the same degree held the property equally. Today it is more commonly used by spouses who take title to the matrimonial home in both of their names and then provide in terms of the title that the predecessor's *pro indiviso* right in the property will pass automatically to the survivor. This is commonly referred to as taking title in joint names, but should not be confused with joint property.

1.11   A distinct form of common property arises under the common law of tenement, whereby each of the proprietors of the flats in the tenement have a right of common property in the common passage and stair within the building.

Management

1.12   As regards management of common property, the consent of all co-proprietors is required to any proposed alteration.[14] In an action regarding any alteration in a common subject, the person opposing an alteration is favoured above the person desiring to give effect to it. In other words, the person prohibiting has a virtual right of veto. An example would be one co-proprietor preventing others from removing tenants unless better rents or better security are offered.[15]

However, this maxim can be overcome in circumstances where necessity demands it. Thus in *Deans v. Woolfson*,[16] for example, where an outside stair of a tenement property common to two proprietors was destroyed it was held that one proprietor was entitled to rebuild the common stair notwithstanding the veto of his co-owner. The maxim did not apply to such a necessary restoration as that being proposed.

---

[14] Covered by the brocard "*in re communi melior est conditio prohibentis*" (the position of the one prohibiting takes precedence).

[15] For this reason a lease granted by the co-proprietors of common property to one of their number is a nullity: *Clydesdale Bank plc v. Davidson*, 1998 S.L.T. 522.

[16] 1922 S.C. 221. This case has recently been disapproved by the Second Division in *Rafique v. Amin*, 1997 S.L.T. 1385. In that case it was held that the control or management of common property is not governed by equitable considerations, and even the most innocuous of proposed alterations requires the consent of all co-proprietors.

Division

Each co-proprietor of common property has an absolute right to insist at any time upon division of the property. This right of division does not, however, apply to the separate type of common property which exists under the law of tenement. Clearly no such right can exist in relation to such common property, which is a necessary adjunct to heritable property owned in parts by a number of people each of whom rely on the common property for access and other purposes. If necessary an action for division can be brought.[17] If the property is, in fact, indivisible, there can be an application for the sale of the property and division of the realised value. As to whether such sale should be conducted by public roup or private bargain, the court has an equitable discretion to effect the sale in whichever way is fairest in the circumstances having regard to the interests of all co-proprietors.[18] Where the property owned in common is a matrimonial home in terms of the Matrimonial Homes (Family Protection) (Scotland) Act 1981, the court's permission must be sought for such a division and sale.[19] In exercising its discretion the court must have regard to all the circumstances of the case, and in particular to the conduct of the parties, their needs and resources, the needs of any child of the family, any business use of the home and whether the spouse seeking the sale decree has offered suitable alternative accommodation.[20] Merely offering half the market value of the property cannot amount to an offer of alternative accommodation, and any offer must be of specific accommodation.[21] It has been held that division and sale should be refused by the court if the defender requires to continue to live there with a child or children of the marriage, at least where the pursuer has failed to offer suitable alternative accommodation[22]; indeed there is authority for the proposition that the only reason for preventing decree being granted is the defender's need to continue to reside in the matrimonial home, at least pending divorce.[23]

1.13

---

[17] *Upper Crathes Fishings Ltd v. Bailey's Executors*, 1991 S.L.T. 747; *sub nom. Upper Crathes Fishings Ltd v. Barclay*, 1991 S.C.L.R. 151 (division of fishings).
[18] *The Miller Group Ltd v. Tasker*, 1993 S.L.T. 207. However, see *Campbells v. Murray*, 1972 S.L.T. 249 where it was held that in modern circumstances public sales were less likely than sales by private bargain to realise the property's best price; *cf. Berry v. Berry (No. 2)*, 1989 S.L.T. 292.
[19] s. 19.
[20] s. 19; discussed more fully in Chap. 12.
[21] *Hall v. Hall*, 1987 S.L.T. (Sh. Ct.) 15.
[22] *Milne v. Milne*, 1994 S.L.T. (Sh. Ct.) 57.
[23] *Berry v. Berry*, 1988 S.L.T. 650.

(d) Common Interest

1.14   Bell defined common interest as:

> "A species of right differing from common property takes place among the owners of subjects possessed in separate portions, but still united by their common interest."[24]

An example of this form of ownership exists in lochs or non-navigable rivers where, because of the parties' common interest in the water, riparian proprietors can take action to prevent unauthorised intrusion on their water. It can also apply to light and air. In *Donald and Sons v. Esslemont and Macintosh Ltd*[25] three proprietors who owned property in the same street as another proprietor were held to have a title to object to the erection of a bridge by this third party which would have linked the properties which he owned on both sides of the street. Their title was based, *inter alia*, on the fact that as members of the community they had a common interest not merely in the surface of the street but in the space above it. It was held that the proposed bridge would be an appropriation of part of that space for private use.

Law of tenement

1.15   The most striking example of common interest operates in the law of tenement. Here we are talking about flatted dwellings generally on two or more storeys owned by separate proprietors who, as well as owning certain parts of the tenement in common property, have a common interest in the preservation of the fabric of the entire tenement.

Normally nowadays the rights and obligations of the owners of flats in tenements are generally determined from their title deeds and the cost of repairs is apportioned by rateable value, equally or according to some other formula. However, in the absence of such provisions the common or customary law of tenement will apply.[26]

(i) Roof

1.16   The roof and the space beneath it[27] are the property of the owner of the highest storey. Top storey owners must make sure they do nothing to impair the roof's efficacy as a shelter from the weather.

---

[24] *Prin.*, §1086.
[25] 1923 S.C. 122.
[26] The state of the law of tenement in Scotland is currently being considered by the Scottish Law Commission: see *Law of Tenement* (Scot. Law Com., Discussion Paper No. 91) (1990). See also K. G. C. Reid, "The Law of the Tenement: New thoughts on old law" (1983) 28 J.L.S.S. 472.
[27] *Taylor v. Dunlop* (1872) 11 M. 25.

They must ensure that it is properly maintained in order to provide this shelter to all the proprietors in the tenement. The lower proprietors have a common interest in the roof which entitles them to enforce the obligation of maintenance on the topmost proprietor.

(ii) Solum

The solum area, which includes the court and back green, belongs 1.17 to the ground floor proprietors, subject to a right of common interest in favour of the upper proprietors, entitling them to resist any injurious alteration (*e.g.* one which undermines support, or the building of anything which would encroach upon their light and air).[28]

(iii) Walls

The owners of each flat have sole property in their own internal 1.18 walls and ownership of that portion of the external walls which bounds their flat. However, the other proprietors have a common interest to prevent damage to the stability of the building. In the case of internal walls between flats there is a right of common property vested in all those persons whose property abuts the wall[29] and other proprietors have a common interest to prevent significant harm to the wall.

(iv) Gables

Initially, it was held that the proprietors of the flats adjoining 1.19 common gables had a common property in the totality of the gable.[30] However, it is now clear that each proprietor is the sole owner of the gable *ad medium filum* with a common interest in the other half.[31] This latter view was confirmed by the Second Division in *Trades House of Glasgow v. Ferguson*[32] where it was held that the proprietor of property with a common gable was responsible to the other proprietor for half the cost of demolition of the wall caused by

---

[28] See generally, *Johnston v. White* (1877) 4 R. 721.
[29] Rankine, *Land-ownership* (4th ed., W. Green, 1909), p. 667. Kenneth Reid has argued that this is not a sensible rule and that it would be better to make each proprietor sole owner to the halfway point with a right of common interest over the other half—"The Law of the Tenement" (1983) 28 J.L.S.S. 472 at 474. There is sheriff court authority to the effect that in the case of a mutual wall each proprietor has a right of property *ad medium filum*. See *Gill v. Mitchell*, 1980 S.L.T. (Sh. Ct.) 48.
[30] *Law v. Monteith* (1855) 18 D. 125; *Rodger v. Russell* (1873) 11 M. 671.
[31] See, for example, *Robertson v. Scott* (1886) 13 R. 1127.
[32] 1979 S.L.T. 187.

loss of support. The loss of support came about when the neighbouring proprietor demolished the top three stories of his tenement and roofed it above the first floor.

(v) Floors and Ceilings

1.20   The floor and ceiling of each flat are divided by a notional line drawn through the mid-line of the joists. In this case neither party is entitled to weaken the floor or ceiling or to expose them to unusual danger of fire. The duties involved here only amount to the proprietors of the lower flats providing support for the proprietors of the upper flats. The upper proprietors, in turn, must provide cover for the lower flats. This duty is in no sense absolute. In *Thomson v. St Cuthbert's Co-operative Association Ltd*[33] the Court of Session was asked to consider whether a ground floor proprietor was liable, without specific proof of negligence, for damage done to an upper flat as a result of the fracture of a cast-iron supporting beam situated within the ground floor. It was held that the law of tenement did not impose absolute duties of mutual support or protection on the proprietors of tenement flats. In order for liability to be established, negligence on the part of the ground floor proprietors had to be proved. This decision was followed in the sheriff court case of *Kerr v. McGreevy*.[34] In this case the proprietor of the lower flat had damaged an upper flat when carrying out alterations authorised under warrant of the dean of guild court. The upper proprietor sought compensation for the damage caused, averring in effect that the lower proprietor owed him an absolute duty. It was held that it had to be shown that the lower proprietor had breached a duty of reasonable care which he owed towards the upper proprietor. Since no breach of such duty was averred the action was dismissed.

(vi) Common Passages and Stairs

1.21   There is no doubt that these are held in common property by all the proprietors in the tenement. However, it is unclear on what basis such property rights are distributed. Rankine argued that ownership should only vest in those proprietors who require to use the passages

---

[33] 1958 S.C. 380. The law of nuisance may also provide a cause of action for loss of support—*Lord Advocate v. Reo Stakis Organisation Ltd*, 1981 S.C. 104. However, where the proprietor is seeking damages for loss of support under the law of nuisance some averments of fault must be made. See the decision of the House of Lords in *RHM Bakeries (Scotland) Ltd v. Strathclyde Regional Council*, 1985 S.L.T. 214.

[34] 1970 S.L.T. (Sh. Ct.) 7.

and stairs for access.[35] More recently, Reid has suggested that the best solution is to accept that each proprietor co-owns the entire passage and stair in equal shares.[36] Neither position is supported by any judicial authority.

The interest in the other flats which owners of flats in tenement property have does not arise from the creation of a series of servitudes, but exists by virtue of being incidents of ownership of tenement property. The rights themselves really stem from the common interest which each proprietor of a tenement flat possesses. As Lord Dunedin explained in *Smith v. Giuliani*[37]:

> "[E]ach proprietor of a flat is proprietor of it, but along with his proprietorship there is linked the common interest in the walls or roof, as the case may be, of the other proprietors and this common interest is not a right of servitude nor of common property, but is a right of a proprietary character."

---

[35] Rankine, *Land-ownership, op. cit.*, p. 677. See also J. G. S. Cameron, "The Law of the Tenement", I Conv. R. 105 and 248 and II Conv. R. 102 at 105.

[36] "The Law of the Tenement" (1983) 28 J.L.S.S. 472 at 475–476.

[37] 1925 S.C. (H.L.) 45.

CHAPTER 2

CLASSIFICATION OF PROPERTY RIGHTS

2.01 There are a number of different ways in which property can be classified. Scots law makes no distinction between personal property for use and property for profit.[1] The law in Scotland protects property whether its basis is in work, creativity or stemming from mere inheritance. The various classifications of the subjects of property which do exist in Scots law serve to explain the nature of different kinds of property as well as having a clear practical function:

    (i) heritable and moveable property;
    (ii) corporeal and incorporeal property; and
    (iii) fungible and non-fungible property.

1. HERITABLE AND MOVEABLE PROPERTY

2.02 The most important division made by Scots law is into property which is heritable and property which is moveable. This classification follows the old Scots law of intestate succession whereby property which was connected with the land went to the heir-at-law (the eldest son), and has attracted criticism as being misleading.[2] The classifications are broadly that heritable property covers land and its pertinents together with all rights in and connected with the land whilst moveable property entails that which by its nature and use is capable of motion or being moved and rights connected with such property. Items may be heritable or moveable according to their nature, by conversion from moveable property to heritage or by the fixing of moveable property to heritage—the law of fixtures.[3]

---

[1] T. Veblen, *The Theory of the Leisure Class* (1925).
[2] Gloag and Henderson, *Introduction to the Law of Scotland* (10th ed., W. Green, 1995) at p. 611; T. B. Smith, *A Short Commentary on the Law of Scotland* (W. Green, 1962), p. 907; W. M. Gordon, *Scottish Land Law* (Scottish Universities Law Institute Ltd/W. Green, 1989), p. 3.
[3] See paras 6.08–6.17.

(1) By Nature

Lands and buildings are clearly heritable. So also are stones and 2.03
minerals and trees[4] so long as they remain part of the ground. Cut
timber, however, is clearly moveable. The natural fruits of the land
which require no constant cultivation, such as grass,[5] are also
heritable until severed. However, there are problems as regards
the exact classification of industrial fruits. Erskine argued that
"those annual fruits which require yearly seed and industry as
wheat, barley etc. are accounted moveable even before separation,
from the moment they are sown or planted".[6] This view would
ensure that an agricultural tenant would have no difficulty in
removing industrial crops which he has sown since they are classified
as items of moveable property. There is contrary authority for the
view that growing crops are heritable in nature until separated by the
tenant, whose right to do so is recognised in law[7]; however this
decision has been doubted subsequently.[8]

(2) By Destination

It is also possible for moveable property to be regarded as heritable 2.04
by destination in cases of succession. This operates on the basis of an
implied intention by the deceased to benefit the heritage at the
expense of the moveable estate. Thus a collection of building
materials piled on the ground which are ready to be added to the
construction would be regarded as heritable.[9] It is unclear whether
the money required to complete an unfinished building after the
owner's death would also be treated as heritable by conversion.[10] It

---

[4] *Paul v. Cuthbertson* (1840) 2 D. 1286.
[5] At one time hay was considered to be a natural crop and so was treated in the
same way as grass: see *Sinclair v. Dalrymple* (1744) Mor. 5421. However, it
would now seem that hay must be treated in the same way as other industrial
crops and may, therefore, be classified as moveable. See *Lyall v. Cooper* (1832)
11 S. 96.
[6] *Inst.*, II, ii, 4. Approved by the whole court, albeit *obiter*, in *Paul v. Cuthbertson*
(1840) 2 D. 1286.
[7] *Chalmer's Tr. v. Dick's Tr.*, 1909 S.C. 761.
[8] *McKinley v. Hutchison's Trs*, 1935 S.L.T. 62.
[9] *Johnston v. Dobie* (1783) Mor. 5443.
[10] In *Malloch v. McLean* (1867) 5 M. 335 it was held that the portion of the
deceased's estate which was required to complete his house, in accordance with
the plans, was, by destination, heritable. This decision has been criticised by
Lord President Clyde in *Fairlie's Trs v. Fairlie's C.B.*, 1932 S.C. 216, who argued
that it should have rested on the notion that the money required was a personal
debt of the deceased. Professor Reid prefers the latter view (*Stair Memorial
Encyclopaedia*, Vol. 18, para. 15).

should be stressed that this concept applies only to the law of succession and has no operation in any other part of Scots property law.

(3) BY ACCESSION

2.05 This principle ensures that an item of property which is moveable in nature and which becomes affixed to heritage can lose its identity as a moveable and become part of the heritable property.[11]

Importance of Heritable/Moveable Classification

2.06   The heritable/moveable division emerges in a variety of contexts, the most important being succession, diligence and as regards the sale and lease of heritage. In all of these situations it is important to know whether an item is classified as heritable or moveable.

(a) Succession

2.07 Prior to 1964, although the heritable property of an intestate passed to male descendants, widows enjoyed a liferent of part of the heritable property of their deceased husband—called *terce*.[12] This right was superseded under the present rules of intestate succession as laid down in the Succession (Scotland) Act 1964,[13] by prior rights. Prior rights entitle the surviving spouse to any house forming part of the deceased's estate up to the value of £110,000, furniture and plenishings up to a value of £20,000 and a financial sum from the remaining estate of £30,000 if there are any issue (children) and £50,000 if the intestate dies without issue.[14]

Whilst it is possible to defeat prior rights by making a will, there are rights from the moveable property which exist irrespective of any will which may have been made. The surviving spouse is entitled to one-third of the moveables and the children also receive one-third— the widow's share is increased to one-half if there are no surviving children and vice versa. Accordingly any person who wishes to ensure that the surviving spouse or children are to receive nothing on their death can only do so at present in Scotland by ensuring that their property is tied up in heritage.

---

[11] The rules which apply to such a change of classification are discussed in more detail at paras 6.08–6.17.

[12] The equivalent right for widowers was a liferent of a proportion of moveables called *courtesy*.

[13] ss. 8 and 9. See D. R. Macdonald, *Succession* (2nd ed., W. Green, 1994), Chap. 4.

[14] These current levels derive from S.I. 1993 No. 2690.

(b) Diligence

Where a creditor is seeking to recover a debt through the use of 2.08
diligence, it is important to know the type of property upon which
the diligence is to be done. There are special forms of diligence which
can only be used in relation to heritable property—inhibition and
adjudication.[15] These allow the heritable creditor valuable rights over
other creditors by providing a high degree of security and ultimately (in
the case of adjudication) the right to acquire the heritable property. The
appropriate legal procedure in relation to corporeal moveable property
is poinding, whereby the goods of the debtor are ascertained and
valued and may be sold under warrant of the court.[16]

(c) Sale and Lease

The heritable/moveable distinction is also important in the case of 2.09
the sale of heritable property as the moveables in the property do not
form part of the sale. The seller is entitled to remove any moveable
property unless the sale contract states otherwise. However, if the
moveable property has become in law a fixture, it is part of the
heritage and may not be removed. In the absence of express agreement there may be disputes over what exactly is moveable. Similarly,
tenants may bring items of moveables onto the property which
become part of the heritage under the rules governing fixtures.
However, in certain circumstances these may nevertheless be removed by the tenant at the end of the lease, since an exception is
made for tenant's trade and ornamental fixtures.[17]

2. CORPOREAL AND INCORPOREAL PROPERTY

A further classification can be made between these kinds of prop- 2.10
erty. This stems from the Latin *corpus*—body:

corporeal—tangible and visible, *e.g.* a car; and
incorporeal—intangible and invisible comprising rights such as
a patent or goodwill.

Combining these two forms of classification any type of property in
Scotland can be categorised into one of four groups:

---

[15] G. L. Gretton, *The Law of Inhibition and Adjudication* (2nd ed., Butterworths, 1996).
[16] G. Maher and D. Cusine, *The Law and Practice of Diligence* (Butterworths, 1990), particularly Chap. 9.
[17] These issues are discussed at paras 6.14–6.17.

(i) corporeal heritable property, *e.g.* land or houses;
(ii) incorporeal heritable property, *e.g.* leases or servitudes;
(iii) corporeal moveable property, *e.g.* bicycle or television;
(iv) incorporeal moveable property, *e.g.* copyrights or trade-marks.

3. FUNGIBLE AND NON-FUNGIBLE PROPERTY

2.11 There is an additional division which can be made by classifying moveable property as either fungible or non-fungible. A fungible is something which is destroyed by being used—such as money, grain or coal—and can be replaced by equal quantities of the same quality. A non-fungible—such as a work of art—is not destroyed in use, has a specific individual value and cannot be replaced by a similar thing.[18] This classification is important where liferent is involved, since the normal rule is that this involves the enjoyment of property without destroying or encroaching upon the substance of the property.[19]

---

[18] Erskine, *Inst.*, III, i, 18, also mentions a horse in this context.
[19] See paras 11.02–11.11.

Chapter 3

CORPOREAL MOVEABLE PROPERTY

1. Nature

Corporeal moveable property consists of those tangible items 3.01
which, as we have noted, are capable of motion and are not
attached in some way to land or buildings. Animals, cars, clothes
and money in cash are all typical instances of corporeal moveable
property.[1]

2. Acquisition

As we have noted possession of property gives certain privileges to 3.02
the possessor.[2] It does not by itself confer ownership, but it may set
up a rebuttable presumption of ownership. In order to obtain
ownership a person must utilise one of the mechanisms noted below.
There are various distinct ways in which moveable property may
be obtained, the majority of which are unique to moveable
property although accession does also operate in relation to heritable property.

(1) Occupation

This is the most primitive way of acquiring property. Moveables 3.03
which have never been owned by any person become the property
of the person who appropriates them, so long as that person
has the intention of becoming owner. Accordingly, any wild
creatures such as animals, birds or fish or even shells or pebbles
can be acquired by the first person to take possession of them—

---

[1] See Chap. 2.
[2] See Chap. 1.

17

quod nullius est fit primi occupantis.[3] Once confined such items remain the property of the person who exercises control over them and to remove them would be theft. The above items are only capable of acquisition through occupation so long as they have never been the property of anyone—known as *res nullius*. Since there is no property right in a *res nullius* until it has been acquired, apart from under statute, it cannot be theft for someone to shoot or otherwise acquire a wild animal which is on the land of another. However, upon the escape of a wild animal these property rights will be lost when the owner ceases to pursue the creature in order to regain possession.[4] It should be noted that there are certain categories of wild animal, such as royal birds and salmon, which belong to the Crown so that rights of property cannot be acquired by occupation. Domestic animals, or marked animals, as well as those creatures with a homing instinct such as bees, pigeons (and hunting birds) remain the property of their owners even when they stray. Complicated issues of proof of original ownership of domestic animals have arisen particularly with cats shuttling between two sets of "owners" unbeknown to the other parties.

3.04   Occupation is not available for property already in the ownership of another. Thus lost property is not covered by the *quod nullius* maxim. The general rule is that the owners of lost articles do not lose possession of them so long as they have the necessary intention of keeping possession or *animus possidendi*. It may be that under Scots common law lost, abandoned or ownerless property goes to the Crown under the maxim *quod nullius est fit domini regis*.[5] There are very few Scottish cases on this issue[6] and it has not attracted the same level of controversy as it has in England.[7] The present law on finding in Scotland is governed by Part VI of the Civic Government (Scotland) Act 1982 which requires the finder of lost or abandoned property to take reasonable care of it and without unreasonable delay to deliver it or report the find to a police officer.[8] It is clear that no right to claim ownership of the lost article is created by the act of finding alone, although in the event of the property not being

---

[3] Stair, *Inst.*, II. i. 33; Erskine, *Inst.*, II, i, 10; Bell, *Prin.*, §§1287 *et seq.*
[4] *ibid.*
[5] See Erskine, *Inst.*, II. i, 12; Bell, *Prin.*, §1290.
[6] See, for example, *Corporation of Glasgow v. Northcote* (1921) 38 Sh. Ct. Rep. 76; and *Dawson v. Muir* (1851) 13 D. 843.
[7] *cf. Bridges v. Hawkesworth* (1851) 21 L.J.Q.B. 75 and *South Staffordshire Water Co. v. Sharman* [1896] 2 Q.B. 44. See also *Hannah v. Peel* [1945] K.B. 509 and *Parker v. British Airways Board* [1982] Q.B. 1004. Note that the English common law rules on treasure trove are to be replaced by a statutory code: Treasure Act 1996.
[8] s. 67(1).

claimed the chief constable has the discretion to give the article to the finder.[9] There is no doubt that the Crown can claim ownership of treasure trove in Scotland so that any treasure hidden under the ground would fall to the Crown and not to the occupier of the land.[10] Equally, Erskine claims that stray cattle that have been abandoned by their owner do not belong to the finder but pass to the Crown as escheat or forfeited goods.[11] Legislation covers certain items such as wrecks which require the appointment of receivers of wrecks by the Department of Trade.[12]

(2) ACCESSION

In this instance a person is given ownership of a new thing through 3.05 his ownership of the original item which has an intimate association with the secondary property[13]—*accessorium sequitur principale.* Thus the owner of an animal also acquires ownership of her off- spring[14] and the owner of a fund of money is entitled to the interest.[15] The former is an example of natural accession because it involves a natural increase in quantity. On the same principle, property can be acquired through the operation of natural forces on land. This could apply where a river gradually alters its course so that new land is exposed or where soil is gradually brought down by a stream and deposited on the banks. The other form of accession involves industrial accession whereby the increase comes about because of some person's industry. There are a number of other forms of industrial accession to which we shall now turn. It should be noted that the legal rules applied in this area lack certainty and consistency so that in some cases it may be difficult to ascertain the true state of the law.[16]

---

[9] ss. 73 and 70(1)(b).

[10] Stair, *Inst.*, II. i. 5; Erskine, *Inst.*, II, i, 12; *Lord Advocate v. University of Aberdeen*, 1963 S.C. 533 where the Second Division preferred to apply the *quod nullius est fit domini regis* maxim as regards the ownership of the "St Ninian's Isle Treasure" rather than the law that once applied in Shetland.

[11] Erskine, *Inst.*, II, i, 12.

[12] Under the Merchant Shipping Act 1995, s. 248, the Department of Trade is given the power to appoint receivers of wreck. The receiver must take possession of any wreck and give notice of this fact so that the owner can claim delivery (ss. 238 and 239). It is an offence to fail to notify the receiver of the existence of a wreck (s. 236) and ownership of unclaimed wrecks is vested in the Crown (s. 241).

[13] Stair, *Inst.*, II. i. 34; Erskine, *Inst.*, II, i, 14–15.

[14] Stair, *Inst.*, II. i. 34; *Lamb v. Grant* (1874) 11 S.L.R. 672.

[15] *Gillespies v. Marshall* (1802) M. App. 1, "Accessorium" No. 2.

[16] See on this point the statement of Lord Ardmillan in *Wylie and Lochhead v. Mitchell* (1870) 8 M. 552, 561.

(3) SPECIFICATION

3.06 The essence of *specificatio* is that where separate items have been
brought together to form a new subject in such a way that the
original elements cannot be returned to their previous state, ownership of this new subject will vest in its creator. This will apply even
although the creator did not contribute any of the materials that
were used in the process.[17] If a new subject is created its owner is
required to restore to the former owner of the separate items a like
quantity and quality, or failing that the price of the material. A good
example of the application of specification is *International Banking
Corporation v. Ferguson, Shaw & Sons*[18] where cotton seed oil and
other substances had been mixed together to make a lard compound.
In an action for damages by the previous owners of the oil, the
Second Division held that on the basis of *specificatio* a new species of
property had been created and that the makers of this new product
had ownership in it and were, therefore, required to compensate the
pursuers for the value of the oil which had been used.

It has been argued that the concept of specification is based on
equity and so can only apply where the maker has acted *bona fide*.[19]

The Scottish courts have applied strictly the requirement that in
the making of the new product the other ingredients must be
destroyed. Thus specification will not apply when the front part
of one car is welded to the rear part of another car since such a car
could be cut into two once more.[20] Equally, market forces alone
cannot create a new species for the purposes of *specificatio*, so that
when work is carried out on a product in order to make it ready for
sale the concept will not apply.[21] The important issue is that there
must be change in the property which involves the disappearance of
the original articles.[22]

---

[17] Stair, *Inst.*, II. i. 41; Erskine, *Inst.*, II, i, 16–17; Bell, *Prin.*, §1298(1).

[18] 1910 S.C. 182.

[19] *per* Lord President Clyde in *McDonald v. Provan (of Scotland Street) Ltd*, 1960
S.L.T. 231 at 232.

[20] *McDonald v. Provan (of Scotland Street) Ltd, supra*, at 231.

[21] See the decision of the Second Division in *Armour v. Thyssen Edelstahlwerke AG*,
1989 S.L.T. 182, reversed on other grounds by the House of Lords at 1990 S.L.T.
891.

[22] *per* Lord McDonald in *North-West Securities Ltd v. Barrhead Coachworks Ltd*,
1976 S.L.T. 99, rejecting the view that *specificatio* could also operate through the
application of consumer credit legislation as expressed by Sheriff Principal
Walker in *F. C. Finance Ltd v. Langtry Investment Co. Ltd*, 1973 S.L.T.
(Sh. Ct.) 11.

(4) Confusion and Commixtion

Confusion is the term applied when liquids come together; commix- 3.07
tion applies to solids. In both cases there is undoubtedly an overlap
with *specificatio*. Where commodities are mixed together and become inseparable, their ownership will be determined by different
rules depending on the character of the commodities. If they are of
the same kind, the mixer does not become the owner of the product.
Instead, the shares are owned in common and are *pro indiviso*
according to the quantity and value of the original contribution.[23]
However, the mixer of the items will acquire ownership if the
substances are different and the process involves the creation of a
new item of property with no possibility of restoring the original
substances to their owners. If the substances are capable of being
returned, then ownership remains with the original owners. Where
two parties agree to produce a new object and contribute work or
material towards this end the new item will be held in common
property corresponding to the value of the contributions.[24]

(5) Other Forms of Accession

(a) Contexture

A typical example of this would arise when materials belonging to 3.08
one person are worked into cloth or some other manufactured
product which belongs to another. If separation cannot take place,
ownership of the item belongs to the manufacturer, who will
be required to compensate the other for its value and may also be
required to make reparation for any damage caused.[25]

(b) Adjunction

This would apply where a person paints or writes on the property 3.09
of another. In the case of a painting, if it is made on the walls of
someone's house the picture will become the property of the house-
owner. Where it is painted on canvas it will belong to the artist
although the owner of the canvas must be recompensed for its
value.[26]

---

[23] Bell, *Prin.*, §1298; Stair, *Inst.*, II. i. 37; Erskine, *Inst.*, II, i, 17.
[24] *Wylie and Lochhead v. Mitchell* (1870) 8 M. 552.
[25] Stair, *Inst.*, II. i. 39.
[26] *ibid.*; Erskine, *Inst.*, II, i, 15.

3. TRANSFER

3.10 Under this heading we are only considering cases where the transfer is made during the grantor's lifetime (*inter vivos*)—there are different rules which apply in the case of transfers after death (*mortis causa*).[27] Under Scots law, transfer of ownership of corporeal moveable property is effected by delivery of the item. No transfer of ownership can be achieved by agreement alone. Writing is commonly used in complicated transactions, but cannot by itself create a real right of ownership: it merely creates a personal obligation to deliver the thing. The critical element is for there to be actual delivery.[28] As Lord President Inglis said in *Clark v. West Calder Oil Co.*[29]: "A mere assignation of corporeal moveables *retenta possessione* (with retention of possession) is nothing whatever but a personal obligation." Moreover, it is also vital for the owner to intend or consent to the transmission and delivery of the thing. Someone other than the owner of the property, or acting without the consent of the owner, cannot generally transfer a good title to the property since they transfer no better a right than they have—explained by the maxim *nemo dat quod non habet.*

3.11 Property in the subject will not pass unless these two elements—intention to transfer and physical delivery—are established. However, it would be legitimate for the parties in a contract of sale of moveables to specify that ownership of the goods will not pass until the full purchase price is paid. In such a case, even although there has been delivery, title will not pass until the purchaser has paid the final instalment.[30] The old traditional Scottish rules have also been affected by the provisions of the Sale of Goods Act 1979. Where the provisions of this Act apply, the rule is that the passing of property does not depend upon the delivery of the subject, but upon the force of the contract and the intentions of the parties.

Reservation of title as described above is also permitted under the Sale of Goods Act 1979. Where title has been reserved to the seller, the buyer in possession of the goods can nonetheless transmit a good title to a third party acting in good faith.[31]

It would now appear to be settled that a reservation of title pending payment of the price by the buyer, or even pending payment by him of all sums due to the seller, is valid and does not offend the

---

[27] D. R. Macdonald, *Succession* (2nd ed., W. Green, 1994).
[28] Under the brocard *traditionibus non nudis pactis dominia rerum transferuntur.*
[29] (1882) 9 R. 1017.
[30] *per* Lord Keith of Kinkel in *Armour v. Thyssen Edelstahlwerke AG*, 1990 S.L.T. 891 at 893.
[31] Sale of Goods Act 1979, s. 25.

provisions of the Sale of Goods Act 1979 which disallow the creation of a security without transfer of possession.[32]

Where title in corporeal moveables is reserved to the seller, it appears that the seller may nevertheless lose ownership through the operation of accession (*i.e.* the irreversible annexation of the goods to other moveable property), though not necessarily through *specificatio* (*i.e.* use of the goods, with other goods, to create a new thing).[33]

(1) British Ships

Special statutory rules govern the transfer of ownership of British 3.12
ships. (A British ship is one which is registered as such.) Whereas previously only ships which were exclusively within the ownership of British nationals or corporations could be registered as British, the law now only requires that a majority interest in a ship is so owned.[34] Registration of ships is now optional, although certain important consequences (including the right to fly the British flag) flow from registration. Ships (except fishing boats) which are less than 24 metres in length and which are exclusively within British ownership qualify as British ships without the need for registration.

Ships are divisible into 64 shares, which cannot be subdivided, so that there can be no more than 64 owners of a ship at any time. Transfer of ownership of the whole of, or of any share in, a British ship must be in writing by bill of sale. Contracts for sale do not require to be in writing.[35] Provided the registrar is satisfied that the ship continues to be a British ship (through majority ownership) he must register the bill of sale in the register, at which point the former owner is divested of title. An earlier registered title has priority over all later registrations. The register is evidence of title to a ship, and not proof of possession.

---

[32] *Armour v. Thyssen Edelstahlwerke AG*, 1990 S.L.T. 891.
[33] See generally, D. L. Carey Miller, *Corporeal Moveables in Scots Law* (W. Green, 1991), Chap. 12.
[34] Merchant Shipping Act 1995, s. 9.
[35] *McConnochie v. Geddes*, 1918 S.C. 391.

CHAPTER 4

INCORPOREAL MOVEABLE PROPERTY

1. NATURE OF INCORPOREAL MOVEABLES

4.01 Incorporeal moveable property covers such things as rights to debts, rights to shares in moveable property, and insurance policies. The constitution and operation of these matters are the subject matter of mercantile or commercial law and here we will limit ourselves to a brief comment on the acquisition and transfer of the property rights involved. In addition there are special protections afforded to those intangible rights which arise from creativity in the artistic, scientific or business spheres. We will look separately at the general principles of acquisition and transfer of property covering all incorporeal moveables, before looking at the specific protections available for patents, copyrights and trademarks.

2. ACQUISITION AND TRANSFER OF OWNERSHIP

4.02 Transfer of ownership of this type of property is called assignation. The person who grants the assignation is known as the cedent, and the person to whom it is granted is the assignee. Previously ownership of incorporeal moveables was believed to require some form of writing, although the rule was not entirely clear. In the absence of any statutory rule governing particular instances, any form of wording, however informal, sufficed. In *Brownlee v. Robb*[1] it was held to be sufficient in an assignation of a life policy to say "I, JR, hand over my life policy to my daughter".

Assignation of incorporeal moveables no longer requires to be in writing, the uncertainty over the existence of a rule having been

---

[1] 1907 S.C. 1302.

removed by Parliament,[2] although it is thought that writing will continue to be used in practice. Writing remains necessary under various statutes for the assignation of life policies,[3] patents[4] and certain other types of incorporeal moveable.

(1) ASSIGNATION

The basic rule is that the holder of an incorporeal right has title to   4.03 transfer ownership whenever he or she wishes. The requirement of writing for such a transfer has been abolished. There are, however, certain incorporeal moveables which cannot be transferred at all. This is the case where the right is personal to the owner by virtue of the legal concept of *delectus personae* (the choice of a person to the exclusion of all others). So in the case of a right to work, for example, there can be no assignation of the contract of employment. The contract only exists between the original parties who actually made it. Nor can there be an assignation of an alimentary provision, since the essence of this is personal to the holder,[5] nor of certain leases.[6]

The right of the assignee is completed in a question with the cedent by delivery of the assignation. This gives the assignee an effective personal right. However, there will have to be intimation to the debtor to ensure a right against him. An incomplete assignation will not entail any transfer of rights, as where an assignee of a lease died before the assignation in his favour was intimated to the landlord.[7] Whilst the cedent by assigning the incorporeal rights guarantees that these exist, this does not mean they will be effectual. Thus there can be no complaint by the assignee of a debt if the debtor turns out to be insolvent.[8] Debt collection agencies deal with this possibility through discounting such rights.

(2) INTIMATION

As already noted, mere delivery of the assignation only deals with   4.04 the rights as between cedent and assignee. As far as making the assignee's rights good against third parties is concerned there must

---

[2] Requirements of Writing (Scotland) Act 1995, s. 11.
[3] Policies of Assurance Act 1867.
[4] Patents Act 1977.
[5] Erskine, *Inst.*, III, v, 2.
[6] See paras 9.22–9.24.
[7] *Smith v. Riddell* (1886) 14 R. 95.
[8] Erskine, *Inst.*, II, iii, 25.

be intimation to those parties. Such intimation completes the assignee's rights. The Transmission of Moveable Property (Scotland) Act 1862 provides that formal intimation may be made by:

> (i) a notary public delivering a certified copy of the assignation to the third party with the certificate of intimation of the notary constituting sufficient evidence of the intimation;
>
> (ii) the holder of the assignation or any person authorised by him transmitting a certified copy by post to the third party with a written acknowledgment by that person being sufficient evidence of such intimation having been duly made.[9]

There are, in addition, other forms of notice or acknowledgment which the law regards as equivalents of intimation—self-proving acknowledgment by the debtor of the assignee's right; citation in an action by the assignee against the debtor; a charge or citation on any diligence against the debtor; production of the assignation in court in an action between them.

Registration of assignation in the Books of Council and Session will not suffice as these are for preservation and diligence and not for publication,[10] nor is reference to the oath of the debtor enough.

(3) Effect of Assignation

4.05 Provided the cedent has power to assign, or has obtained any necessary consent from the creditor, the assignee steps into the cedent's shoes and succeeds to the cedent's rights and obligations. Thus every right competent to the cedent is competent to the assignee and the assignee acquires the right to sue or defend a legal action to the same extent as the cedent.[11] However, the assignee cannot obtain any higher right by the assignation than that possessed by the cedent. Thus if the rights of the cedent are flawed it is just as lawful to raise these objections against the assignee unless there is personal bar.[12] Ineffectual assignations have been held to cover loss of a settlement on remarriage,[13] and an insurance policy where the original policyholder had made untrue statements as to his health and drinking habits.[14] However, the above rules do not apply

---

[9] s. 2.

[10] *Tod's Trs v. Wilson* (1869) 7 M. 1100; *Cameron's Trs v. Cameron*, 1907 S.C. 407.

[11] These rights are expressed in the latin maxim *assignatus utitur jure auctoris*.

[12] *Scottish Equitable Life Ass. Soc. v. Buist* (1877) 4 R. 1076 at 1081, affd, (1878) 5 R. (H.L.) 64.

[13] *Johnstone-Beattie v. Dalziel* (1868) 6 M. 333.

[14] *The Scottish Widows' Fund v. Buist* (1876) 3 R. 1078.

to latent claims. An assignee who takes in good faith and for value is not affected by latent trusts or equitable claims affecting the right of the cedent. Such claims undoubtedly affect the rights of the cedent but do not affect an onerous assignee. This point was established in *Redfearn v. Somervail*[15] where a man who was apparently the owner of a share in a private company assigned this in security for a private loan. In fact the share in the private company was held as trustee for the firm of which he was a partner. The creditor took the share in the honest belief that he was the true owner and intimated his right. In a competition between the assignee's creditor and the trustee's firm the assignee's claim was upheld. This was on the basis that the dispute was not between the debtor in the obligation and the assignee, but between the assignee and a beneficiary under a trust whose claim was collateral to the transaction which had transferred the share.

3. INTELLECTUAL PROPERTY

(1) COPYRIGHT

(a) Nature of Copyright

The present law on copyright in the United Kingdom is regulated 4.06 by the Copyright, Designs and Patents Act 1988. Copyright is a property right which applies to three kinds of work:

    (i) original literary, dramatic, musical or artistic works;
    (ii) sound recordings, films, broadcasts or cable programmes; and
    (iii) the typographical arrangement of published editions.[16]

Such a right comes into being automatically without any formality as soon as the relevant work is created, and restricts to the owner of the work the right to do certain acts in the United Kingdom which are discussed below.[17] However, in the case of literary, dramatic or musical works copyright does not subsist unless and until it is recorded in writing or otherwise.[18] The phrase "literary work" is defined broadly to cover not only any work, other than a dramatic

---

[15] (1813) 5 Pat. App. 707.
[16] See generally, s. 1(1)(a)–(c). As far as a typographical arrangement of published editions is concerned it is clear that this is intended to cover the way in which the words or symbols are laid out. See s. 8.
[17] s. 2.
[18] s. 3(2).

or musical work, which is written, spoken or sung but also any table or compilation and any computer program.[19] "Artistic work" means a graphic work, photograph, sculpture or collage, irrespective of artistic quality, a work of architecture or a work of artistic craftsmanship.[20]

4.07   Owners of copyright have the exclusive right to do the following acts in the United Kingdom.[21] These are to copy the work[22]; to issue copies of the work to the public[23]; to perform, show or play the work in public[24]; to broadcast the work or include it in a cable programme service[25] and to make an adaptation of the work or do any of the above matters in relation to an adaptation.[26] A person other than the copyright owner who does any of these acts without the permission of the copyright owner will infringe copyright. A wide definition of copying is provided in the legislation. In the case of literary, dramatic, musical or artistic works copying involves reproducing the work in any material form (including storage by electronic means).[27] It is made clear that a still photograph might infringe copyright in a film.[28] The protection against copying any typographical arrangement of a published work means making a facsimile copy of the arrangement.[29] This definition is wide enough to include not only photocopying but also transmissions by means of fax machines.

There are, however, certain acts which may be done in relation to copyright works which do not involve any infringement.[30] The various permitted acts must be construed independently of each other.[31] There is a defence of "fair dealing" so far as research, private study, criticism, review and news reporting are concerned

---

[19] s. 3(1). "Dramatic work" includes a work of dance or mime, and a "musical work" is a work consisting of music excluding any words or action intended to be sung, spoken or performed with the music.

[20] s. 4(1).

[21] s. 16(1)(a)–(e).

[22] s. 17.

[23] s. 18.

[24] s. 19.

[25] s. 20; it has been held that the incorporation by the owners of one newspaper in their Internet website of headlines appearing in another newspaper's website and giving access to stories in that other newspaper's website constituted a prima facie infringement of s. 20, being the broadcasting or inclusion of a copyrighted work in a cable programme service: *Shetland Times Ltd v. Wills*, 1997 S.L.T. 669.

[26] s. 21.

[27] s. 17(2).

[28] s. 17(4).

[29] s. 17(5).

[30] See generally, s. 28 and Chap. III.

[31] s. 28(4).

(provided in the case of criticism, review or news reporting a sufficient acknowledgment of the original is given).[32] In the case of education, copyright in a literary, dramatic, musical or artistic work is not infringed so long as it is done in the course of or in preparation for instruction, provided the copying is done by a teacher or student and is not by means of a reprographic process.[33] However, there are special licence arrangements which enable educational establishments to make reprographic copies from published literary, dramatic or musical works without infringing copyright.[34] There are also a variety of acts exceptionally permitted within educational establishments.[35] In addition there are a range of special rights in relation to copyright material available to those involved in libraries and archives[36] as well as in public administration.[37]

The 1988 Act also introduced a right in the author of a copyright   4.08 literary, dramatic, musical or artistic work to be identified as author and for the director of a copyright film to be identified as director.[38] Rights arising from such identification are known as "moral rights" and include the right to object to false attribution of work,[39] the right to privacy of certain photographs and films,[40] and the right to object to derogatory treatment of one's work.[41] A person will only infringe the right of identification if the author or director has asserted his right in due manner.[42] There are exceptions where no right to identification can be asserted. These arise in the case of computer programs, the design of a typeface and any computer-generated work[43] as well as where the copyright vests in the employer.[44] There are also a variety of actions which do not infringe the moral right[45] including the reporting of current events, incidental

---

[32] ss. 29 and 30.

[33] s. 32(1).

[34] s. 36. In addition, an educational establishment can copy up to 1 per cent of any work in any quarter year.

[35] See s. 34 (performing, playing or showing work in the course of activities of an educational establishment) and s. 35 (recording by educational establishments of broadcasts and cable programmes).

[36] See ss. 37–44.

[37] Copyright is not infringed by anything done for the purposes of parliamentary or judicial proceedings or the proceedings of a Royal Commission or statutory inquiry—sections 45 and 46.

[38] Chap. IV.

[39] s. 84.

[40] s. 85.

[41] s. 80.

[42] s. 78.

[43] s. 79(2).

[44] s. 79(3).

[45] s. 79(4) and (5).

inclusion in an artistic work, sound recording etc., as well as examination questions, parliamentary and judicial proceedings and Royal Commissions.

(b) Duration of Copyright

4.09   Copyright in literary, dramatic, musical or artistic works expires at the end of 70 years from the end of the calendar year in which the author dies.[46] As far as sound recordings are concerned, copyright lasts for 50 years from the end of the calendar year in which the recording was released, although in the case of an unpublished recording copyright subsists only for 50 years from the date in which it was made.[47] A sound recording is "released" when it is first published, played in public, broadcast or included in a cable programme service. Copyright in a film expires at the end of 70 years from the calendar year in which the last of the film's principal director, screenplay author, dialogue author or composer of the film's score dies.[48] Copyright in broadcasts and cable programmes expires at the end of 50 years from the end of the calendar year in which the broadcast was made or the programme was included in a cable programme service.[49] Copyright in a typographical arrangement of a published edition expires at the end of 25 years from the end of the year in which the edition was first published.[50]

In addition to copyright itself, any person who publishes for the first time a previously unpublished work in respect of which copyright protection has expired has a property right known as a publication right. This right, which is said to be equivalent to copyright, subsists for 25 years from the end of the calendar year of first publication.[51]

(c) Ownership of Copyright

4.10   The Act makes it clear that the author is the creator of the work[52] and declares that such a person is the first owner of the copyright.[53] The copyright of works produced by employees in the course of their

---

[46] s. 12(1): 70 years was substituted for the previous 50 years by the Duration of Copyright and Rights in Performances Regulations 1995.
[47] s. 13A, inserted by the Duration of Copyright and Rights in Performances Regulations 1995.
[48] s. 13B, inserted by the Copyright and Rights in Performances Regulations 1995.
[49] s. 14(1).
[50] s. 15.
[51] Copyright and Related Rights Regulations 1996.
[52] s. 9(1). For the rules for identifying the author in the case of sound recording, film, broadcast, cable programme or typographical arrangement of a published edition, see s. 9(2)(a)–(d).
[53] s. 11(1).

employment belongs in the first place to the employer, subject to any agreement to the contrary.[54] Ownership of copyright generally carries with it the exclusive right to sue for infringement of the copyright.

(d) Transfer of Copyright and Moral Rights

Copyright is transmissible by assignation, by will or by operation 4.11 of law as moveable property.[55] An assignation is not effective unless it is in writing and signed by or on behalf of the assignor.[56] No particular form of words is required. Copyright may be assigned partially, either in respect of one of the bundle of rights which would otherwise be exclusive to the copyright owner, or in respect of part of the time for which the copyright shall subsist. Where a work is unpublished at the author's death and the work itself is bequeathed in terms of the deceased's will, the copyright will pass with it. Moral rights are not assignable[57] although they may be transmitted on death by will or on intestacy.[58]

(e) Remedies for Infringement of Copyright

An infringement of copyright is actionable by the copyright 4.12 owner[59] in the Court of Session. In any action for infringement of copyright the owner may seek relief by way of damages, interdict or count, reckoning and payment.[60] An owner also has the right to apply to the court (in this case, including the sheriff court) for an order that the infringing copy be delivered up to him.[61] There are also limited rights to seize infringing copies and other articles.[62]

(2) PATENTS

(a) Nature of a Patent

A patent is a monopoly right given to inventors to prevent others 4.13 making or using their inventions. The law regulating patents is to be found primarily in the Patents Act 1977. This Act protects inventors from infringement of their patent rights and sets out a procedure by

---

[54] s. 11(2).
[55] ss. 90 and 177.
[56] s. 90(3).
[57] s. 94.
[58] s. 95.
[59] s. 96.
[60] s. 96(2).
[61] s. 99.
[62] s. 100.

which applications for a patent can be dealt with by the Patent Office. Unlike copyright, where protection is provided by copyright law as soon as the work is created, an invention will only be protected through the existence of a patent once the inventor has sought and obtained such a right. A patent may be granted for an invention only if the following conditions are satisfied. First, the invention must be new[63] and an invention is new if it does not form part of the state of the art.[64] The state of the art comprises all matter (whether a product, a process, information about either or anything else) which has at any time before the date of the application been made available to the public by written or oral description, by use or in any other way.[65] Secondly, it must involve an inventive step.[66] An inventive step is something which is not obvious to a person skilled in the art, having regard to any matter which forms part of the state of the art.[67] Thirdly, it must be capable of industrial application[68] by being made or used in any kind of industry, including agriculture.[69] Furthermore, it must not otherwise be excluded by the Act.[70]

The Act does not define an invention although it does make it clear that certain things cannot be the subject of a patent application. These include:

(i) a discovery, scientific theory or mathematical method;
(ii) a literary, dramatic, musical or artistic work or any other aesthetic creation whatsoever (a matter for copyright law);
(iii) a scheme, rule or method for performing a mental act, playing a game or doing business, or a computer program; and
(iv) the presentation of information.[71]

Further, a patent cannot be granted for an invention the publication or exploitation of which would be generally expected to encourage offensive, immoral or anti-social behaviour or for any variety of animal or plant or any essentially biological process for the production of animals or plants, not being a micro-biological process or the product of such a process.[72]

---

[63] Patents Act 1977, s. 1(1)(a).
[64] s. 2(1).
[65] s. 2(2).
[66] s. 1(1)(b).
[67] s. 3.
[68] s. 1(1)(c).
[69] s. 4(1).
[70] s. 1(1)(d).
[71] s. 1(2)(a)–(d).
[72] s. 1(3).

(b) Application for a Patent

As far as the Patents Act is concerned, the act of making an 4.14
invention confers no rights upon the inventor. The onus is upon
the inventors, or a person acting on their behalf, to apply to the
Patent Office for patent rights. Any such application must contain
a request for the grant of a patent, a specification containing a
description of the invention in a manner which is clear enough
and complete enough for the invention to be performed by a
person skilled in the art, a statement of claim and any drawing
where appropriate and an abstract.[73] The date of filing of a patent
application is crucial because it sets a priority date giving that
inventor precedence over any similar applications by others which
are submitted at a later date.[74] The details of the application
must be published and advertised in the journal of the Patent
Office.[75]

Thereafter, the inventor may request that the Patent Office
appoint an examiner to conduct a preliminary examination and
search to ensure that the application complies with all the formal
requirements of the Act (*i.e.* is it accompanied by a specification and
claim and an abstract?).[76] If the applicant wishes the application
process to continue, a request must be made for a substantive
examination which is the critical stage in the award of a patent.
It is at this stage that the examiner will determine the substantive
issues pertaining to the patent application—whether the invention is
novel, involves an inventive step, is capable of industrial application
and is not otherwise excluded by the Act—and will report on these
matters to the Comptroller-General.[77] If the examiner reports that
the application complies with the requirements of the Act, the
comptroller will grant the applicant a patent.

(c) The Effect of a Patent

A patent is initially awarded for four years, and may be extended 4.15
on an annual basis to a maximum duration of 20 years.[78] Any patent
and any right in or under it is incorporeal moveable property.[79] As
such it is capable of being assigned to third parties, so long as the
assignation is subscribed in accordance with the Requirements of

---

[73] s. 14(2) and (3).
[74] See generally, s. 5.
[75] s. 16(1).
[76] s. 17.
[77] s. 18.
[78] s. 25(1).
[79] s. 31(2).

Writing (Scotland) Act 1995, and of being used as security.[80] A licence may also be granted by a proprietor of a patent for the working of the invention by others.[81] Where a patent is granted to two or more persons, each has an equal undivided share in the patent. Each can do any act which would otherwise be an infringement without the consent of the others, but none of those entitled can assign a share in the patent without such consent.

The basic right conferred on the inventor by the patent is a right to take action against any person who infringes its terms either directly or indirectly. Direct infringement arises when a person, without the consent of the proprietor of the patent, makes, disposes of, offers to dispose of, uses or imports a product or keeps it for disposal or some other purpose.[82] A similar prohibition applies to a patented process.[83] Patent rights are also infringed directly if someone uses the process or offers it for use when they know, or it is obvious to a reasonable person in the circumstances, that its use is without the consent of the proprietor.[84] There is an indirect infringement if a person, while the patent is in force and without the proprietor's consent, supplies or offers to supply a person with the means, relating to an essential element of the invention, of putting it into effect.[85]

(d) Remedies for Infringement

4.16   Proprietors of patents have the right to seek interdict in the Court of Session to prevent the defender infringing the patent and a declarator that the patent is valid and has been infringed. They can also obtain damages in respect of infringements or an account of profits and an order requiring the defender to deliver up or destroy any products which entail an infringement of the patent.[86]

(3) TRADE MARKS

4.17   At common law a person has no property right in a trade name,[87] although there may be circumstances where a person may have a cause of action for passing-off if another person uses that name

---

[80] s. 31(3) and (6).
[81] s. 31(4).
[82] s. 60(1)(a).
[83] s. 60(1)(b) and (c).
[84] s. 70(1)(b).
[85] s. 60(2).
[86] s. 61(1).
[87] See the judgment of Lord President Dunedin in *Charles P. Kinnell and Co. Ltd v. A. Ballantine and Sons*, 1910 S.C. 246 at 251.

fraudulently or to cause avoidable confusion. Essentially, in such a case the person who argues that the trade name has been infringed would have to establish that the name has become so associated with that person's particular goods that they are regarded in the market as theirs.[88] However, there is also statutory regulation of trade marks. The Trade Marks Act 1994 obliges the registrar to maintain a register of trade marks[89] and to enter:

(i) all registered trade marks;
(ii) notifications of assignations and transfers; and
(iii) such other matters as may be prescribed.[90]

A person who wishes the protection of the Act may register a trade mark in respect of particular goods or classes of goods with the comptroller. The registration of a trade mark is for a period of 10 years and can be renewed for further periods of 10 years.[91] Registration as proprietor of a trade mark in respect of any goods generally gives that person the exclusive right to the use of that trade mark in relation to those goods and entitles the proprietor to prevent others using the trade mark or implying that they have a right to use it.[92]

A registered trade mark is incorporeal moveable property and as such is transmissible by assignation, will or operation of law.[93] Where a registered trade mark is owned by two or more persons, none of them can grant a licence to use the registered trade mark, or grant a security over it, without the consent of the other owners. It may be transmitted in connection with the sale of the goodwill of a business or on its own. Any assignation of a registered trade mark must be in writing and signed by the assignor.[94] All assignations must be registered, and an unregistered assignation is ineffective against a third party who acquires a competing interest in or under the trade mark in ignorance of the assignation.[95]

4.18

---

[88] See generally, W. J. Stewart, *Delict and related Obligations* (2nd ed., W.Green, 1993), paras 3.7–3.13.
[89] A trade mark is defined by s. 1 of the 1994 Act as "any sign capable of being represented graphically which is capable of distinguishing goods or services of one undertaking from those of other undertakings. A trade mark may, in particular, consist of words (including personal names), designs, letters, numerals or the shape of goods or their packaging".
[90] Trade Marks Act 1994, s. 63.
[91] s. 42.
[92] s. 9.
[93] s. 24.
[94] s. 24(3).
[95] s. 25.

CHAPTER 5

FORMS OF LANDOWNERSHIP IN SCOTLAND

1. FEUDAL LANDHOLDING IN SCOTLAND

(1) ORIGINS AND DEVELOPMENT

5.01 As the White Paper *Land Tenure in Scotland: A plan for reform* stated in 1969[1]:

> "Most land in Scotland is held today on a system of tenure which has its origin in medieval times. This system is feudal tenure which, in its practical operation in the latter half of the present century, is far removed from its beginnings in a feudal society. A feature of that society was the practice whereby a landowning nobleman would grant to a loyal follower the right to a piece of land in return for service: this service would commonly take the form of an obligation to arm and to fight in wars in which the overlord became engaged."

This form of tenure first appeared in Scotland around the time of the twelfth century. It was developed under English influence, particularly during the reign of David I (1124–1153) of Scotland. It depends on an hierarchical structure, with the monarch as ultimate lord. Each landholder appeared in this hierarchical chain and was known as a vassal or feuar which meant he was required to pay certain homage to his lord and ultimately the monarch because of his position as "paramount superior".

5.02   In the beginning, the system of feudal tenure in Scotland developed through the King granting tracts of land to his supporters for the assistance they had given him in wars, etc. In return for this grant, the grantee paid homage and service to the

---

[1] Cmnd 4099.

King. This homage symbolised the relationship of "lord" and man, and the idea of service formed the basis for the legal classification of the tenure.[2] Moreover, it also ensured that the grantee's title was conditional and not absolute since the grantor retained an interest in the land.

The whole system was based on a personal grant of land to the King's servant. As a result of the personal nature of the relationship, when feudal tenure was in its infancy, the grant was revocable during the grantee's life. This gradually changed to revocation on the grantee's death, until ultimately the law developed to permit the land to pass to the grantee's heir. A further aspect of the personal nature of the relationship was that the feudal system forbade the substitution of another for the original grantee. This was on the basis that, since the grant was in theory personal, the superior was entitled to insist on retaining the vassal in the chain. If the vassal wished to dispose of his land then he could subinfeudate, *i.e.* become the lord of the next individual by adding a further link to the chain. This contrasts with the English law, where subinfeudation was forbidden by the statute *Quia Emptores* of 1290. In any case, in later times in Scotland, substitution tended to be more prevalent than subinfeudation. However, even when there was substitution of a new vassal for a previous owner, given the pervasive and personal nature of the feudal system, the superior had to approve this substitution of vassals. This was called "entry" and entailed the superior either offering a fresh feudal grant to the new vassal or confirming the continuance of the original feudal grant which had been made to the old vassal. Nowadays obtaining a duly recorded or registered title to the property also ensures entry.[3]

In later times, grants of land were sold in return for both a purchase price and a fixed annual payment to the superior known as the feu duty. Following changes introduced by the Land Tenure Reform (Scotland) Act 1974 it is incompetent to impose a new feu duty in a deed executed after September 1, 1974. In addition, where a feu is conveyed for valuable consideration (typically on sale), after this date the feu duty (so long as it is allocated) is deemed to be redeemed, and the redemption money forms a real burden secured on the feu in favour of the superior. The amount required to redeem a feu duty is calculated according

5.03

---

[2] For a discussion of the older forms of feudal tenure see W. M. Gordon, *Scottish Land Law* (W. Green, 1989), paras 2–07 to 2–18.
[3] This process was rationalised by the Titles to Land Consolidation (Scotland) Act 1868, and is a matter which really relates to conveyancing.
[4] Land Tenure Reform (Scotland) Act 1974, s. 5.

to a statutory formula.[4] There is also provision for voluntary
redemption of feu duty by a proprietor of the feu serving notice
on the superior at any term of Whitsunday or Martinmas.[5] The
fact that there is no feu duty, however, in no way affects the
feudal relationship. The feudal nature of the tenure is otherwise
preserved and the superior is still entitled to impose and enforce
certain restrictions on the use of the land.

(2) FEUDAL RELATIONSHIP TODAY

5.04 Let us look at a situation where a landowner, X, who owns an estate
directly from the Crown, decides to sell part of it to a building
company for housing development. Traditionally, along with the
sale price a feu duty would have been imposed, since the concept of
the feudal chain necessitated the existence of a feu duty. However, as
we have seen, in any sale after September 1, 1974 no feu duty may be
imposed. The builder, Y, will then proceed to build a housing estate
and, on completion, each house will be feued to buyers A, B, C, and
D. In the course of these transactions we have built up a chain as
shown below.

Feudal Relationships

(Ultimate superior)	Crown
(Superior to Y)	Landowner X
(Superior to A, B, C, D)	Building Firm Y
(Feuars or vassals)	Owners A, B, C, D

This chain can extend for as long as the land will bear it.

(3) RIGHTS AND RELATIONSHIPS OF SUPERIORS AND FEUARS

5.05 The nature of the feudal relationship permits the superior to impose
certain conditions known as "real conditions" on the feuar's ownership.[6] These might include restrictions on the feuar's use of the
property. Thus, in the above example it may be a condition of the feu

---

[5] Now May 28 and November 28 respectively: Term and Quarter Days (Scotland)
Act 1990, s. 1.
[6] See Chap. 8.

granted to Y that Y is to build only houses, and not a shopping plaza, etc. The superior may also retain certain of the property rights associated with the land such as ownership of, and the right to work, minerals. Similarly, when Y conveys the houses to A, B, C and D there might well be a stipulation that no garages are to be erected in the gardens of the houses, or that no house may be used as an office or pub. Such conditions run with the land and therefore, so far as unimplemented or continuing, bind all successive owners of the *dominium utile* (see below).

All of this is possible because, in feudal theory, ownership of the land is divided between the superior and the feuar. The feuar is the owner of the land for practical purposes, but the superior retains a less tangible right of ownership, which allows the superior to enforce the feuing conditions and (if appropriate) collect the feu duty. The rights acquired by the feuar are collectively called the *dominium utile*, and the rights retained by the superior are known as the *dominium directum*. These rights can be summarised as follows:

> *dominium directum*—empowers the superior to enforce the conditions of the grant;
>
> *dominium utile*—gives the feuar exclusive right of possession and enjoyment of the land so long as the feuing conditions are respected;
>
> *dominium plenum*—this is the totality of all rights in the land, and exists where there is no feudal relationship.

In each of the transactions described above, certain rights have 5.06 been granted in return for the performance of certain duties, principally (before 1974) the payment of feu duty. Although A, B, C and D acquire ownership (in the sense of the *dominium utile*), Y has not given up its entire interest in the land. Y still has an interest in ensuring that the feuing conditions are observed, and any appropriate feu duty paid timeously. If a feuar should fail to comply with any of the feuing conditions (including the payment of feu duty) the superior is entitled to recover possession of the property. This is achieved by obtaining a "declarator of irritancy" from the court, the effect of which is that the feuar forfeits the feu and loses all right in the land. In obtaining a declarator of irritancy, however, the superior will forego all arrears of feu duty.

(4) HOW A FEUDAL GRANT IS EFFECTED

An original feudal grant can be effected by one of three writs—feu 5.07 charter, feu disposition and feu contract. The first two deeds are unilateral and are signed only by the granter. The latter of the two is the most common form of feudal grant in modern times. Apart from the feu contract being bilateral, there was very little difference between the three types of deed. More important in the modern context is the question of infeftment. Before a person is entitled to exercise feudal rights that person must be infeft. In the old days this involved "delivery of the sasine" where there was a symbolic delivery of the land through a ceremony conducted on the property. Later, infeftment took place by recording an instrument of sasine (a document, separate from the feu deed itself, narrating the circumstances and terms of the feudal grant) in the land registers. The conveyancing reforms of the nineteenth century[7] permitted the recording of the feudal grant or deed of transfer itself, rather than an instrument of sasine, in the land registers. Since the Land Registration (Scotland) Act 1979, registration of title will suffice in order to create an effective feudal right. As we shall see, it is the registration of title which creates a real right over the property vested in the feuar.

(5) Reform

5.08 The Scottish Law Commission[8] have confirmed their intention to work towards the complete abolition of the feudal system, and its replacement with a system of absolute ownership, and aim to issue a report on the matter by 1999.

2. Other Forms of Landownership in Scotland

5.09 There are three other forms of landholding in Scotland. These are allodial landholding, contracts of ground annual and long leases.

(1) Allodial Land

5.10 Although most of the land in Scotland is held under feudal tenure, there are alternative forms of landholding which probably account for about 20 per cent of the total. The most important of these is allodial land. Unlike feudal tenure, allodial landholding does not rely on the doctrine of "universal derivative tenure". There is no

---

[7] See in this regard the Titles to Land (Scotland) Act 1858 and the Titles to Land Consolidation (Scotland) Act 1868.

[8] *Fifth Programme of Law Reform* (Scot. Law Com. No. 159 (1997)).

derivation of rights through the feudal chain back to the sovereign. Thus allodial property is property which is owned absolutely without acknowledgment of any superior owner.

There are five types of allodial land, as described below:

(a) The Property of the Crown

The paramount superior can clearly have no superior. Moreover, since all land held under feudal tenure can ultimately be derived back to the Crown, the Crown is entitled to the superiority when no other superior can be ascertained. However, this form of landholding not only encompasses Crown superiorities but covers Crown lands as well. Thus land which has never been feued or which has reverted to the Crown also falls under this head.   5.11

(b) The Property of the Prince of Scotland

This was settled on the eldest son of the sovereign by Act of Parliament in 1469.[9]   5.12

(c) Churches, Churchyards, Manses and Glebes

These were exempted from the annexation of Church property after the Reformation.[10] In any case, Scots common law recognised that parish churches and churchyards were held by the heritors of the parish under allodial title.[11] By the Church of Scotland (Property and Endowments) Act 1925, churches and manses became the property of and vested in the General Trustees of the Church of Scotland[12] and churchyards were transferred to parish councils.[13] A glebe is that portion of land and other heritable rights which a parish minister is entitled to in addition to his stipend, and its exact ownership is subject to regulations made by the Scottish Ecclesiastical Commissioners.[14] It would appear that only churchyards are now truly allodial.[15]   5.13

(d) Udal Land

This is the land held in Orkney and Shetland, where the owner does not owe any obligations or duties to a superior landholder.   5.14

---

[9] For a discussion as to whether these lands are genuinely allodial, see W. M. Gordon, *Scottish Land Law* (W. Green, 1989), para. 3–17.

[10] 1587 Act c. 29.

[11] Stair, *Inst.*, II. iii. 4; Erskine, *Inst.*, II, iii, 8.

[12] s. 28.

[13] s. 32.

[14] s. 30.

[15] See *Stair Memorial Encyclopaedia*, Vol. 18, para. 47; Gordon, *op. cit.*, paras 3–11 to 3–16.

Erskine stated that udal land is held by natural possession and might
be proved by witness without there being any title in writing.[16] This
anomalous form of tenure arose from the fact that Orkney and
Shetland were transferred to Scotland in 1468 in security for the
unpaid part of Princess Margaret's dowry to James III of Scotland.
The islands were formally annexed to the Scottish Crown in 1472
when the balance remained unpaid. The Act of 1567[17] declared that
neither Orkney nor Shetland should be subject to the common law
of Scotland but should continue to have their own laws. Gradually
the municipal law has been extended to cover Orkney and Shetland.
To this extent, there has been a conflict between the udal law of
Orkney and Shetland and the municipal law of Scotland, with the
municipal law generally winning the day. However, in *Lord Advocate v. Balfour*[18] it was declared that the Crown is not deemed to
have been the original proprietor in the islands and so could not
claim ownership of salmon fishings.

In *Lord Advocate v. University of Aberdeen*[19] the doctrine "*quod
nullius est fit domini regis*" ("that which is the property of nobody,
belongs to our lord the King") which is feudal in origin, was applied
to give ownership of the "St Ninian's Isle Treasure" to the Crown.
To this extent, there is some doubt as to the exact status of udal
rights to land.[20]

(e) Lands Compulsorily Purchased

5.15   When lands are compulsorily acquired under various statutes,
most notably the Lands Clauses Consolidation (Scotland) Act 1845,
all intermediary superiorities (*i.e.* apart from that of the Crown) are
terminated, and any feu duty is treated as having been redeemed. In
this respect the acquired lands are sometimes said to be allodial.
Since the Crown's ultimate superiority appears to survive, however,
it is probably more correct to classify such lands as truly feudal,[21]
albeit they are allodial for all practical purposes.

(2) Contracts of Ground Annual

5.16 The second form of non-feudal tenure arises under a contract
whereby a stipulated annual payment is due perpetually from the

---

[16] *Inst.*, II, iii, 18.
[17] c. 48.
[18] 1907 S.C. 1360.
[19] 1963 S.C. 533.
[20] For a more detailed discussion of udal law see *Stair Memorial Encyclopaedia*
(1989), Vol. 24.
[21] See Gordon, *op. cit.*, paras 3–18 to 3–21.

lands and secured as a real burden over them. This contract of ground annual does not create a feudal relationship between the parties, but merely a personal obligation on the owner to pay the ground annual with the ground being used as security. It is, therefore, the contract and the security which it creates which oblige the purchaser to pay the ground annual. Payment depends on a creditor-debtor relationship, rather than on a feudal one.

The reason for the existence of the contract of ground annual was that prior to 1874, when the Conveyancing (Scotland) Act was enacted, the right to sub feu was prohibited in lands held under burgage tenure (a particular form of tenure found in towns). The Land Tenure Reform (Scotland) Act 1974 prohibits the imposition of new ground annuals in deeds executed after September 1, 1974. There is also provision in the Act[22] for both the voluntary and compulsory redemption of ground annuals.

(3) LONG LEASES

The Registration of Leases Act 1857 provided that leases of over 20 years' duration (previously 31 years)[23] which had been recorded in the General Register of Sasines were to be effectual against singular successors of the lessor even though the lessee had not entered into possession. Thus the 1857 Act provided an alternative method of acquiring occupation of land without resorting to the concept of feudalism, and it was often used as a basis for transferring land rights when there was a prohibition on subinfeudation.

5.17

Once recorded, a long lease permits occupiers the same sort of enjoyment of their property as they would be given under the terms of a feudal grant. There are now two[24] requirements which must be fulfilled before a long lease can be recorded. First, the deed executing the transfer must be attested in accordance with the provisions of section 6 of the Requirements of Writing (Scotland) Act 1995, and, secondly, the period of the lease must exceed 20 years.

---

[22] ss. 4 and 5.
[23] Amended by the Land Tenure Reform (Scotland) Act 1974, Sched. 6, para. 1.
[24] Formerly, the subjects let could not exceed 50 acres (except in the case of mines). This was repealed by the Land Tenure Reform (Scotland) Act 1974, s. 18 and Sched. 6, para. 5.

CHAPTER 6

ACQUISITION AND DISPOSAL OF HERITAGE

1. ACQUISITION OF HERITABLE PROPERTY

6.01 There are a number of ways in which title to heritable property can be acquired. It may be acquired originally, either by occupation or by prescription; by accession; or derivatively. Original acquisition by occupation may be appropriate for non-feudal land[1] but cannot apply to feudal land since, as was noted in Chapter 5, in feudal theory all land is held from the Crown. This means that mere possession (for example by a squatter) does not confer any rights of ownership under Scots law. Original acquisition by prescription is considered in the following section. Current property ownership may be extended by accession where there is an accumulation of silt carried downstream or a river or sea recedes.[2] Property ownership is acquired derivatively through the transfer of an *ex facie* valid title followed by the recording of that title in a property register in order to create a real right of ownership. The process of transfer of title to heritable property, and the systems of registration of title operating in Scotland, are considered further below.

(1) ORIGINAL ACQUISITION BY OPERATION OF PRESCRIPTION

6.02 Real rights of ownership can also be acquired under the rules of positive prescription. This is appropriate where, in relation to sasine titles, a title has been recorded *a non domino* (by a non-owner) and, in relation to titles registered in the Land Register, in the small number of cases where state indemnity has been excluded. In either case, the passage of time perfects the previously challengeable title and extinguishes any possible right of challenge

---

[1] Erskine, II, i, 11.
[2] Stair, *Inst.*, II. i. 35; Erskine, *Inst.*, II, i, 14; Bell, *Prin.*, §935.

44

or extinguishes the title of any former owner. The law on positive prescription is contained in the Prescription and Limitation (Scotland) Act 1973.

In order for positive prescription to apply, the land in question must be possessed by the party acquiring title (and, if appropriate, by his or her singular successors) for a continuous period of 10 years. The relevant possession must be open, peaceable and without judicial interruption, so that possession acquired by force, fear or stealth will not suffice. Possession in this regard may be either natural or civil. Furthermore, the possession must be founded upon the recording (or, in relation to land in an operational area for the purposes of land registration, the registration) of a deed which is valid *ex facie* and not forged, and which is sufficient in its terms to constitute a title to the land in question. In particular, the title must include a description which is capable of being construed as including the land in question (often referred to as a description which is *habile* to include the land). In conveyancing practice this deed, upon which prescriptive possession is based, is known as the foundation writ.

In relation to land to which land registration applies, possession must be founded upon registration of an interest in land in the Land Register subject to an exclusion of indemnity by the Keeper. If indemnity is not excluded, prescription cannot operate. Furthermore, prescription cannot operate if the registration proceeded upon a deed which was, to the knowledge of the registered proprietor at the time of registration, forged. Unlike sasine titles, where prescription confers a title where there was none previously, prescription in relation to interests registered in the Land Register frees the title from the risk of rectification of the register, and thus perfects a previously voidable title. In respect of both sasine and registered titles, the effect of positive prescription is to render a previously defective title "exempt from challenge".

Other rights are acquired by positive prescription based on 20 years' continuous, open, peaceable possession without judicial interruption. Thus a right of positive servitude or a right of way can be established through possession for this longer period provided, in the case of a positive servitude, the possession is founded upon a deed which is sufficient in its terms (whether expressly or by implication) to constitute the servitude. The period of positive prescription is also 20 years in the case of the acquisition of an interest in the foreshore, or in any salmon fishings, from the Crown.

6.03

(2) NEGATIVE PRESCRIPTION

6.04 Certain rights and obligations related to heritable property can also be affected by negative prescription. The 1973 Act created two negative prescriptions, the long negative prescription of 20 years and the quinquennial (five-year) short negative prescription. Negative prescription of either kind operates to extinguish a relevant obligation which has subsisted for the appropriate period of time without a relevant claim having been made in relation to it and without its subsistence having been acknowledged by the party owing it.

Thus, the obligation to pay rent or feuduty is extinguished if not claimed within the short negative prescription of five years. Only the obligation to make a particular payment prescribes, however: the relationship between the parties (landlord and tenant or superior and vassal) is unaffected, as is the obligation to make future payments.

6.05 Various rights relating to property are extinguished by the long negative prescription. This includes the right of an adjacent proprietor to object to a use of land which constitutes an actionable nuisance, and the right of a party to exercise a servitude right over property. However, real rights of ownership in land and tenants' real rights under recorded leases are imprescriptible and cannot be lost through non-use. Any right exercisable as a *res merae facultatis* (*i.e.* one whose exercise is at the discretion of the party entitled to do so) is also imprescriptible, and this includes the right to collect rent or feuduty, though not the right to a particular instalment of rent or feuduty (which as we have seen can be extinguished by the short negative prescription). Finally, the public's right of navigation in rivers cannot be extinguished by negative prescription.

(3) DERIVATIVE ACQUISITION BY TRANSFER OF TITLE

6.06 This is by far the most common means of acquiring title to heritable property in Scotland. In theory the process is two-fold. In the first stage of the process the infeft proprietor (*i.e.* the party in whom the title is currently vested) and the intending transferee enter into a contract for the transfer of the property. The conclusion of a legally binding agreement between them creates a personal right in favour of the transferee to have the title transferred to him. The contract by itself does not effect a transfer of ownership. In the second stage the transferee registers an executed disposition (or deed of transfer) in his favour in the appropriate property register, thereby acquiring a real right of ownership or becoming "infeft". Ownership transfers at the point of registration of the transferee's title, and not before.

Some commentators have argued (largely on the basis of one

judicial comment on the matter)[3] that there exists an intermediate stage, coinciding with delivery of the executed disposition to the purchaser or transferee, in which the transferee enjoys a quasi-real right, which can be made real by the act of registration, and the transferor retains only a bare title without any continuing right to deal with the property. Such a possibility has now been firmly rejected by the court in *Sharp v. Thomson*.[4] The courts have accepted the concept of the so-called "unitary theory of ownership" of Scottish heritable property, the effect of which is that there can be only one real right of ownership in property at any given time.[5]

(4) Contracts for the Transfer of Heritable Property

Contracts to buy and sell heritable property were previously *obliga-* 6.07 *tiones literis* and so required probative writing to be effectual. That category of contract has now been abolished[6] and although a contract for the creation or transfer of an interest in land must still be in writing, it is considered formally valid if it (or each of the constituent parts of it) is signed by the person(s) entering into it. No special form of words is required,[7] but the exchange of missives (or formal letters) which constitute the contract should encapsulate the terms and conditions of the sale. Acceptance of an offer by fax is effective to conclude a binding contract.[8] At this stage the parties owe personal obligations to each other based upon the missives. To complete the purchaser's right to the property, there must be delivery and registration of a disposition (deed of transfer) signed by the seller.

A contract for the transfer of heritable property has a number of legal consequences. First, it creates a personal right against the seller for delivery of a valid disposition, and the buyer may be entitled to sue the seller on the contract for damages if he fails to do so. Secondly, risk (of damage to, or destruction of, the property pending

---

[3] Lord President Emslie's *obiter dictum* in *Gibson v. Hunter Home Designs Ltd,* 1976 S.C. 23 to the apparent effect that title transferred to a purchaser upon delivery of an executed disposition in his favour is now almost certainly permanently discredited in light of the decision of the House of Lords in *Sharp v. Thomson,* 1997 S.L.T. 636.

[4] The Inner House analysis of the law on this point, reported at 1995 S.L.T. 837, was not disturbed by the House of Lords which, although allowing the appeal from the Inner Court's decision, did so on a point of statutory interpretation only.

[5] For a useful review of the state of the law on this matter post-Sharp, see K. G. C. Reid's, "Jam Today: *Sharp* in the House of Lords", 1997 S.L.T. (News) 79.

[6] Requirements of Writing (Scotland) Act 1995, s. 1.

[7] A. J. MacDonald, *Conveyancing*; J. H. Sinclair, *Handbook of Conveyancing Practice in Scotland* (3rd ed., 1995).

[8] *McIntosh v. Allan*, 1997 S.C.L.R. 1171.

completion of the transfer of title) automatically passes to the buyer under Scots law when such a contract is entered into[9] unless the transfer of risk is delayed by the operation of a suspensive condition in the contract, or the parties agree that risk is to remain with the seller until the date on which the purchaser takes entry to the property.

6.08   Two further aspects of a contract for the transfer of heritable property merit comment. First, problems have arisen as to conditions in the missives being superseded by the terms of the disposition. The issue was highlighted in *Winston v. Patrick*[10] where there had been a sale of a bungalow with an extension. The missives indicated that the seller warranted that all local authority requirements in relation to the property had been fulfilled. This clause was not repeated in the disposition of sale. It transpired that a building warrant had not been obtained and the purchasers sued in damages for breach of contract on the basis that the sellers had not constructed the extension in accordance with their obligations under the missives. The Second Division considered that the clause did not incorporate any personal obligation on the seller to do anything in the future. At best the clause was merely a statement as to the condition of the property at the date of the missives. This meant that although the purchaser could found on the warranty prior to delivery of the disposition, once the disposition had been delivered no action of damages for breach of contract could be entertained. The result of this case was the widespread use of clauses indicating that the missives were not to be superseded by the disposition. Extensive litigation[11] on the same point followed over a period of years, and the law was far from certain. Parliament has recognised this problem and, based on recommendations made to it by the Scottish Law Commission, has passed the Contract (Scotland) Act 1997 which provides that delivery of the disposition will not in future supersede the terms of the missives unless the parties have expressly agreed that it shall. This applies from June 21, 1997. The 1997 Act also deals with another point related to missives—known as the prior communings rule—which meant that when a contract was reduced to writing it was not competent to lead parole or informal written evidence to rebut the terms of the written contract. For the future the presumption that a contract reduced to writing by the parties contains all of the agreed terms is a rebuttable one, and oral or written evidence may be used to prove otherwise. Parties will,

---

[9] *Sloans Dairies Ltd v. Glasgow Corporation*, 1977 S.C. 223; 1979 S.L.T. 17.
[10] 1980 S.C. 246.
[11] For an excellent summary of the litigation and the academic literature on this subject, see *Stair Memorial Encyclopaedia* (1988), Vol. 6, para. 566.

however, be able to include within the contract a statement that all agreed terms have been included in it, and such a statement shall be conclusive.

The second problem is whether or not certain items attached to the property are included in the sale. Where the missives are silent on a disputed item the rules relating to fixtures apply. An item is a fixture if the moveable is so affixed to the heritage as to become a part of the heritable property. This is another application of the law of accession which was discussed earlier in this book. If an item is not a fixture it remains a moveable and so would not be covered by the missives so far as they specifically relate to heritage. The law of fixtures was explained by Lord Chelmsford in *Brand's Trustees v. Brand's Trustees*.[12] He said that the meaning of the word fixture is:

"[A]nything annexed to the [heritage], that is, fastened to or connected with it, not in mere juxtaposition with the soil. Whatever is so annexed becomes part of the [heritage], and the person who was the owner of it when it was a [moveable] loses his property in it, which immediately vests in the owner of the soil."

An article which meets these requirements would be a fixture and 6.09 would be regarded as being part of the heritage. In the *Brand's Trustees* case the Lord Chancellor stated that there were two general rules in relation to the law of fixtures. The first of these rules is that whatever is fixed to the heritage becomes part of the heritable property and belongs to the heritable owner. To this rule there are no exceptions. The second rule is that once something has become part of the heritage it cannot be removed by someone other than the heritable proprietor. However, the law recognises certain exceptions to the second rule, particularly in relation to the right to remove trade fixtures which a tenant has erected in the course of trade.

Under *Brand's Trustees* the test for considering whether a moveable had become heritage was based upon the degree of affixation.[13] It has been argued that this approach, which concentrates solely upon affixation, runs contrary to the previous Scots law where account was also taken of the presumed intention of the parties.[14] It

---

[12] (1876) 3 R. (H.L.) 16.

[13] In *Cliffplant Ltd v. Kinnaird*, 1982 S.L.T. 2 the Inner House relied solely on the degree of affixation in deciding whether the article in that case was heritable. This part of the decision has been overruled by a Full Bench in *Scottish Discount Co. v. Blin*, 1985 S.C. 216.

[14] K. G. C. Reid, "The Lord Chancellor's Fixtures" (1983) 28 J.L.S.S. 49. See also the earlier decisions in *Fisher v. Dixon* (1843) 5 D. 775; *Dowall v. Miln* (1874) 1 R. 1180.

was thereby possible to have some regard to the relationship of the parties when deciding whether or not the article was a fixture.[15] In *Scottish Discount Co. v. Blin*[16] it was held that the question as to whether an item is a fixture should not be resolved solely on the basis of the degree of physical attachment but regard should also be paid to a number of other factors including the intention of the party who attached it and the relationship between the parties involved.

(a) Manner of Attachment

6.10   It is now clear that the court must consider other factors beyond the simple issue of physical attachment. In the *Blin* case the Lord President declared that the correct test was that spelled out by Professor Gloag in the 1929 edition of the *Encyclopaedia of the Laws of Scotland*.[17] Thus, as well as the degree and extent of attachment, the following other elements should also be considered: whether the article can be removed *integre, salve et commode, i.e.* without the destruction of itself as a separate thing, or of the soil or building to which it is attached; whether its annexation was of permanent or quasi-permanent character; whether the building to which it is attached was specially adapted for its use; how far the use or enjoyment of the soil or building would be affected by its removal[18]; and the intention of the party attaching it. This intention must be discovered from the nature of the article and the building and the manner in which it is affixed. It is not to be proved by extrinsic evidence or deduced from the fact that the relationship is one of landlord and tenant.

It is impossible to lay down any exact rules as to what constitutes a fixture. Each case will depend on its own facts and circumstances. However, the greater the attachment of an article (particularly if this involves dismantling it in order to remove it), the more likely it is that the item will be a fixture irrespective of the intention of the party attaching it. On the other hand, it is possible for an article to be a fixture without there being any physical attachment. For example, in *Howie's Trustees v. McLay*[19] it was held that five lace looms bolted to an iron soleplate attached by its own weight to the floor were heritable. However, in such a case the burden of proof is on the person who

---

[15] In *Syme v. Harvey* (1861) 24 D. 202 greenhouses which had been erected by a market gardener were held to be moveable largely because they had been erected by a tenant in the course of trade.

[16] 1985 S.C. 216.

[17] See Vol. 7, paras 362 and 363.

[18] In this regard see *Christie v. Smith's Exr*, 1949 S.C. 572 where one reason why a summerhouse was held to be heritable was because of the gap that was left in a boundary wall when it was removed.

[19] (1902) 5 F. 214.

asserts that the article is heritable to prove it is so.[20] Moreover, there are
some types of fixture where there need be no physical attachment
whatsoever: these are constructive fixtures, such as a key, which is
constructively annexed because it is accessory to the heritage.

The purpose of the affixation is also relevant. Was the aim of the 6.11
attachment to improve the heritage, or to permit the better enjoyment of the moveable itself? Even though a moveable is attached to
the heritage to a considerable degree, it will not become heritable
unless the purpose of the annexation is to improve the heritage. This
means that carpets nailed to floors or pictures hung on walls do not
become fixtures despite the fact that they are attached to heritage,
since the purpose of the attachment is to aid display of the moveables, not to improve the heritage.

(b) Right of Removal

This may well be a matter which the parties will consider expressly 6.12
in their contract, and the terms of that contract would normally be
accepted by the court in relation to any disputes over removal.
However, the terms of such a contract would only bind the parties to
it and may not affect third parties. In *Hobson v. Gorringe*[21] it was
held that the terms of a hire-purchase agreement which permitted
the owner to remove a fixture if the hirer defaulted in his payments
did not affect the rights of the hirer's mortgagee to claim the article
since he had rights over the heritage. This general approach has
found some favour in Scotland although it may be the hire-purchase
agreement could be examined where the question whether the article
is a fixture is in fine balance.[22] If there is no express agreement over
removal, the court is likely to take into account the relationship of
the parties before deciding whether the fixture can be removed. This
principle applies in a variety of relationships—seller and purchaser
and landlord and tenant are the most important.

(i) Seller and Purchaser

This is clearly a case where the terms of a contract are likely to 6.13
determine any right of removal. Where there is no term in the
contract of sale the courts have generally considered that the fixture
should remain with the heritage. The courts have concluded that the
most important consideration is whether the fixture can be removed
without injury to itself and to the heritage.[23] Some guide to the

---

[20] *Holland v. Hodgson* (1872) L.R. 7 C.P. 328.
[21] [1897] 1 Ch. 182.
[22] See in particular the judgment of Lord President Emslie in *Scottish Discount
Co. v. Blin*, 1985 S.C. 216 at 234–235.
[23] *Jamieson v. Welsh* (1900) 3 F. 176.

courts' approach can be gleaned from the rating cases under the
Lands Valuation Acts. In *Cowans v. Assessor for Forfarshire*[24] one
reason why the court considered that grates, gas fittings, chande-
liers, blinds, curtain poles and picture rods could not be removed
was that not only were they for the comfortable enjoyment of the
house, but they were necessary in order to render it habitable.

(ii) Landlord and Tenant

6.14   In this situation considerations of public policy have given the
tenant a larger right to remove a fixture. This was accepted in the
Brand's Trustees case, where the Lord Chancellor explained that a
limited right of removal was given to tenants particularly in the case
of trade fixtures. The reason why tenants are given greater rights of
removal is in order to encourage them to improve the property
which they are occupying. There is some incentive for tenants who
know that they can take away the improvements made to the
property during their occupation. The law divides fixtures removable by a tenant into three groups: trade fixtures, ornamental
fixtures and agricultural fixtures.

6.15   **(1) Trade Fixtures**. It has long been established that a tenant may
remove fixtures which he has attached to the heritage for the
purposes of his trade. In *Syme v. Harvey*[25] it was held that since
a number of greenhouses had been constructed by a market gardener
for the purpose of his trade, they could be removed on the expiry of
the lease. However, this case was decided before the *Brand's Trustees*
case and seems to be based on the view that the articles retained their
moveable characteristics. Nonetheless, even *Brand's Trustees* recognises that tenants may at the end of the lease remove trade fixtures
which they have erected.

6.16   **(2) Ornamental Fixtures**. In this situation the tenant is also given
limited rights of removal. In *Spyer v. Phillipson*[26] it was held that a
tenant could remove an ornamental fixture so long as it was for the
better enjoyment of the article itself.

6.17   **(3) Agricultural Fixtures**. It seems that the common law was less
favourable to the tenant in the case of agricultural fixtures.[27] To
some extent, this is now regulated by statute. The Agricultural

---

[24] 1910 S.C. 810.
[25] (1861) 24 D. 201.
[26] [1931] 2 Ch. 183.
[27] Rankine, *The Law of Leases in Scotland* (3rd ed., W. Green, 1916), pp. 301–302.

Holdings (Scotland) Act 1991 declares that any engine, machinery, fencing or other fixture affixed by the tenant, any building erected by him, remain the property of the tenant and are removable by him for up to six months after the expiry of the lease, on making good any damage caused by the removal.[28]

(5) ACQUIRING A REAL RIGHT TO HERITABLE PROPERTY

As we saw above, a contract for the transfer of heritable property 6.18 confers only a personal right on the buyer. In order to convert that into a real right (*i.e.* one which is enforceable not just against the seller, but against the whole world) the buyer must complete his title by registering his title in the appropriate property register: either the Register of Sasines or the Land Register of Scotland.

Transfer of ownership of heritable property is achieved by means of a document (usually a disposition, although if a new feudal estate is being created it may be a feu contract, a feu charter or a feu disposition) which is executed by the person transferring the title. Since the effect of the disposition is to transfer rights in heritable property, the disposition must be in writing and be executed in accordance with the provisions of the Requirements of Writing (Scotland) Act 1995. In practice this usually means that the last page of the disposition, and any attached plan or other annexation, should be signed by the granter in the presence of a single witness, who should also sign the last page: Requirements of Writing (Scotland) Act 1995, ss. 3 and 7. For dispositions executed before August 1, 1995 the common law rules, particularly the need for two witnesses, must have been complied with. Once the disposition has been delivered to the buyer (usually in exchange for payment of the price) the buyer must complete his title by registration, and thereby acquire a real right to the property. The process of registration of title is considered below.

2. IMPACT OF LAND TENURE REFORM (SCOTLAND) ACT 1974

(1) INTRODUCTION

The Land Tenure Reform (Scotland) Act 1974 has had a major 6.19 impact upon the operation of the feudal system. However, like the Conveyancing and Feudal Reform (Scotland) Act 1970, which will be discussed in Chapter 8, the 1974 Act did not bring about

---

[28] s. 18.

the abolition of the feudal system, but merely created a number of mechanisms for the eventual elimination of feu duty. The 1974 Act provided that there would be no payment of feu duty in new feus created after September 1, 1974, and also provided for the redemption of existing feu duties. These are dealt with in two ways. First, the Act allows a feuar to redeem an allocated feu duty at any time: and secondly, it requires sellers of heritable property to redeem their feu duty prior to the sale of their properties.

(2) PROHIBITION OF FEU DUTY IN NEW FEUS

6.20 The Act provides that no deed executed after the commencement of the Act (September 1, 1974) shall impose a feu duty. The section also adds that any feudal grant made after September 1, 1974 shall have effect as if the grant were subject to feu duty.[29] In other words the 1974 Act only abolishes the payment of feu duty and does not otherwise affect the feudal relationship between superior and feuar.

(3) OPTIONAL REDEMPTION OF FEU DUTY

6.21 There is provision that any proprietor of a feu may, at any term of Whitsunday or Martinmas, redeem the feu duty which would otherwise fall due.[30] In order to redeem the feu duty the feuar must:

(i) give to the superior or his agent a notice of redemption as prescribed in Schedule 1 of the Act; and
(ii) pay to the superior such a sum of money as would, if invested in 2½ per cent Consolidated Stock at the middle market price at the close of business last preceding the date occurring one month before the appropriate term, produce an annual sum equal to the feu duty, and also any amount of feu duty unpaid in respect of the property.[31]

The effect of redemption is to terminate the obligation to pay the feu duty for the future, but the feu continues in all other respects.

---

[29] s. 1.
[30] s. 4(1).
[31] s. 4(2).

(4) COMPULSORY REDEMPTION OF FEU DUTY ON SALE

There is provision for the compulsory redemption of feu duty on sales **6.22**
of heritable property after September 1, 1974.[32] Where the property is
transferred for "valuable consideration" the seller is obliged to
redeem the feu duty before giving entry to the purchaser. The Act
requires the person who was the proprietor of the feu (the seller) to
pay to the superior the necessary redemption money computed once
again in relation to the price of 2½ per cent Consolidated Stock one
month before the redemption date (which is taken to be the date of
entry under the conveyance of the property).

Once the redemption date has passed, the purchaser is entitled to
give to the superior a notice of redemption. Two months after the
notice has been given the feu duty which was payable on the feu
ceases to exist. This applies even where the seller has failed to make
the necessary payment to redeem the feu duty. The superior, however, is still permitted to raise an action against the seller or his
representatives for recovery of the redemption money and any
interest which has accrued should the seller have failed to redeem
the feu duty. It is only by order of the court that the superior can
seek the redemption money from the purchaser when the seller has
failed to make the necessary redemption and the court will order this
only when it is not reasonably practicable to recover the money from
the seller or his representatives.

This procedure only applies to allocated feu duties.[33] Redemption **6.23**
by law does not apply in the case of a *cumulo* feu duty which has not
been allocated among the several feuars. This fact restricts the effect
of the redemption procedure because it would not apply to tenement
property, for example, where the property is under *cumulo* feu duty.
Here no redemption can be made on the sale of one of the tenement
flats unless the feu duty is first allocated under the procedure
specified in the Conveyancing and Feudal Reform (Scotland) Act
1970.[34]

(5) APPLICATION TO GROUND ANNUALS

These rules in relation to feu duty also apply in the case of ground **6.24**
annuals. No deed executed after September 1, 1974 shall impose a
ground annual and there are also provisions which authorise the
voluntary and compulsory redemption of ground annuals.[35]

---

[32] s. 5.
[33] s. 5.
[34] ss. 3–5.
[35] s. 2.

3. LAND REGISTRATION IN SCOTLAND

(1) THE MOVEMENT FOR REFORM

6.25 Demands for reform of the feudal land system in the past have centred on the system of land registration. Since the start of the twentieth century there have been constant demands for reform with the objective of creating a system of registration where only the title to the property need be registered.

In 1910 a Royal Commission under the chairmanship of Lord Dunedin examined "the expediency of instituting in Scotland a system of registration of title" and, although the report of the Commission did not recommend the immediate introduction of registration of title, it did make certain recommendations for reform.[36] In 1959 the Secretary of State for Scotland appointed a departmental committee under the chairmanship of Lord Reid to look at statutory conveyancing reforms. The report of this Committee[37] in 1963 recommended the creation of an expert committee to consider possible amendments to conveyancing statutes and also that another expert committee should be appointed to devise details of a scheme for registration of title. This recommendation led to the appointment of an expert committee, chaired by Professor G. L. F. Henry of Edinburgh University.[38] This was asked to work out details and provide the material for a Registration of Title Bill. To facilitate its work it carried out a pilot scheme in the Registers of Scotland.

The Report of the Henry Committee, published in 1969, set out in detail a proposed scheme for registration of title, and this scheme eventually formed the basis of the Land Registration (Scotland) Act 1979. The provisions of this Act are being brought into effect in Scotland over a lengthy period and it was hoped that land registration would cover the whole of Scotland by the early 1990s.[39] This turned out to be overly optimistic.[40] Consequently, before examining registration of title, it is necessary to look at the system of the recording of writs in Scotland which it will ultimately replace.

---

[36] Cd. 5316.
[37] Cmnd 2032.
[38] *Report on the Scheme for the Introduction and Operation of Registration of Title to Land in Scotland*, Cmnd 4137 (1969).
[39] See Bulletin section (1984) 29 J.L.S.S. 303.
[40] See para. 6.29.

(2) WRIT REGISTRATION

(a) General Register of Sasines

Traditionally, deeds affecting heritable property were recorded in 6.26
the General Register of Sasines. This Register has been since its
inception the chief security in Scotland of the rights of land and
other heritable property. The Register dates back to the Act of the
Scots Parliament 1617 c. 16, but it is now regulated by the Land
Registers (Scotland) Act 1868.

Where appropriate, recording any deed affecting heritable property in this Register creates a real right over the property. This act
transforms a personal right against the seller into a real right which
is effective against the whole world. The Register of Sasines is one of
14 Registers in Scotland. In 1978 more than 270,900 writs were
presented for recording in the Register. This number was increasing
every year, but has started to drop off considerably as new areas of
Scotland become affected by the 1979 Act.

(b) Recording of Writs

The Register of Sasines was divided into 33 divisions which 6.27
correspond with the former local county areas. A presentment book
for each county is kept in the Public Office. When a deed was
presented for registration, the following details were entered in the
Book:

- (i) the daily running number;
- (ii) date and hour of presentment;
- (iii) name of the writ;
- (iv) name of the person to or by whom the writ is granted;
- (v) the signature of the presenter;
- (vi) the name of the solicitor sending the writ to be recorded.

A minute of abridgment of the writ was thereafter made up, and
details entered in the minute book. In addition, each writ was
photographed and bound together in order of presentation in a
record volume and indexed. These volumes are open to public
inspection.

Each writ was also entered on a search sheet: this is where the deed
is ledgerised under the property or registration unit. All the entries in
the minute book were posted under the separate headings of the
property to which the deeds respectively referred, and the description of the property formed the heading of the related search sheet.
The search sheet was necessary in order to find the deeds in the
register.

(c) Why Reform was Needed

6.28   This system had worked very satisfactorily since 1617, but the register was not geared to the volume of transactions which were taking place in Scotland every year. It was also a register of deeds, rather than one of title. Registration could also be rather cumbersome. The Land Registration system was introduced to overcome these difficulties.

(3) LAND REGISTRATION (SCOTLAND) ACT 1979

6.29 There are three preliminary points that need to be made about this Act:

  (i) it implements the recommendations of the Henry Committee with its introduction of a system of title registration in Scotland[41];
  (ii) it creates a new property register—the "Land Register of Scotland"—under the management and control of the Keeper of the Registers of Scotland;
  (iii) this reformed register is map-based (rather than deed-based as was the Sasine Register).

The first area to move over to registration of title was Renfrew when the land registration system became effective there on April 6, 1981. Subsequently the system has been extended to Dumbarton, Lanark, Glasgow, Stirling, West Lothian, Fife, Aberdeen, Kincardine, Ayr, Dumfries, Wigtown and the Stewartry of Kirkcudbright. It will be the next century before the process of changeover is completed.

6.30   The reformed system centres around the issuing and recording of a "land certificate" after application for registration has been made to the Keeper.[42] The certificate is the title sheet of the property, which is registered in the Land Register. It is drawn from a description based on the Ordnance Survey Map. Once the title sheet is recorded, a real right will be given to the person registered as entitled to that interest in land. Once an area starts to operate the new Register, the only method of creating interests in land is by registration of title in it.

---

[41] For criticisms of the scheme which was introduced by the 1979 Act see K. G. C. Reid, "New Titles for Old" (1984) 29 J.L.S.S. 171 and "Registration of Title: The draftsman's part" (1984) J.L.S.S. 212 and the replies by the Keeper (1984) 29 J.L.S.S. 175 and 216.
[42] See generally, the Land Registration (Scotland) Act 1979, Pt I.

CHAPTER 7

INCIDENTS OF LANDOWNERSHIP

Ownership of land carries with it the right to use and enjoy the 7.01
property as well as the right to exclude others. In addition, a
landowner acquires certain incidental rights. Some of these are truly
incidents of possession; others are incidents of landownership, such
as the right to support. Although a landowner has the exclusive right
to use and enjoy the property, the exercise of his or her rights is
subject to the competing rights of neighbours and others in the
community.[1] This chapter considers the most important incidents of
possession and landownership.

1. POSSESSION

It has already been noted in Chapter 6 that mere possession of 7.02
heritage creates no rights of property under Scots law. Possession
based on an appropriate title can however operate, under the rules of
positive prescription, to cure a defective title.[2] In addition possession
can have several important consequences. First, a person who is in
possession of heritage has the right to defend that possession, or
recover it if lost, using the possessory remedies. Of the specific or
nominate remedies the most important is the action of removing.[3]
This action entitles the pursuer to recover possession from a person
who claims to have a title to possess, or who had a title to possess,
and refuses to give up possession. The other and general possessory
remedy is interdict, which is available to prohibit any act which
amounts to an invasion or threat of invasion of the pursuer's legal
rights. It can be used as a means of preventing one person from
continuing to occupy or repeating any occupation of another

---

[1] See Chap. 8.
[2] See paras 6.02–6.03.
[3] For a discussion of the other specific remedies see W. M. Gordon, *Scottish Land
Law* (W. Green, 1989), paras 14–15 to 14–30.

person's lands.[4] Where a possessory remedy is sought, the requisite possession must have lasted uninterrupted for at least seven years,[5] be open and peaceful and be based upon some sort of written title. This could be a feu title, but a lease would suffice.[6]

Secondly, possession brings certain benefits provided it is bona fide. A bona fide possessor of land is one who, although not truly the proprietor of the property which he possesses, believes himself to be such on probable grounds and with a good conscience.[7] The possession must be based on some colourable title so that a person cannot have bona fide possession where there is no title and no reason to believe that a title exists. A bona fide possessor enjoys the following rights:

    (i) ownership of the fruits of the thing possessed during the period of bona fide possession (in respect of heritage, the fruits include rents and feu duties);

    (ii) the right to recompense for improvements made to the property;

    (iii) no liability to the true owner for violent profits (whereas a possessor acting in bad faith would be liable to account for all the profits the true owner could have made if not denied possession).

2. RIGHTS OF SUPPORT

7.03 Arising *ex lege* as an incident of landownership, a right of support is enjoyed by a landowner to the extent necessary to uphold the land in its natural state. Every property is entitled to both subjacent and adjacent support, so that if any operations beneath the property or on neighbouring property affect the level of support, the landowner is entitled to damages for surface damage without the need to prove negligence.[8] However the landowner's right is simply the right to sue for loss of support; owners do not enjoy a positive right to claim support.[9] A fresh right of action arises on each occasion that damage is caused to the land.[10] As well as damages to compensate for any appreciable damage to the land, the landowner may seek interdict to prevent the operations continuing. Although the right to support is a

---

[4] N. R. Whitty, "Positive and Negative Interdicts" (1990) 35 J.L.S.S. 510.

[5] *per* Lord Cowan for the Second Division in *Colquhoun v. Paton* (1859) 21 D. 996 at 1001.

[6] *McDonald v. Dempster* (1871) 10 M. 94.

[7] Erskine, *Inst.*, II, i, 25.

[8] *per* Lord Justice-Clerk Thomson in *Angus v. National Coal Board*, 1955 S.C. 175 at 181.

[9] W. M. Gordon, *Scottish Land Law, op. cit.*, para. 6–83.

[10] *Darley Main Colliery Co. v. Mitchell* (1886) 11 App. Cas. 127.

natural right and exists without express stipulation, it can be renounced by the party entitled to it. Thus, where a superior reserves in a feu grant the right to work and carry away the minerals beneath the ground and the feuar agrees that such operations shall not result in liability for damage caused to the surface, interdict cannot be obtained to prevent the superior working the minerals even where doing so is causing damage to the feuar's property.[11]

There is no natural right of support for buildings which have been erected on the land. However, a right of support can be acquired, either by express grant or reservation when minerals are severed, or more commonly by implication. Where buildings have already been erected when the ownership of the minerals under the land is severed, a right to sue for any damage caused may be implied. The grant or reservation of the minerals will be presumed to have been made on the basis of the level of support which the buildings previously received. However, if the buildings are erected after the minerals have been severed no right of support for those buildings can be implied, since this would increase the burden of support beyond what the parties originally contemplated. However, if the minerals are reserved when the land is conveyed for a specific purpose which is likely to result in a need for increased levels of support, a right to such support as is necessary for that purpose will be implied.[12]

A proprietor may also have a right of action, in terms of the law 7.04 of nuisance, against the activities of a neighbour which lead to a withdrawal of support.[13] The Coal Mining Subsidence Act 1991 also grants rights to owners by placing a duty on the British Coal Corporation to conduct remedial works or pay for such works where subsidence damage to land or buildings is caused by the loss of support through coal mining operations.

3. RIGHTS IN WATER

The Crown exercises considerable rights in water, particularly as 7.05 regards the sea and tidal rivers. These will be discussed later in this chapter when we consider the *regalia*. This section of the chapter will be concentrating upon the rights of landowners who have a quantity of water upon their properties.

---

[11] *Buchanan v. Andrew* (1873) 11 M. (H.L.) 13; see also *White v. Wm. Dixon Ltd* (1883) 10 R. (H.L.) 45.

[12] *Caledonian Ry Co. v. Sprot* (1856) 2 Macq. 449; *North British Ry v. Turners Ltd* (1904) 6 F. 900.

[13] *Lord Advocate v. Reo Stakis Organisation Ltd*, 1982 S.L.T. 140. This issue is discussed more fully in Chap. 8.

(1) RIVERS AND STREAMS

7.06 Riparian proprietors[14] (*i.e.* those who own the land on either side of the river) have certain rights over the water which flows through or alongside their properties. The nature of their rights depends upon whether the river is navigable.

(a) Navigable Rivers

7.07   In the case of tidal navigable rivers, the bed or *alveus* belongs to the Crown. The public enjoy rights of navigation and fishing, and are entitled to moor boats on the river so long as this is not on a permanent basis.[15] Any activity (such as the mooring of fish farm cages) which causes material interference with the public's right of navigation can be interdicted.[16] In the case of non-tidal navigable rivers, the public enjoys a right of navigation, although the *alveus* and banks are the property of the riparian owners.

   Frequently, the courts are required to decide whether a right of navigation exists. In *Wills' Trustees v. Cairngorm Canoeing and Sailing School*[17] it was made clear that rights of navigation are not constituted in the same way as public rights of way over land. The correct approach is not only to consider the theoretical navigability of the river, but also to identify a regular, habitual use as a channel of communication or transportation since time immemorial (customarily for 40 years). Moreover, since the right of navigation is an imprescriptible right it cannot be lost by non-use. In *Wills' Trustees*, the House of Lords concluded that, as since time immemorial the public had used the river for the purpose of floating logs down to the sea, a right of navigation had been established. However, given the nature of the use (the floating of logs to the sea), the right of navigation only operated in relation to traffic going downstream.

7.08   The extent of the right of navigation depends upon the physical capacity and quality of the river. The key issue is whether and to what extent the river is capable of coping with the public's right of passage. In *Wills' Trustees*, Lord Wilberforce declared as follows:

   "[T]he fact that some stretch of water is navigable or passable by some acrobatic tour de force does not establish a public right of passage. Thus, again, the establishment of a public right of passage does not open the door to every kind of user which

---

[14] See *Marquess of Breadalbane v. West Highland Ry Co.* (1895) 22 R. 307.
[15] *Crown Estate Commissioners v. Fairlie Yacht Slip Ltd*, 1979 S.C. 156.
[16] *Walford v. David*, 1989 S.L.T. 876.
[17] 1976 S.C. (H.L.) 30.

physical prowess or exorbitant technology may make possible. The right is one for the ordinary public to use conformably with the nature of the river as water flowing past other people's lands."[18]

The public's right of navigation is therefore essentially one of passage. Nonetheless, the public may also acquire certain incidental rights[19] such as the right to moor or anchor boats so long as these are exercised on a wholly temporary basis consistent with the right of passage which is being exercised.[20] Equally, the riparian proprietors retain the right to use the *alveus* so long as they do nothing which interferes with or obstructs navigation.[21]

(b) Non-Navigable Rivers

Rights in these are truly incidents of landownership, and so there 7.09 are no public rights. Where a single proprietor owns the land on both sides of a stream or river, he owns the surface, bed and banks. Where the stream constitutes a boundary between two properties in separate ownership, each owns the bed of the stream, so far as *ex adverso* (alongside) his own property, to the *medium filum* (centre line of the river). Riparian proprietors also enjoy a common interest to ensure that the flow of water is not affected adversely by the activities of other riparian proprietors (principally those further upstream). Thus a riparian landowner must not interfere with the character or quality of the water, nor do anything which diminishes or increases its flow.[22]

Every proprietor is entitled to take water from the stream for primary purposes (*e.g.* drinking water for people or animals) and for domestic purposes (*e.g.* washing), even though the effect is to diminish or even exhaust the supply of water. Any surplus must be returned to the stream by proprietors within their own lands. Water cannot, however, be taken from the stream for secondary purposes (*e.g.* for a manufacturing process) if the rights of the riparian proprietors downstream are infringed either as to quality or flow. On the other hand, there would be nothing intrinsically unlawful in a proprietor using water for secondary purposes so long

---

[18] 1976 S.C. (H.L.) 30 at 124. See also the speech of Lord Fraser of Tullybelton at 169.

[19] The issues are summarised by Lord McDonald in *Scammell v. Scottish Sports Council*, 1983 S.L.T. 463.

[20] *Campbell's Trs v. Sweeney*, 1911 S.C. 1319; *Leith-Buchanan v. Hogg*, 1931 S.C. 204.

[21] *Orr Ewing and Co. v. Colquhoun's Trs* (1877) 4 R. (H.L.) 116.

[22] *Young and Co. v. Bankier Distillery Co.*, 1893 20 R. (H.L.) 76.

as there is sufficient water left for other owners. A riparian proprietor can obtain an interdict to prevent another affecting the flow of a river or stream or polluting it.[23] However, if a person has been drawing water for secondary purposes without any objection by other riparian proprietors for the period of the negative prescription (20 years)[24] this would prevent the other proprietors raising an objection at a later date.

(2) WATER NOT IN A DEFINITE CHANNEL

7.10 Water lying on the surface of land, in a bog or percolating through the ground is part of the land (*pars soli*) and belongs to the landowner if appropriated by him. Thus a landowner is entitled to extract for manufacturing purposes, by means of sinking a well, water percolating through the ground even although the water, if not intercepted, would join a watercourse and thereafter be extractable only in the limited circumstances described above.[25] Surface water may lawfully be discharged on to lower lands owned by a different proprietor if it naturally drains in that direction. The proprietor of the lower land must receive the flow of water, although he cannot insist on its continuance. However, the proprietor of the higher land may not increase the flow through pumping operations or by artificially altering the flow.[26] Nor is he entitled to discharge polluted water onto someone else's land.[27]

(3) LOCHS

7.11 If a loch is surrounded completely by the lands of one owner he has full rights of ownership in the loch and fishing rights over it. If the loch is surrounded by lands belonging to several proprietors there is a presumption that the loch is owned in common. Each proprietor has exclusive ownership over the bed of the loch *ex adverso* their lands up to the centre point of the loch. They share rights of navigation and fishing and can use the water for primary purposes. If the loch has a stream running out of it, the proprietors of the loch must not prejudice the rights of the stream's riparian proprietors.

---

[23] For the statutory rules on pollution see the Rivers (Prevention of Pollution) (Scotland) Acts 1951 and 1965 and the Control of Pollution Act 1974, as amended by the Water Act 1989 and the Environment Act 1995.
[24] Prescription and Limitation (Scotland) Act 1973, s. 8.
[25] *Milton v. Glen-Moray Glenlivet Distillery Co.* (1898) 1 F. 135.
[26] *Young and Co. v. Bankier Distillery Co.* (1893) 20 R. (H.L.) 76.
[27] *Montgomerie v. Buchanan's Trs* (1853) 15 D. 853.

A sea loch is treated as an extension of the sea. The Crown owns the *alveus*, the public enjoy rights of navigation, and the landowners whose properties lie *ex adverso* the loch acquire no rights of property.

4. RIGHTS IN MINERALS AND MINES

In Scots law a person is deemed to own property from the sky to the 7.12 centre of the earth (*a caelo usque ad centrum*). This means that, as well as owning the surface of the land, an owner also owns the airspace above it and the ground underneath it. There are, however, certain exceptions to the principle, notably:

(i) The right of aeroplanes to pass over property (see para. 7.16).

(ii) The right to gold and silver which belong to the Crown as part of the *regalia minora*. As such they are capable of being alienated by the Crown, and the Royal Mines Act 1424 c. 12 creates a procedure for the sale of the right to work precious metals in return for a royalty payable to the Crown.

(iii) Ownership of coal and the right to mine for it is vested in the British Coal Corporation under the provisions of the Coal Industry Act 1994.

(iv) Petroleum and natural gas rights, which vest in the Crown under the provisions of the Petroleum (Production) Act 1934.

Apart from the above exceptions, owners of property are entitled to the minerals lying underneath their properties. If a property is sold or feued the rights to the minerals pass with the property on sale unless the seller or superior expressly reserves the minerals from the sale or grant. Alternatively, a landowner may convey a right to minerals to another party as a separate transaction, or a right to minerals may be created by 10 years' open and uninterrupted possession on a suitable title amounting to positive prescription.[28] Thus the landowner's prima facie right to the minerals under the land can be severed by express grant or reservation or through prescriptive use.

The law does not define the word mineral. The definition depends upon the facts of each case, and in particular much will depend upon the intentions of the parties when the minerals were severed.[29] However, as a rule of thumb a mineral is any substance which is known in the vernacular by mining engineers, commercial people

---

[28] Prescription and Limitation (Scotland) Act 1973, s. 1.
[29] *Borthwick-Norton v. Gavin Paul and Sons*, 1947 S.C. 659.

and landowners in the locality as a mineral.[30] The substance should also be distinct from the ordinary subsoil of the area and be exceptional in its character, use and value.[31] A person who obtains the rights to minerals should also ensure that the necessary ancillary rights, such as a right of access and provision for storage and removing of the minerals, are also provided, since these will not necessarily be implied by the common law.

7.13   The above rules do not apply in the case of railways. Under the provisions of the Railway Clauses Consolidation (Scotland) Act 1845 (as amended) a railway is not entitled to the minerals under land purchased for the purposes of railway construction. Only those minerals which must be dug out or taken away in the construction belong to the railway company. Others carrying on mining operations close to a railway line must respect an "area of protection" extending to 40 yards or other prescribed distance on either side of the railway line.

5. NUISANCE

7.14 Landowners have the right to prevent any offensive or intolerable behaviour by others which affects their enjoyment of their property. Although the right to complain of a nuisance is an incident of landownership, the law of nuisance itself has developed as a branch of the law of delict. The classic definition was given by Professor Bell in *The Principles of the Law of Scotland*. He declared that:

> "whatever obstructs the public means of commerce and intercourse, whether in highways or navigable rivers, whatever is noxious or unsafe, or renders life uncomfortable to the public generally, or to the neighbourhood: whatever is intolerably offensive to individuals in their dwelling-houses, or inconsistent with the comfort of life, whether by stench (as the boiling of whale blubber), by noise (as in a smithy on an upper floor), or by indecency (as a brothel next door), is a nuisance."[32]

The essence of a nuisance is that it abuses a person's natural rights of property. As well as covering the situation where a neighbour infringes one's natural rights of enjoyment and use of land, it is also broad enough to cover what is, in effect, a public nuisance. In other words, it is broad enough to cover matters which refer not to the neighbourhood but which affect the public generally. Thus in

---

[30] *Borthwick-Norton, supra; Caledonian Ry Co. v. Glenboig Union Fireclay Co. Ltd,* 1911 S.C. (H.L.) 72.

[31] *Borthwick-Norton, supra.*

[32] §974.

Slater v. McLellan[33] the owner of a traction engine travelling on the highway was held to have committed a nuisance when he allowed sparks to be emitted by the engine, causing surrounding trees and houses to be damaged. The most common forms of nuisance in Scotland involve breaches of the law of neighbourhood. This often involves pollution, the emission of noise or heat or the causing of vibrations. In addition, a person whose building has suffered loss of support as a result of activities carried out by a neighbour may have an action in nuisance without the need to demonstrate interest as required for a normal loss of support action.[34] Nuisance is considered more fully in Chapter 8.

6. ENCROACHMENT

As we have seen, in terms of the maxim *a caelo usque ad centrum*, 7.15 ownership of land generally extends both above and below its surface. A proprietor would have a cause of action where there is any temporary or permanent encroachment upon or below the surface of his land or in the airspace above it. A proprietor can take action, for example, if a neighbour's trees should overhang his property,[35] or the jib of a crane should pass overhead.[36] A person's property rights would also be infringed when roots from a neighbour's tree penetrate through onto one's land. Encroachment also occurs if the owner of minerals attempts to extract them from under a person's property without having the necessary title or permission to work them. The usual remedy for encroachment is interdict to prevent the encroachment continuing or recurring.

There is a statutory exception to freedom from encroachment. In 7.16 terms of the Civil Aviation Act 1982 aeroplanes have the right to pass over property without the risk of liability for trespass or nuisance, provided they fly at a height which is reasonable in all the circumstances.[37] However, if material loss or damage is caused to any person or property by an aircraft, or anything falling from an aircraft, the owner of the plane is liable for such damage without proof of negligence.

---

[33] 1924 S.C. 854.
[34] *Lord Advocate v. Reo Stakis Organisation Ltd*, 1982 S.L.T. 140. But see now *RHM Bakeries (Scotland) Ltd v. Strathclyde R.C.*, 1985 S.L.T. 214.
[35] *Halkerston v. Wedderburn* (1781) Mor. 10495.
[36] *Brown v. Lee Constructions Ltd*, 1977 S.L.T. (Notes) 61 (interdict granted on the basis of trespass).
[37] s. 76; discussed in *Steel-Maitland v. British Airways Board*, 1981 S.L.T. 110.

7. TRESPASS

7.17 The law of trespass is a concomitant of a property owner's freedom of use and enjoyment of his property. Trespass is any temporary intrusion or entering upon the property of another without permission. Trespass can be committed on foot, or by an animal, or by use of a bicycle or vehicle. The proprietor of land may warn any person who is trespassing thereon but may not eject a trespasser forcibly unless the trespasser occasions or threatens violence on the proprietor or does damage to the property.[38] If the landowner requires to use force he can only use such force as is reasonably necessary in the circumstances. Although damages can be claimed for damage done to the property by a trespasser, the principal remedy is interdict.

The court will only award interdict if there is a threat or probability of continuance or repetition of the trespass. Interdict is, therefore, discretionary.[39] In *Hay's Trustees v. Young*[40] the principal reason why the court refused interdict was because repetition of the entry on the pursuer's lands was not to be expected. Neither will an interdict be granted where the trespass is having a minimal impact on the property (application of the *de minimis* rule). In *Winans v. Macrae*[41] a landholder was refused interdict when he attempted to stop a pet lamb belonging to a cottar straying onto his lands. The court considered that this was a *de minimis* situation and that other remedies existed beyond interdict.

7.18 A proprietor's right to prevent trespass on land is subject to one major limitation. As Professor Bell has put it: "the exclusive right of a landowner to use his property as he pleases yields wherever public interest or necessity requires that it should yield."[42] This means that at common law it is permissible to trespass during an emergency such as in the case of fire, or in pursuit of a criminal, or to obtain evidence in connection with a crime[43] or to avoid danger. The English courts have held that this exception does not extend to a permission to homeless people to enter property since otherwise no one's house would be safe from intrusion.[44] There are also a number of statutory rights of entry for public officials.[45]

---

[38] *Wood v. North British Ry* (1899) 2 F. 1.
[39] See, for example, *Plessey Co. plc v. Wilson*, 1983 S.L.T. 319.
[40] (1877) 4 R. 398.
[41] (1885) 12 R. 1051.
[42] *Prin.*, §956.
[43] *Shepherd v. Menzies* (1900) 2 F. 443; *Southern Bowling Club v. Ross* (1902) 4 F. 405.
[44] *Southwark LBC v. Williams* [1971] Ch. 734.
[45] See, for example, the Rights of Entry (Gas and Electricity Boards) Act 1954, s. 2 (grant of warrant by sheriff to enter premises by force) as amended by the Electricity Act 1989 and the Gas Act 1995; Health and Safety at Work etc. Act 1974, s. 20 (right of inspectors to enter premises without permission).

Although under Scots law trespass does not normally give rise to criminal proceedings, there are particular Acts which allow certain public bodies to prosecute trespassers. Further, the Trespass (Scotland) Act 1865 makes it a criminal offence for a person to lodge in any premises, or occupy any land, without the consent and permission of the owner.

8. PROPERTY RIGHTS OF THE CROWN

There are certain rights in heritable property which are presumed to be owned by the Crown. Two specific forms of Crown ownership are recognised by Scots law. 7.19

(1) REGALIA MAJORA

Rights to the *regalia majora* are held by the Crown in trust for public purposes. It is impossible for these rights to be alienated to anyone else by the Crown. They are more in the way of a right of sovereignty than one of property. 7.20

(2) REGALIA MINORA

These rights are in Crown ownership also. In this case the Crown does possess a property right which can be alienated to others. 7.21

Examples of these two groups of rights are given below.

The Sea

The sea below the foreshore and within the territorial limit,[46] as part of the *regalia majora*, belongs to the Crown in trust for the public rights of navigation and fishing. 7.22

The Foreshore

This area encompasses the shore between the high and low water marks of ordinary spring tides. The foreshore is an example of Crown property where both the *regalia majora* and the *regalia minora* apply. Thus the Crown possesses two specific rights. First, it has a right of sovereignty which means that the foreshore is vested in the Crown in trust for public purpose. This right cannot be 7.23

---

[46] Now 12 international nautical miles—Territorial Sea Act 1987, s. 1(1)(a).

alienated. The public purposes recognised by this right include a right of navigation and of fishing. The right of navigation also covers certain ancillary rights such as the right to anchor or moor so long as this is done in the course of passage. The right of navigation does not extend to the laying of fixed moorings because this is not incidental to the public's right of passage but involves the provision of a facility which a vessel may use from time to time.[47] It is probable that the public also has a right to use the foreshore for recreation purposes. The other right to the foreshore vested in the Crown is a right of property. Although the Crown is taken to own the foreshore, it can be alienated to another by the Crown. It can be alienated to an adjacent proprietor, for example, if he has been given a specific grant of ownership from the Crown. Such a grant need not refer to the foreshore in specific words.[48] Equally, the foreshore can be acquired by prescriptive possession based on a habile title.[49] If the foreshore is owned by someone other than the Crown, that person must recognise the rights of the public to use the foreshore for navigation, fishing, etc.

Navigable Rivers

7.24   Rivers which are navigable and tidal are the property of the Crown in trust for the public's right of passage. The law applying to rivers and lochs was discussed above.

Ferries, Ports and Harbours

7.25   These rights are part of the *regalia minora* and belong to the Crown but can be alienated to others by express grant or by operation of prescription. Thus they can be items of private property so long as the owner allows the public access to them, for which access the proprietor is often entitled to charge.

 ### Salmon Fishing

7.26   Salmon fishing is a separate feudal right which is vested in the Crown. As part of the *regalia minora* it can be granted by the Crown to a subject either by express grant or through a general grant with exercise of the right for the prescriptive period. As we have seen, this is 20 years.[50]

---

[47] *Crown Estates Commissioners v. Fairlie Yacht Slip Ltd*, 1979 S.C. 156.
[48] *Lord Advocate v. Wemyss* (1899) 2 F. (H.L.) 1.
[49] Prescription and Limitation (Scotland) Act 1973, s. 1(1) and (4). The prescriptive period is 20 years when the positive prescription is pleaded against the Crown.
[50] For a more detailed discussion of this topic see W. M. Gordon, *Scottish Land Law, op. cit.*, paras 8–49 to 8–75.

CHAPTER 8

RESTRICTIONS ON LANDOWNERSHIP

Ownership of land in society involves certain limitations flowing 8.01
from the potential conflict between the rights of different landowners as well as other members of the public. These restrictions
stem from individual agreements, from the law protecting amenity
and from statutory schemes on the use of land and the protection of
certain economically disadvantaged groups like tenants, the homeless or, traditionally, women.

1. RESTRICTIONS BY AGREEMENT

(1) PERSONAL BURDENS ON LAND

It is open to any landowner to enter into any agreement with any 8.02
other person to provide lawful rights to that other person over the
landowner's property. Such an agreement would give rise to
personal rights—only the parties to the agreement are bound
by such arrangements. An agreement to allow a person to fish
on one's property would be personal to the angler and would not
bind any subsequent purchaser of the land. It is possible by
agreement to create rights which bind later owners of land
provided that these meet certain requirements. These are known
as "real burdens".

(2) REAL BURDENS ON LAND

Under the feudal system the superior is permitted to lay down 8.03
restrictions on the use of the property by the feuar. These restrictions
are generally referred to as real burdens or, more properly, real
conditions.[1] Real burdens are conditions which permanently run
with the land irrespective of the fact that the original granter and
grantee have long ceased to have an interest in the property.

---

[1] K. G. C. Reid, "What is a Real Burden?" (1984) 29 J.L.S.S. 9.

Typically a real burden is imposed by the superior on the feuar's use of the land. Real burdens could, for example, prohibit the feuar from using the property as "a factory, warehouse, office or piggery". They could even restrict the use of the property to a dwelling-house for one family only. Indeed, the real burden could cover almost anything, even down to a requirement that the subjects be insured at a certain minimum value.

In *Tailors of Aberdeen v. Coutts*[2] the Court of Session laid down seven requirements which a restriction must satisfy before it is given the status of a real burden. Any condition which does not meet the requirements of these seven rules may apply to the original superior and feuar who created it, but it will not affect singular successors of either of them. Since the principal feature of a real burden is that it runs with the land and does not only affect the parties who created it, a restriction will not apply to all successors of the original granter and grantee unless it satisfies the rules as laid down in the *Tailors of Aberdeen* case.

(a) Clear Intention

8.04   To constitute a real burden or condition effectual against singular successors no technical words are required, but the words that are used must clearly show an intention to affect the property itself and not merely the grantee.

In *Tailors of Aberdeen* the Court of Session declared that it was not necessary that any technical forms of words should be employed in order to create the real burden. The grant need not even declare that the burden is real, or that it should be inserted in all future grants or that it attaches to singular successors. It is sufficient if the intention of the parties is clear.

(b) Acceptable Purpose

8.05   The burden or condition must not be contrary to law or public policy; useless or vexatious; too vague; nor inconsistent with the nature of the property.

(i) Contrary to Law or Public Policy

8.06   Where the real burden is so created that its performance would require the commission of an unlawful act, or if it is of such a nature that its performance would give the superior a monopoly, the real burden will be struck down as being illegal or contrary to public policy. So a condition which required the feuar to maintain a brothel

---

[2] (1840) 1 Rob. App. 296.

on his property, or which required the feuar to grind all his grain at the superior's mill, would not be enforceable. In *Yeaman v. Crawford*[3] where there was a stipulation that the feuars were to have all their blacksmith work done at the barony blacksmith, the real burden was struck down as being contrary to public policy. In a more modern case, *Aberdeen Varieties v. James F. Donald*,[4] a company had sold one of its theatres to another company with a restriction which was declared to be a real burden that the theatre could not be used in all time coming for any stage play. Singular successors of the seller sought to enforce this restriction. One reason why the condition was struck down in the Inner House was that it was unlawful because, if enforced, it would mean the imposition of a perpetual commercial monopoly. This case would suggest that it will be difficult for a seller to create a real burden for the sale of a business since any restriction as to use may be construed as bestowing monopoly powers in the seller.[5]

(ii) Useless or Vexatious

In *Tailors of Aberdeen* a condition which required every singular 8.07 successor of the feuars to grant personal obligations to the superior for payment of feu duty was held to be both unnecessary and vexatious. This was because the payment of feu duty is implied by feudal law, hence the condition served no actual purpose.

(iii) Inconsistent with the Nature of the Property

This point is illustrated in *Beckett v. Bissett*[6] where Beckett 8.08 claimed that the exclusive rights of shooting she alleged she possessed over Bisset's property constituted a real burden. Her action failed, however, because Lord Blackburn determined that one cannot convert a right of shooting into a separate tenement under the guise of a real burden. As far as he was concerned, the right alleged to be created was "inconsistent with the nature of the species of property and so was not enforceable".[7]

(c) Specific Wording

The burden or condition must be specific, and will be construed 8.09 strictly *contra proferentem* (*i.e.* against the party seeking to apply it). The real burden must be specific in all the material requirements

---

[3] (1770) Mor. 14537.
[4] 1939 S.C. 788. Appeal on the question of competency—1940 S.C. (H.L.) 52.
[5] *Phillips v.Lavery*, 1962 S.L.T. (Sh. Ct.) 57.
[6] 1921 S.L.T. 33.
[7] *ibid.*

necessary to enforce it as a legal obligation. Thus in a number of cases
the real burden has been struck down because the words which created
it were susceptible to a doubt as to the superior's intention. So in
Murray's Trustees v. St Margaret's Convent Trustees[8] the proprietors
of a piece of property in a villa area granted a condition over it in favour
of the proprietor of an adjoining house. This condition bound the
proprietors of the property and their successors not to erect on the
property any building "of an unseemly description". A singular
successor of the granter proposed to build a four-flatted tenement.
The other proprietor sought interdict to prevent the building going
ahead. The House of Lords held that the restriction against the erection
of an unseemly building was too vague and indefinite to be valid as a
restraint against the use of property. In a later case, *Kirkintilloch Kirk
Session v. Kirkintilloch School Board*,[9] "a perpetual right of occasional
occupation" was held to be too vague.

Similarly an obligation "to maintain the supply of water in the mill
lade to provide adequate flow to cleanse and drain . . . the mill lade . . . to
the satisfaction of" the benefited proprietor was rejected as being
imprecise[10] since amongst other things it was not made clear at what
flow the supply of water was to be maintained. By contrast a restriction
not to "carry on . . . any operation of any description that the (superior)
may deem objectionable" was accepted as being capable of enforcement since it could be read as a limitation on uses which would create,
for example, smells, smoke, excessive noise or other immediate and
direct effects upon surrounding properties.[11] The court indicated that
the effects of such uses must be shown to be real and substantial rather
than mere expressions of opinion or taste.[12]

It is also the case that the court will, if at all possible, construe the
burden in order to take the least possible constraint from the
restriction. In *Kemp v. Magistrates of Largs*[13] a proprietor of a
piece of land in Largs adjoining the harbour wished to build an
amusement arcade. His superior, the Burgh of Largs, objected on
the basis that this would be in contravention of their feu right
whereby the use to which the property could be put was restricted to
works necessarily connected with the harbour. The House of Lords

---

[8] (1906) 8 F. 1109; 1907 S.C. (H.L.) 8; contrast with *McNeill v. Mackenzie* (1870)
   8 M. 520 on alterations to roof and chimney tops which were not to be made in
   such a way as to be "an annoyance or offensive to the proprietors or occupants
   of any of the houses in [the] street"—a restriction which was held to be
   enforceable.
[9] 1911 S.C. 1127.
[10] *Lothian R.C. v. Rennie*, 1991 S.L.T. 465.
[11] *Meriton Ltd v. Winning*, 1995 S.L.T. 76.
[12] *ibid.* p. 80.
[13] 1939 S.C. (H.L.) 6.

held that the granter had not clearly signified his intention that the land should be subject to a real burden against the use of the property for any other purpose than the maintenance of a harbour.

(d) Clear Financial Obligation

If the burden refers to the payment of money, the amount must be 8.10 definite and the creditor identifiable.[14] In *Tailors of Aberdeen* the feuars were required to pay a proportion of two-third parts of the expense of forming and enclosing the area in the middle of the town square and of upholding it in good repair. This was held not to be a real burden because it was made up of an obligation to pay an indefinite sum of money. While the creditor must be stated and clearly identified, there is no requirement that they need actually be named. In *Erskine v. Wright*[15] a real burden was accepted by the court in favour of children who were not named but whose parents were.

(e) Record in Register of Sasines or Land Register

The real burden or condition must be recorded in the General 8.11 Register of Sasines or the Land Register of Scotland. Failure to record a real burden in the General Register or Land Register means that the condition will attach only to those persons who were parties to the original contract.

(f) Supporting Clauses not Necessary

There is no need in the feudal grant to fence the burden or condition 8.12 with irritant or resolutive clauses which grant rights to the superior to recover possession of the land if the real burden is breached. Although these clauses are generally inserted in feudal grants they are not strictly necessary because they are implied by feudal law.

(g) Interest Needed for Enforcement

The party seeking to enforce a real burden must not merely have a 8.13 title to do so but an interest as well. This question must be examined in relation both to the superior and to co-feuars.

(i) The Superior

The superior's title to enforce a real burden will generally be based 8.14 on the contract contained in the feudal grant. This is really a question of fact rather than law and the presumption for this

---

[14] This rule is obviously subject to the provisions of the Land Tenure Reform (Scotland) Act as regards the redemption of feu duty.
[15] (1846) 8 D. 863.

discussion is that the superior has the necessary title. The question of interest is rather more complicated. The rule is that, in any court action that the superior wishes to take to prevent the contravention, his or her interest to take the action is assumed to exist. It has been stated in a number of cases that the existence of the feudal relationship is prima facie evidence of the superior's interest. In *Macdonald v. Douglas*,[16] for example, Lord Justice-Clerk Grant declared that:

> "So far as the superior's interest is concerned, it was not disputed that, prima facie, a vassal in consenting to be bound, concedes the superior's interest and that the onus is on the vassal to prove that, owing to some change of circumstances, any legitimate interest which the superior may originally have had has ceased to exist."

It is clear, therefore, that the onus is upon the feuar to rebut the presumption in favour of the superior's interest to enforce the real burden. This would be achieved by showing that there has been a change of circumstances. As Lord Watson declared in *Earl of Zetland v. Hislop*[17]:

> "Prima facie, the vassal in consenting to be bound by the restriction concedes the interest of the superior; and, therefore, it appears to me, that the *onus* is upon the vassal who is pleading a release from his contract to allege and prove that, owing to some change of circumstances, any legitimate interest which the superior may originally have had in maintaining the restriction has ceased to exist."

8.15   There can be no doubt that there is a heavy onus on a feuar seeking to prove a change in circumstances. In *Earl of Zetland* the superior sought to enforce a condition which prevented feuars using their premises for retailing spirits or as eating-houses without the superior's consent. Here a feuar argued that a substantial increase in the population of the town covered by the restriction amounted to a change in circumstances. Lord Watson accepted that an increase in population could be an element in estimating the change. He went on to state as follows:

> "If all the dwelling-houses, save one, in a particular street were by license of the superior used for the sale of liquor, I can conceive that the superior might have difficulty in showing a legitimate interest to prohibit the sale of liquor in that one house. But I am at a loss to understand why the existence of a

---

[16] 1963 S.C. 374.
[17] (1882) 9 R. (H.L.) 40 at 47.

whole street of public-houses in one part of the burgh should disable him from enforcing the prohibition in a street of villa dwellings in another quarter of the town."[18]

The crucial point here is that the change of circumstances must be material and the onus is on the vassal to prove the loss of the superior's interest.

Equally, in *Howard De Walden Estates Ltd v. Bowmaker Ltd*[19] the First Division held that the test as to whether the feuar had proved that the superior had lost his interest to enforce the conditions of the feu was whether the original residential character of the neighbourhood and every part of it had been wholly lost by a change in circumstances. In this case the feuars were unable to prove that the superior had lost his interest despite the fact that over one-third of the houses in the street were no longer used as dwelling-houses (which their feudal grant required them to be). In this instance, it should be noted, there was no feuing plan. Where, however, there is a feuing plan and an instance of acquiescence occurs, the superior's interest may well be lost in respect of all plots.

There is clearly a very high burden on the feuar to prove the necessary loss of interest. Moreover it would seem that the interest of the superior need not be patrimonial or even beneficial.[20] In *Menzies v. Caledonian Canal Commissioners*[21] it was held that the Commissioners could prevent a hotel being built which would have been in contravention of the conditions of the feu. This condition had been inserted in the feudal grant in order to prevent the workers on the canal getting drunk during working hours. The court concluded that the superior had an interest in ensuring that the canal was used safely by securing the sobriety of those who worked on the canal. 8.16

It is also possible to prevent the superior taking action to enforce feuing conditions by showing that the superior has acquiesced in earlier contraventions by the feuar. Thus the superior may be personally barred from enforcing a real burden if a material breach of the conditions has been knowingly allowed to take place and to subsist for some substantial time. The matter has been put succinctly:

"A superior who stands by and knows of and allows the vassal to incur considerable expense in doing that to which objection may be taken as a contravention of a restrictive feuing condition is barred from objecting at a later stage to that particular contravention."[22]

---

[18] (1882) 9 R. (H.L.) 40 at 51.
[19] 1965 S.C. 163.
[20] *cf. Earl of Zetland v. Hislop* (1882) 9 R. (H.L.) 40.
[21] (1900) 2 F. 953.
[22] *Greenwell v. McColl*, 1964 S.C. 106.

8.17   The law on acquiescence was outlined in *Ben Challum Ltd v. Buchanan*.[23] The feuar in this case was obliged by his feu charter to erect a dwelling-house and shop with suitable offices. It was also stated that he should not alter nor add to these buildings without the superior's written consent. Over a period of 12 years the feuar erected five petrol pumps and a wooden bungalow for fodder storage without the consent of the superior. After a further 17 years the superior's successor decided to raise an action against the erection of the petrol pumps and the bungalow. The feuar argued successfully that the superior had acquiesced in the breach of the feuing conditions that the ground unbuilt on should remain so and that there should be no erection of further buildings. In the course of their decision the First Division outlined the necessary factors for acquiescence as follows:

  (i) It must be shown that the superior knew that it was being disregarded.

  (ii) There must be more than mere silence on the part of the superior. It must be shown that the superior actually permitted the feuar to proceed to incur expense (in that case, the cost of structural alterations).

(ii) Co-feuars

8.18   Normally it is only the superior who has the interest and right to enforce the conditions of the feu but a neighbouring feuar may have a right to sue provided there is a *jus quaesitum tertio* (*i.e.* the right of a third party to sue). The right to sue rests on some element of mutuality of rights and obligations between the feuars. The issue was discussed by the House of Lords in *Hislop v. MacRitchie's Trustees*[24] where it was stressed that a *jus quaesitum tertio* will not be established easily. There are three routes whereby co-feuars can establish they have *jus quaesitum tertio*:

  (i) by express grant from the superior;
  (ii) by implication from the feudal deeds;
  (iii) by agreement among the co-feuars.

In *Hislop* Lord Watson examined the existing law and made the following points:

  (i) The fact that the same condition appears in feu charters derived from the same superior coupled with a substantial interest in its observance does not create a right to sue. Thus

---

[23] 1955 S.C. 348.
[24] (1881) 8 R. (H.L.) 95.

a right to sue cannot be created simply because co-feuars share common conditions.

(ii) The right can be created either expressly or by implication from the feudal grant. An express right will be created where the superior stipulates expressly in the several feudal grants that each vassal will have a right to sue. A right to sue can also be created by reasonable implication from a reference in each feudal grant to a uniform plan of building or a common feuing plan or where an area is feued subject to certain general conditions that must be inserted in all sub-feus.

It is also possible for a *jus quaesitum tertio* to be created where the feuars agree amongst themselves that each may enforce the conditions against the others.

Thus it is clear that the mere fact that there are several feus adjoining or in close proximity to one another and possessing a common superior does not of itself permit any one of them to enforce compliance with the conditions of the feu. For a *jus quaesitum tertio* to exist there must be a very clear inference to be drawn from the titles that this was the intention. It is not enough that neighbouring properties hold of the same superior on titles containing similar or even identical conditions. A simple undertaking given by superiors to insert similar burdens in the titles to neighbouring properties when such properties came to be feued has not been taken as sufficient to establish mutuality.[25]

It is not enough that a co-feuar will be prejudiced by the contravention of the feuing conditions or that the superior concurs in the action. In *Hislop v. MacRitchie's Trustees*[26] it was held that the consent and concurrence of the superior did not give a co-feuar a right to object where a right to sue could not be set up either expressly from the feu grant or by implication. The fact that the grants given to the co-feuars contained the same restrictions did not give them a right to sue. 8.19

The rights of the superior and of co-feuars to sue are independent and separate rights. The right of the superior rests upon a contract created by the feudal grant, whereas the right of a co-feuar is more in the nature of a proper servitude.[27] This means that a loss of an interest to sue by the superior will have no effect upon co-feuars. In *Lawrence v. Scott*[28] it was held that the fact

---

[25] *McCarthy and Stone (Developments) Ltd v. Smith*, 1995 S.L.T. (Lands Tr.) 19 at 25.

[26] (1881) 8 R. (H.L.) 95.

[27] *per* Lord Watson in *Hislop v. MacRitchie's Trs* (1881) 8 R. 95 at 102.

[28] 1965 S.L.T. 390.

that the superior neither authorised nor complained about a breach of feuing conditions did not prevent a co-feuar from suing on the basis that a *jus quaesitum tertio* had been expressly conferred upon him in the feudal grant. Co-feuars who enjoy a right to sue may become personally barred from suing through acquiescence. However, this will depend upon the extent of the harm and its seriousness for the relevant objector. Thus the fact that there have been breaches of feuing conditions in other parts of the area feued to which the co-feuar has not objected will not necessarily bar that person from complaining in the case of breaches closer to home.[29]

8.20　Where property is merely disponed rather than feued, there is also the possibility of a right to sue. Hence, where other disponees have breached conditions of their sale, similar rules to those which affect co-feuars will be applied.[30]

(3) Discharge and Variation by the Lands Tribunal for Scotland

8.21　It is clear from the above discussion that feudal law made it difficult for feuars to avoid their feudal conditions. At common law a feuar may obtain a waiver of a particular feuing condition from the superior or, more radically, a charter of *novodamus* may be arranged which involves a re-grant of the feu with the offending conditions omitted or altered. Alternatively, the feuar may seek a declarator that the superior no longer has an interest to enforce the condition.[31] As we saw in earlier chapters, various aspects of the feudal system (such as feu duty and land registration) have been the subjects of public concern and ultimately legislative amendment. The operation of feuing conditions has been the subject of particular scrutiny in the twentieth century.

The White Paper, *Land Tenure in Scotland: A Plan for Reform*,[32] published in July 1969, examined the feudal system in some detail. It criticised the system as being both autocratic and obsolete and considered that in cases where the superior had no real concern for the amenity of the area the only basis upon which a superior was likely to enforce feuing conditions was financial. Moreover, since in

---

[29] *Mactaggart and Co. v. Roemmele*, 1907 S.C. 1318.
[30] *Nicholson v. Glasgow Blind Asylum*, 1911 S.C. 391; *SCWS v. Finnie*, 1937 S.C. 835.
[31] See, for example, *Menzies v. Caledonian Canal Commissioners* (1900) 2 F. 953. This right cannot be exercised by the tenant of a feuar—*Eagle Lodge Ltd v. Keir and Cawder Estates Ltd*, 1964 S.C. 30.
[32] Cmnd 4099.

the great majority of cases superiors no longer lived in the area there was no real pressure on them to ensure that the conditions of the feudal grant were being complied with. The White Paper argued that the answer did not lie in minor patchwork reforms. It was convinced that the feudal system should be replaced by a new system altogether. The suggested solution was that on an appointed day existing feuars who were owners of the *dominium utile* should be declared to own their lands in terms of some new form of absolute ownership.[33]

As a direct result of the White Paper's criticisms, the Conveyancing and Feudal Reform (Scotland) Act was enacted in 1970. This Act also implemented many of the proposals contained in the earlier Halliday Report[34] but did not bring about the abolition of the feudal system as the White Paper of 1969 had advocated. Instead, it provided a completely new way of discharging the land conditions which were an integral part of the feudal system. Sections 1 and 2 of this Act provided an opportunity for disputed land conditions to be referred to the Lands Tribunal for Scotland for possible discharge or variation.

(a) Constitution

The Lands Tribunal was created by sections 1 to 4 of the Lands 8.22 Tribunal Act 1949. In Scotland, however, the Lands Tribunal did not actually come into being until March 1, 1971 when an Order in Council brought into force the relevant provisions of the 1949 Act for Scotland. The Lands Tribunal is made up of professional people of two types—lawyers who deal with the purely legal points and surveyors who can value the property and consider claims for compensation. It is usual for the Tribunal to sit in pairs consisting of one lawyer and one surveyor, although larger tribunals have been convened. If necessary, cases are decided by vote with the chairman having a casting vote in the case of a tie. The procedure which the Tribunal is to follow is laid down in the Lands Tribunal for Scotland Rules 1971.[35]

(b) Jurisdiction

The Tribunal has jurisdiction over the discharge and variation of 8.23 "land obligations". A land obligation is defined in section 1(2) as an obligation relating to land which is enforceable by a proprietor of an interest in land, by virtue of his being such proprietor, and which is

---

[33] See also the Green Paper, *Land Tenure Reform in Scotland*, published by the Conservative Government in 1972.

[34] *Conveyancing Legislation and Practice*, Cmnd 3118 (1966).

[35] S.I. 1971 No. 218.

binding upon a proprietor of another interest in that land, or of an interest in other land, by virtue of his being such proprietor. The definition covers not only land conditions as set up under the rules as laid down in *Tailors of Aberdeen*, but also other obligations in feu grants which, although not created real, or lacking the precision of a real burden, are nevertheless binding upon successive feuars as inherent conditions of the grant. Private servitudes both positive and negative are also included, as are obligations created in deeds of declaration of conditions and registered long leases. Typical examples of such conditions are restrictions on the use of the property to residential; limitations on the number of buildings which can be erected; and requirements for any alterations to be approved by the superior.

However, excluded from the definition are feu duties and other periodic payments of money, rights to work minerals, obligations imposed by the Crown for the protection of royal parks, gardens or palaces, obligations created for military purposes and obligations under statutes relating to agriculture.[36] The Act also excludes all land obligations which are less than two years old.[37] An application for variation or discharge cannot be brought prior to the expiry of two years after the date of creation of the relevant land obligation.[38] The two-year period is computed from the date of delivery of the relevant disposition which creates the land obligation.[39]

(c) Right of Hearing

8.24   The Lands Tribunal can only hear cases from those people who are "burdened proprietors" as defined in the Act. A burdened proprietor petitions the Tribunal, requesting it to vary or discharge the land obligation where the obligation is enforced upon that property by a "benefited proprietor". The legislation provides that any other person who appears to be affected by the land obligation or by its proposed variation or discharge may be heard in relation to any application.[40] The affected person must, however, in support of any written objections attend the hearing in person to state their views in order that they may be cross examined on behalf of the applicant. Otherwise their written objections will not be looked at by the Tribunal.[41]

---

[36] 1970 Act, s. 1 and Sched. 1.
[37] 1970 Act, s. 2(5).
[38] 1970 Act, s. 2(5).
[39] *Watters v. Motherwell D.C.*, 1991 S.L.T. 2.
[40] 1970 Act, s. 2(2).
[41] *Scott v. Wilson*, 1993 S.L.T. (Lands Tr.) 51.

The phrases "benefited proprietor" and "burdened proprietor" are defined as follows:

(i) A benefited proprietor is a proprietor of an interest in land who is entitled by virtue of his being such a proprietor to enforce the obligation (*e.g.* the superior or proprietor of a dominant tenement).[42]

(ii) A burdened proprietor is a proprietor of an interest in the land upon whom, by virtue of his being such a proprietor, the obligation is binding (*e.g.* the feuar or proprietor of the servient tenement).[43]

If the Tribunal should vary or discharge the obligation, the benefited proprietor may be entitled to compensation.

(d) When Obligations may be Varied or Discharged

The Act gives the Tribunal directions as to when it has authority 8.25 to vary or discharge a land obligation. It can only do so when it is satisfied that one or more of the following conditions have been met[44]:

(i) by reason of changes in the character of the land affected by the land obligation or of the neighbourhood or other circumstances which the Tribunal deems material, the obligation is or has become unreasonable or inappropriate[45]; or

(ii) the obligation is unduly burdensome compared with any benefit resulting or which would result from its performance[46]; or

(iii) the existence of the obligation impedes some reasonable use of the land.[47]

A burdened proprietor can petition the Lands Tribunal on each one of these three grounds—they are not mutually exclusive. The burden of a restriction is not to be assessed by considering circumstances which are purely personal to the applicants, so that where applicants wished to make alterations to their property because of the health of one of the joint owners, this was not relevant in terms of the 1970 legislation.[48]

---

[42] A co-feuar with a *jus quaesitum tertio* is also a benefited proprietor.
[43] 1970 Act, s. 2(6).
[44] s. 1(3).
[45] s. 1(3)(a)
[46] s. 1(3)(b).
[47] s. 1(3)(c).
[48] *Stoddart v. Glendinning*, 1993 S.L.T. (Lands Tr.) 12.

(e) Right to Award of Compensation

8.26   As noted, if the Tribunal discharges the land obligation it can
award compensation to the benefited proprietor. The Tribunal
can award compensation in one of two cases[49]:

> (i) as a sum to compensate for any substantial loss or disad-
> vantage suffered by the benefited proprietor in consequence
> of the variation or discharge[50]; or
> (ii) as a sum to make up for any effect which the obligation
> produced at the time when it was imposed, in reducing the
> consideration then paid or made payable for the interest in
> land affected by it.[51]

The mere fact that the granting of waivers is a source of income does
not mean that compensation will be granted for loss of such a source
where there is a variation or discharge.[52]

(4) VARIATION OR DISCHARGE THROUGH CHANGE OF CHARACTER[53]

(a) Introduction

8.27   Section 1(3)(a) deals with cases where a change in character in the
neighbourhood has taken place subsequent to the imposition of the
land obligation and which has affected the amenity of the property
rendering the obligation unreasonable or inappropriate. There are
three issues here—changes in the character of the land; changes in
the neighbourhood; and other circumstances deemed material by the
Tribunal.

(b) Change of Character of Land

8.28   Generally, an obligation will be discharged under this provision
where it can be established that the land has become useless in terms
of the purpose for which the obligation was originally created. Mere
convenience to the applicant will not suffice.[54] By the same token,

---

[49] s. 1(4).
[50] s. 1(4)(a).
[51] s. 1(4)(b).
[52] *Harris v. Douglass*; *Erskine v. Douglass*, 1993 S.L.T. (Lands Tr.) 56 at 59 and
discussed at para. 8.38.
[53] s. 1(3)(a).
[54] Contrast *Solway Cedar Ltd v. Hendry*, 1972 S.L.T. (Lands Tr.) 42 (restriction to
eight houses in a development and proposal for one more house) and *Ross and
Cromarty D.C. v. Ullapool Property Co. Ltd*, 1983 S.L.T. (Lands Tr.) 9 (jetty no
longer used by the public)—both unsuccessful applications.

actions of the superior may lead to changes enabling a discharge. Typically, a restriction that buildings adjacent to a railway station be used only as an auction mart became inappropriate once the transport of livestock by rail had ceased.[55] Here British Rail had objected to the discharge despite the changes which had rendered the location of the auction mart irrelevant.

A change in the profitability of the use of the land will not necessarily lead to a discharge. In *Bolton v. Aberdeen Corporation*[56] the applicant owned a grocery shop in Aberdeen and sought discharge of a condition which prevented him opening as a betting shop. He claimed that because of increased competition his profits as a grocer had slumped. However, the Tribunal denied discharge because the land continued to have an economic use as a grocery shop.[57]

(c) Changes in the Neighbourhood

This question was considered in *Main v. Lord Doune*[58] where there was a restriction against the use of the property for anything other than residential purposes. The feuar wished to open up a nursery on the property. This, clearly, was prohibited under the terms of his feudal grant. It was shown that one side of the Edinburgh New Town crescent where the feuar lived was no longer residential but that the other side retained its residential character. The Tribunal could see no reason why, when a particular small section of a large feu has lost its residential character, it should be said that any of the adjoining parts which had not done so should be deemed to have acquired a non-residential character. Thus the Tribunal concluded that the burdened proprietor had not shown a change in the residential character of the neighbourhood and so discharge was refused on this ground. This case sets a very high standard for change of character but the same approach seems to have been favoured in later cases.[59] The other issue under this head is for the tribunal to identify the "neighbourhood". In this regard the Tribunal will look at all the circumstances in identifying the area of protection of the obligation.[60]

8.29

---

[55] *United Auctions (Scotland) Ltd v. British Railways Board*, 1991 S.L.T. (Lands Tr.) 71.

[56] 1972 S.L.T. (Lands Tr.) 26.

[57] See for a more recent parallel approach to the question of profitability under s. 1(3)(c): *Miller Group Ltd v. Gardner's Executors*, 1992 S.L.T. (Lands Tr.) 62.

[58] 1972 S.L.T. (Lands Tr.) 14.

[59] *Pickford v. Young*, 1975 S.L.T. (Lands Tr.) 17; *Cameron v. Stirling*, 1988 S.L.T. (Lands Tr.) 18.

[60] *Bolton v. Aberdeen Corp.*, 1972 S.L.T. (Lands Tr.) 26.

(d) Changes in Social Habits

8.30	Although section 1(3)(a) relates to changes in the character of the
land, the Tribunal may also grant discharge where there are other
circumstances which the Tribunal thinks material. This was discussed in *Murrayfield Ice Rink v. Scottish Rugby Union*[61] where the
proprietors of an ice rink applied for discharge of a land obligation
which prevented them from using the premises as a supermarket.
The application was opposed by the superior, the SRU. The ice rink
proprietors argued on the basis of section 1(3)(a) that there were
other circumstances which rendered the obligation unreasonable or
inappropriate. It was claimed that there had been a change of social
habits over the years and that there had been a decline in demand for
ice sports. The Tribunal, however, could find no evidence of this.
According to the Tribunal, if there was such a decline it was prior to
1960 when the land obligation was imposed in the feu grant.
Consequently they refused discharge on this ground. The Tribunal
did admit, however, that a change in social habits and public taste
might constitute other material circumstances.

Discharge was successful under section 1(3)(a) in *Manz v. Butter's Trustees.*[62] In this case a hotel in the High Street in Pitlochry
was prohibited from selling liquor since its founding in 1924.
Discharge was sought under section 1(3)(a) since Pitlochry had
now become a major tourist area. The Tribunal accepted that
changes in the type of visitor going to the area and changes in
social habits regarding drink meant that the obligation could be
discharged.[63] It was pointed out by the Tribunal, however, that a
prohibition against liquor might still be reasonable in a particular
area. However, the case does illustrate that a change in social
habits can be deemed material circumstances and bring about a
discharge under section 1(3)(a).

(5) VARIATION OR DISCHARGE THROUGH UNDUE BURDEN[64]

8.31	The Act also provides a test based on whether any benefit would
be provided by the discharge of the obligation. This test does not
depend upon the personal circumstances of the burdened proprietor. The test is objective in terms of the locality. This point
was made clear in *Murrayfield Ice Rink* where the Tribunal was at
pains to point out that the fact that a discharge to allow a

---

[61] 1972 S.L.T. (Lands Tr.) 20, approved by the Inner House at 1973 S.L.T. 99.
[62] 1973 S.L.T. (Lands Tr.) 3.
[63] See also *Owen v. Mackenzie*, 1974 S.L.T. (Lands Tr.) 11.
[64] s. 1(3)(b).

supermarket in place of a failing ice rink enterprise would benefit the burdened proprietor did not automatically mean that it would bring benefit to the locality. The Tribunal's approach to this test is best illustrated in *Bolton*. Under this head, Bolton claimed that his land obligation was unduly burdensome on him because as a grocer he was making far smaller profits than he would make as a bookmaker. The Tribunal did not accept this contention, however, and were not satisfied that Bolton's decline in profits was due to the restrictive land obligation. It could also have been due to Bolton's personal skills as a grocer. Thus the mere fact that the land would become more profitable if the obligation were discharged is not of itself sufficient grounds under section 1(3)(b).[65] This was emphasised in a case involving the conflict between neighbours' amenity in having no building on a piece of adjacent land and the denial of profit to the burdened proprietor from being unable to build houses. The fact that the restriction prevented a profitable use of the land in question did not satisfy this test where there were competing tangible amenity benefits to non-development.[66]

(6) VARIATION OR DISCHARGE BECAUSE REASONABLE USE IMPEDED[67]

This has proved to be the most fruitful ground on which an 8.32 applicant can obtain discharge or variation of a land obligation. It should be noted that where there is an obligation to obtain consent for a particular use of land it is the very existence of the obligation which impedes the use and it is not impeded only by the way in which the benefited proprietor exercises the right to give or withhold consent.[68] The Tribunal has identified four central issues under the reasonable use test.

(a) Is there a Need for the Proposed Change of Use?

Murrayfield Ice Rink has made it clear that this question must be 8.33 looked at in all the circumstances. In it, the Tribunal asked itself whether wholesale and retail trade at the ice rink was a reasonable use of the land in all the circumstances. The Tribunal discovered that adequate vehicular access to the ice rink as an "island site" could not

---

[65] *Sinclair v. Gillon*, 1974 S.L.T. (Lands Tr.) 18.
[66] *The Miller Group Ltd v. Gardner's Exrs*, 1992 S.L.T. (Lands Tr.) 2.
[67] s. 1(3)(c).
[68] *Ramsay v. Holmes*, 1992 S.L.T. (Lands Tr.) 53 at 58 disapproving dicta in *British Bakeries (Scotland) Ltd v. City of Edinburgh D.C.*, 1990 S.L.T. (Lands Tr.) 33.

be arranged. There was also no proof that adequate parking space would be available to meet the increased traffic generated by a supermarket. Consequently, the Lands Tribunal held that the relevant land obligation was not presently impeding some reasonable use of the land and that the proposed supermarket was not reasonable in all the circumstances.

On the other hand, in *Main*[69] the restriction was found to impede a reasonable use of the land. This was because it was proved to the satisfaction of the Tribunal that the provision of a nursery in the locality would fulfil a social need.

(b) Would the Discharge Provide a Beneficial Utilisation of Land?

8.34   This was a question which the Tribunal considered in *West Lothian Co-operative Society Ltd v. Ashdale Land and Property Co. Ltd.*[70] The case concerned certain disused shop and residential property in Broxburn which had been sold with the intention of building a factory. The feuing conditions in question, however, required that certain derelict buildings be maintained on the feu and also prevented the premises being used as a factory. The Tribunal granted discharge under section 1(3)(c) because the requirement that the buildings be maintained impeded the redevelopment of the feu. Similarly, where land was simply lying unused and posing a possible danger to children playing there, then a servitude which had no prospect of being utilised was discharged.[71] The servitude right was for the purpose of a play area bordering the garden of the burdened proprietor. No playground had been built nor was contemplated. The local authority did not consider the land suitable for such a purpose.

(c) Has Planning Permission Been Obtained?

8.35   It is relevant to the applicant's case if planning permission has been obtained for the proposed change in use. In *Main*[72] planning permission had already been obtained for the proposed nursery. The Tribunal took this into account when considering whether the land obligation impeded a reasonable use of the land. It has been suggested that where the local authority has imposed a restriction in a disposition of land on what are really planning grounds, and where planning permission has subsequently been granted for a development covered by the restriction, there cannot be many circumstances in which it

---

[69] 1972 S.L.T. (Lands Tr.) 14.
[70] 1972 S.L.T. (Lands Tr.) 30.
[71] *Spafford v. Brydon*, 1991 S.L.T. (Lands Tr.) 49.
[72] 1972 S.L.T. (Lands Tr.) 14.

would be reasonable to maintain the restriction.[73] It cannot be assumed, however, that the exemption of a proposal from the need to apply for planning permission means such a development is always to be regarded as constituting a reasonable use of the land.[74]

(d) How will the Amenity of the Area be Affected by the Discharge?

This is the most common ground of objection to applications under section 1 (3)(c). The superior or other affected persons, such as local residents, may object on the basis of a consequent loss of amenity if the obligation is discharged. The question of whether a reasonable use of the land is impeded will be looked at in the light of all the circumstances including the impact on the amenity of the benefited premises.[75] In *Bolton*[76] the application was also rejected under this ground. The Tribunal agreed with the position that Aberdeen Corporation had adopted, that the restriction on betting shops was necessary to uphold the amenity of the area. This question was also considered in *Smith v. Taylor*.[77] In this case there was an application for discharge of an obligation which forbade the sale of liquor in a private hotel. The feuar sought discharge in order to obtain a liquor licence for the hotel. There were objections to the discharge from a number of neighbouring proprietors because of the noise and smell and increase in traffic and the parking of cars which licensed premises would create. The Tribunal considered that it was helpful to the applicant's case that his property had already been used without objection as a private hotel and boarding house.

8.36

(7) POWER OF ADDITION

Under section 1(5) the Tribunal has the power when varying or discharging a land obligation to add or substitute any such provision as appears to it to be reasonable as a result of the variation or discharge and as may be accepted by the applicant. The Tribunal has been able to use this procedure as a way of protecting the amenity of the area or preserving privacy as where they imposed a two-storey height restriction and requirement for a screening copse.[78] Certain

8.37

---

[73] *British Bakeries (Scotland) Ltd v. City of Edinburgh D.C.*, 1990 S.L.T. (Lands Tr.) 33 at 36.

[74] *Stoddart v. Glendinning*, 1993 S.L.T. (Lands Tr.) 12 at 17.

[75] *Tully v. Armstrong*, 1990 S.L.T. (Lands Tr.) 42.

[76] 1972 S.L.T. (Lands Tr.) 26.

[77] 1972 S.L.T. (Lands Tr.) 34.

[78] *Crombie v. George Heriot's Trust*, 1972 S.L.T. (Lands Tr.) 40; see also *Bruce v. Modern Homes Investment Co. Ltd*, 1978 S.L.T. (Lands Tr.) 34 on ground regrading.

considerations, however, will be treated as beyond the remit of the Tribunal such as questions of road safety outwith the area of a servitude right of way.[79]

(8) COMPENSATION[80]

8.38   For compensation to be awarded under section 1(4)(i) the loss or disadvantage must be substantial. The 1970 Act does not, however, contemplate waiver payments under the name of "compensation" where there is no loss or disadvantage such as reduction in value of land or loss of amenity as a result of any proposed development.[81] In *Smith v. Taylor*,[82] for example, the surrounding householders claimed compensation for the increased noise and smells that would be created by a licensed hotel. Their claims were successful and they were awarded compensation of between £100 and £800 depending on their proximity to the boarding house. Equally, compensation may be awarded under this head where the discharge is likely to lead to a depreciation in the value of premises.[83] However, compensation will not be awarded simply because the discharge of the obligation means that the superior will not receive the amount of money that a waiver of the obligation would provide.[84] Where a superior retains no interest in the area and the interest in enforcing land conditions is simply to extract as much money as possible in return for granting waivers, compensation has been refused.[85] Seeking money beyond administrative expenses for such waivers has been treated as vexatious and unreasonable. In addition, under section 1(3)(c) only, discharge or variation must be refused if, due to exceptional circumstances, money would not adequately compensate the benefited proprietor.[86]

8.39   The second ground upon which compensation can be awarded is as a sum to make up for any effect which the obligation produced, at the time of its imposition, in reducing the consideration paid. The basic issue here is whether the superior charged a lower feu duty on the basis of the obligation which has now been discharged. In *Manz v. Butter's Trustees*[87] the Tribunal held that the superiors

---

[79] *Spafford v. Brydon*, 1991 S.L.T. (Lands Tr.) 49.
[80] s. 1(4).
[81] *Harris v. Douglass; Erskine v. Douglass*, 1993 S.L.T. (Lands Tr.) 56 at 59.
[82] 1972 S.L.T. (Lands Tr.) 34.
[83] *Co-operative Wholesale Society v. Ushers Brewery*, 1975 S.L.T. (Lands Tr.) 9.
[84] *West Lothian Co-operative Society v. Ashdale Land and Property Co. Ltd*, 1972 S.L.T. (Lands Tr.) 30.
[85] *Harris v. Douglass; Erskine v. Douglass*, 1993 S.L.T. (Lands Tr.) 56.
[86] s. 1(4).
[87] 1973 S.L.T. (Lands Tr.) 2; *West Lothian Co-operative Society, supra*.

were not entitled to compensation under section 1(4)(ii) because they had failed to prove that a lower feuing rate was charged in 1924 when the land was first feued than would have been charged if the relevant feuing conditions had not been imposed. It is very rare for compensation to be awarded under this head.

(9) SERVITUDES OVER LAND

As in other areas of Scots law, much of the law on servitudes is 8.40
derived from Roman law.[88] A servitude has been defined by Bell as:

> "[A] burden on land or houses, imposed by agreement—express or implied—in favour of the owners of other tenements: whereby the owner of the burdened or 'servient' tenement, and his heirs and singular successors in the subject, must submit to certain uses to be exercised by the owner of the other or 'dominant' tenement or must restrain in his own use and occupation of the property."[89]

A servitude is, therefore, nothing more than a burden on heritable property in favour of the "dominant" tenement. The benefit granted to the owner of the dominant tenement is not personal, but is derived from the ownership of the dominant tenement. Thus a servitude is always praedial, that is, it is real and binds singular successors. Personal rights of skating, shooting, fishing, etc., are not servitudes but privileges, which subsist only as personal licences.

Servitudes are divided into two groups, positive and negative:

(i) A positive servitude permits the owner of the dominant tenement to do a positive act, such as walk over the servient tenement or pasture cattle there.

(ii) A negative servitude allows the owner of the dominant tenement to prevent or restrain the servient tenement from doing some action.

(a) Essentials of a Servitude

(i) There must be two tenements owned by diffeı̣̇at persons,[90] 8.41
both comprising subjects which are corporeal heritable property, and which are neighbouring or reasonably adjacent to one another.

(ii) There must be benefit to the dominant tenement, for this is

---

[88] Just., *Inst.* ii. 2. 3.

[89] Bell, *Prin.*, §979.

[90] As to whether a servitude can be created in favour of a tenement held by a tenant, see W. M. Gordon, *Scottish Land Law* (W. Green, 1989), para. 24–09.

the reason for the existence of the servitude. Thus the servitude must benefit the land and not merely be for the personal advantage of the holder of the dominant tenement.[91]

(iii) When a servitude is created by express grant, the words creating it must be unambiguous, definite and precise.[92] Since a servitude is a restraint on the freedom of property, strict construction will be applied of any document purporting to set it up.[93]

(b) Creation of a Servitude

8.42   There are four ways of creating a servitude.

(i) Express Grant

8.43   This is the only way that a negative servitude can be created, since prescriptive possession is out of the question and other methods would be almost impossible to establish where the operation of the servitude involves something not taking place. The document creating the servitude must satisfy the Requirements of Writing (Scotland) Act 1995.[94] There is no need for the agreement to be registered in the General Register of Sasines or Land Register. However, if it is a positive servitude it may be difficult to show that it was intended to apply to singular successors of the grantor. However, in theory at least, a person who acquires the dominant tenement can exercise the rights created by the servitude so long as there has been inspection of the property and inquiry followed by possession. Since in the case of a negative servitude there is no question of possession if the agreement is not recorded, it would not otherwise come to the notice of singular successors.

(ii) Implied Grant

8.44   This is an exceptional method by which a servitude can be created since it means placing a burden on another property as well as a benefit to the dominant tenement, and this would impinge upon the concept of freedom of property. Typically, a positive servitude may be created in this way if the property was originally owned by one person and the parts were later sold separately so that a servitude of

---

[91] *Patrick v. Napier* (1867) 5 M. 683.
[92] See, for example, *Fearnan Partnership v. Grindlay*, 1992 S.L.T. 460.
[93] See the speech of Lord Reid in *Hunter v. Fox*, 1964 S.C. (H.L.) 95.
[94] See, for example, *Safeway Food Stores Ltd v. Wellington Motor Co. (Ayr) Ltd*, 1976 S.L.T. 53.

access out of necessity would have to be implied. Such an implied servitude would have to be absolutely necessary or, at least, reasonably necessary for the comfortable enjoyment of the dominant tenement.[95]

(iii) Express or Implied Reservation

In this case, both tenements must have been in ownership of the 8.45
one person and later separated. This would occur when a seller sells off part of the land and reserves certain servitude rights which appear on the deed of conveyance. It is also possible to reserve a servitude right impliedly but this is seldom upheld.[96] It will be implied where there is necessity. An implied reservation cannot be set up, however, where the right sought is merely for the more comfortable or convenient enjoyment of the retained subjects, because this would be a derogation from the disponer's own grant.[97]

(iv) Prescription

Where there has been an actual use of a servitude and possession 8.46
for 20 years, continuously, openly, peaceably and without judicial interruption, a positive servitude will be created.[98] It may be possible to establish the servitude without proof of actual possession for 20 years. So long as for most of this period the relevant possession can be proved, the court will be prepared to infer use for the entire period of the positive prescription.[99] If acquired in this way, the kind of servitude created is determined by the prescriptive possession which has been established.

(c) Positive Servitudes

These may be either *urban* (affecting buildings in town or country) 8.47
or *rural* (affecting lands).

(i) Urban Servitudes

These can be further classified into various types.

(1) Support. Two servitudes of support are recognised, stemming 8.48
from the civil law:

---

[95] Contrast *Cochranes v. Ewart* (1860) 22 D. 358 (particularly *per* Lord Chancellor Campbell (1861) 23 D. 3) with *Fraser v. Cox*, 1938 S.C. 506.
[96] *Fergusson v. Campbell*, 1913 1 S.L.T. 241—water as an adjunct to a mill lade.
[97] Rankine, *Land-ownership* (4th ed., W. Green, 1909), p438. See also *Fergusson v. Campbell, supra.*
[98] Prescription and Limitation (Scotland) Act 1973, s. 3.
[99] *McGregor v. Crieff Co-operative Society*, 1915 S.C. (H.L.) 93.

tigni immitendi—the right to insert, into the wall of the servient tenement, a beam or other structural member forming part of the dominant tenement and to maintain it there and renew it when necessary;

oneris ferendi—the right of the dominant tenement to rest beams on the wall of the servient tenement and to have whole rooms resting on the other's tenement. There is an implied duty on servient owners to maintain their individual tenement.

8.49   **(2) Stillicide**. This is a right of eavesdrop which allows the dominant tenement proprietor to discharge rainwater from his roof onto the tenement which is servient, although this is likely to be overridden in practice by the restrictions imposed by the law of nuisance.

(ii) Rural Servitudes

Again these can be classified.

8.50   **(1) Fuel, feal and divot**. This is a right to dig peat for fuel and to take clods for fencing and roofing. Under this servitude there is implied a right of access to the locality. The right may be restricted to such parts of the servient tenement as is sufficient for the needs of the dominant tenement. The access is to be extensive enough to allow the relevant materials to be carted away.

8.51   **(2) Pasturage**. This servitude confers on the dominant tenement the right to pasture stock on the servient tenement, or, more frequently, on common ground.[1] If it is created by express grant, but no numbers are specified, the extent of the right is measured by the benefit to the dominant tenement. In practice, where common ground is concerned, since there are likely to be several dominant tenements their rights are determined either by rentals or the stock each can winter.

(3) Water

8.52   *Aquaehaustus*. This servitude allows the owner of the dominant tenement to take water to one tenement for his use. It often exists so that the dominant owner can take water for cattle, but it may apply for other purposes. The owner of the servient tenement may use the water, at least for primary purposes, provided the dominant tenement is left with the appropriate entitlement.

8.53   *Aqueduct*. This is the right to lead water over the servient tenement. There is implied a right of access for the dominant tenement in

---

[1] *Fraser v. Secretary of State for Scotland*, 1959 S.L.T. (Notes) 36.

order that the works can be maintained. This form of servitude is generally linked with the right to rest a weir on the servient tenement. It was held in *Central Regional Council v. Ferns*[2] that a servitude of aqueduct could be created by implication through the existence of legislation. In such case the owner of the servient tenement was not entitled to do any act which materially interfered with the dominant proprietor's right of access to the works.

(4) Passage. This form of servitude exists in four degrees—footways; 8.54 horse roads; drove roads and carriageways. A grant of wider use covers the narrower uses also so that, for example, a right of carriageway implies a right of footway. The type of passage the dominant servitude possesses will depend on the grant or the type of possession which has been exercised. The right may be restricted to use for a particular purpose, *e.g.* to go to a church or a mill, etc. A right of carriage road permits the dominant owner to use cars over it. The servient tenement can erect gates over the road but may not lock them. In some circumstances the course of a servitude road may be altered if provision is made of a substitute equally convenient to the dominant owner.[3] The extent of the dominant proprietor's right of access falls to be determined by reference to a person of average strength and agility and takes no account of the fact that a person may be disabled.[4] The fact that gates were erected to keep in livestock did not amount to an obstruction. The solution suggested for affected disabled owners was to use their right to enter the servient tenement to execute works to maintain the servitude and alter or adapt the gates.

(5) Other rural servitudes. Other rights have also been recognised 8.55 as rural servitudes, for example, bleaching, quarrying stone and taking sand and gravel. The modern development rights to run a pipeline through land, or an electricity or telephone line over it, are dealt with under the Pipelines Act 1962. This grants bodies wishing to construct such pipelines the authority compulsorily to acquire the necessary rights.

(d) Negative Servitudes

These are rights which do not require the dominant owner to 8.56 perform any acts, but exist to prevent or restrain some action by the servient owner (*in non faciendo*). They are of three types—light, air and prospect. As a general rule they restrict the otherwise natural

---

[2] 1979 S.C. 136.
[3] See, for example, *Magistrates of Rutherglen v. Bainbridge* (1886) 13 R. 745.
[4] *Drury v. McGarvie*, 1993 S.L.T. 987.

right of the servient owner to build where and as high as he chooses on his own property and thus block his neighbour's windows.

A servitude *non aedificandi* prevents the construction of any building, however harmless, while a servitude *altius non tollendi* permits the servient owner to build to a certain height.

These servitudes are always construed in favour of the servient tenement. Thus in one case, *Craig v. Gould*,[5] there was a prohibition against building higher than 10 feet "in order to preserve the lights" of the dominant owner. It was held that the servient owner could build up to 10 feet even although by so doing he blocked some windows of the dominant tenement. A servitude *non officiendi* is less specific. It restrains the owner of the servient tenement from constructing a building which interferes with the dominant owner's view.

(e) Enjoyment of Servitudes

8.57   Certain principles have been decided over the years governing how these restrictions of the ownership rights of the servient tenement should be exercised by the owner of the dominant tenement. These have been summarised by the House of Lords[6] as follows:

  (i) the owner of the dominant tenement may exercise the right not only for the purpose of the use to which the tenement is then being put but also for any other lawful purpose;
  (ii) the right must be exercised reasonably and in a manner least burdensome to the servient tenement;
  (iii) for the better enjoyment of the right, the dominant owner may improve the ground over which that right extends, provided there is no substantial alteration nor prejudice to the servient tenement;
  (iv) a servitude right of access is for the benefit of the dominant tenement and not for other adjoining tenements.

(f) Transmission of Servitudes

8.58   Servitudes have nothing to do with the superior/vassal relationship. They run with the land, and a singular successor of the dominant tenement automatically has a right to them if followed by infeftment (the recording of title in the Register of Sasines or Land Register) or by possession and enjoyment by the owner of the dominant tenement.

---

[5] (1861) 24 D. 20.
[6] *Alvis v. Harrison*, 1991 S.L.T. 64 at 67.

(g) Extinction of Servitudes

Servitudes can be extinguished in the following ways: 8.59

(i) Express Discharge or Renunciation

Such renunciation must be by the dominant owner in accordance 8.60
with the terms of the Requirements of Writing (Scotland) Act 1995.
This will bind singular successors to the dominant tenement. Like
the rules for creation of a servitude there is no need that the deed of
renunciation be recorded in the Register of Sasines or Land Register. However, it is preferable to register such a deed particularly
when the original grant creating the servitude has been recorded.

(ii) Confusio

This arises where both tenements come into the ownership of the 8.61
one person. In such a case the servitude disappears and does not
revive if the tenements are later separated. However, this presumption may be rebutted if it can be established that the properties were
held on separate titles.[7]

(iii) Negative Prescription

If a positive servitude has not been exercised or a relevant claim 8.62
made by the owner of the dominant tenement for a continuous
period of 20 years the servitude will be extinguished.[8] The time will
run from the last date when the owner of the dominant tenement
exercised the right. Equally, a negative servitude will cease to exist
where the dominant tenement has failed to enforce it for 20 years. In
this case, the time is calculated from the date of the first contravention by the servient tenement which went unchallenged.

(iv) Acquiescence

This occurs where the owner of the dominant tenement evidences 8.63
by his conduct an intention to give up the right so that subsequently
he is personally barred from enforcing it.

(v) Change of Circumstances

The servitude will be extinguished if either the dominant or the 8.64
servient tenement is destroyed. In such a case there must be total
destruction for the servitude to disappear. If there is merely a

---

[7] Bell, *Prin.*, §997. See *Donaldson's Trs v. Forbes* (1839) 1 D. 449. *Cf. Walton Bros v.
Magistrates of Glasgow* (1876) 3 R. 1130.
[8] Prescription and Limitation (Scotland) Act 1973, s. 8.

temporary unfitness of either tenement the servitude will simply be suspended until the necessary remedial action is taken. Servitudes may also be affected by the compulsory requisition of the servient tenement. In such a case the servitude will be suspended until the property is returned to private hands.

(vi) Statute

8.65   It is possible that a statute which provides for the compulsory acquisition of the servient tenement will declare that the land is to be free from any servitudes. In any case any servitude which is incompatible with the compulsory purchase is likely to expire.

(10) PUBLIC RIGHTS OF WAY

8.66   A public right of way is not a servitude, but a right whereby the public can pass from one public place to another along a definite route. It is usually acquired by use for the prescriptive period of 20 years. The Prescription and Limitation (Scotland) Act 1973, s. 3(3) makes it clear that the use possessed by the public must be open, peaceable and without judicial interruption and declares that once the 20-year period has expired a right of way will exist and be exempt from legal challenge. Where a right of way is established as a public right of way, it is not necessary that the use made of it be restricted to use from one end to the other. The proprietors of land along the course of the right of way are entitled to use the road for access to their properties.[9] If the road as a whole ceases to run from one public place to another, the established rights of use enjoyed by proprietors along the road for access to their own properties are not, thereby, lost.[10]

The difference between a servitude and a public right of way was discussed in *Ayr Burgh Council v. British Transport Commission.*[11] Here, the cattle market was approached through railway property. The council, as proprietors of the local cattle market, raised an action of interdict against British Rail from levying a charge against cars, etc., making use of the British Transport Commission's livestock bank beside the cattle market. The council based their case on the fact that they had acquired a public right of way for the purpose of getting to the cattle market. They also claimed that if no public right of way could be set up they had acquired a private servitude of access either by prescription or agreement. The court held that as the market was open only four days a week and was closed at nights, no

---

[9] *McRobert v. Reid*, 1914 S.C. 633.
[10] *Lord Burton v. Mackay*, 1995 S.L.T. 507.
[11] 1955 S.L.T. 219.

public right of way could be set up since the essence of a public right of way is that the public place should be kept open for passage by the public at all times. The court also held that no servitude right of way in favour of the public was known to Scots law since the essence of a servitude is to benefit one particular property, *viz* the dominant tenement.

Rights of way are basically extinguished in the same ways as servitudes.[12] Where a public right of way is asserted by use, however, the owner cannot stand by and expect that inaction will be taken as good nature or tolerance. If the access is merely at the owner of the land's goodwill then the public must be made aware of the fact so that they know that the route is being used by permission not as of right.[13]

2. LAW OF NEIGHBOURHOOD

The social nature of property ownership was recognised by the common law in two major forms prior to the emergence of statutory limitations on what property owners could do with their heritage. Initially the option of freedom of property dominated and for any limitation an element of malice was required. However, this was modified in the doctrine of nuisance which merely limited property owners to using their property in such a way as not to harm the property rights of others. This is in accordance with the maxim *sic utere tuo ut alienum non laedas* (so use your property as not to injure that of another). Whilst this provided the basis for complaint, it relied for its effectiveness on active complaints and litigation. It was greatly supplemented by regulation by public officials on behalf of the community in the form of statutory nuisance on a national basis in Scotland from 1867 onwards.

8.67

(1) THE USE OF ONE'S PROPERTY WITH MALICE AGAINST NEIGHBOURING PROPERTY (*IN AEMULATIONEM VICINI*)

The common law prohibits any use of property where the sole benefit is to harm neighbouring property without there being any benefit to the property owner.[14] The spite or malice involved must be proved rather than merely assumed. Fishing beyond the mid-point

8.68

---

[12] See W. M. Gordon, *Scottish Land Law* (W. Green, 1989), paras 24–147 to 24–154.

[13] *Cumbernauld and Kilsyth D.C. v. Dollar Land (Cumbernauld) Ltd*, 1993 S.L.T. 1318.

[14] Lord Watson questioned the existence of such a concept in *Mayor of Bradford v. Pickles* [1895] A.C. 587 at 598. His statement must be considered *obiter* and cannot be reconciled with later Scottish decisions. See also "Reparation", in *Encyclopaedia of the Laws of Scotland* (1931), Vol 12, paras 1076–1078.

of a river was taken to amount to malicious use against the rights of
the owner of the opposite bank in *Campbell v. Muir*.[15] More
recently, in *More v. Boyle*[16] the act of closing a waterpipe running
through a garden was accepted as coming within the bounds of
aemulatio. Here there was a dispute about a repair to the water
supply and the response of the defender thereafter was to excavate in
his garden and close up the pipe supplying his neighbours including
the pursuer. Proof before answer was allowed.

(2) NUISANCE UNDER THE COMMON LAW

8.69   Owners are restricted by the common law of Scotland to using their
property in such a way as not to harm others' enjoyment of their
property. Property owners are entitled to an environment free from
pollution. This covers physical discomfort—smoke, smells, noise or
vibration—as well as things offensive to decency.[17]
   The broad approach is whether or not the acts complained of
interfere with the enjoyment of life of another property owner.
The proper angle of approach is from the standpoint of the victim
of the loss or inconvenience rather than from the standpoint of
the alleged offender.[18] What is acceptable conduct has varied
between different times and different geographical locations.
Whether a particular act or omission amounts to a nuisance is
largely a question of neighbourhood, circumstance and degree.
Typically the important element of the locality will mean that
what is a nuisance in a residential area need not be a nuisance in
an industrial estate. Some activities might be dealt with by either
the criminal law or by the relevant environmental protection
legislation. Nevertheless, there is no limitation on the use of
the common law merely because the activities complained of
are illegal or subject to regulation by statutory agencies. Indeed,
given the unwillingness of the courts to interfere with discretionary powers given to the police and local authorities the common
law of nuisance may prove a crucial mechanism of control, as can
be seen by the successful interdict secured against the erection of
the stands for the Edinburgh Military Tattoo in *Webster v. Lord
Advocate*.[19]

---

[15] 1908 S.C. 387.
[16] 1967 S.L.T. (Sh. Ct.) 38.
[17] See the classic definition of nuisance provided by Professor Bell, *Prin.*, §974, and
quoted in full in Chap. 7.
[18] *per* Lord President Cooper in *Watt v. Jamieson*, 1954 S.C. 56 at 57.
[19] 1984 S.L.T. 13—although this was suspended for 6 months to allow existing
contractual obligations to be met and for a negotiated settlement to be secured.

The complainer at common law may seek interdict as well as damages and, where appropriate, restitution. It is now clear that where nuisance is claimed some reference to fault or *culpa* must be made.[20] The right to complain about a nuisance can be lost through consent and acquiescence, although this may not be easy to establish.[21] In addition, the right of a property owner to object may be lost through the operation of the period of the negative prescription which is 20 years[22] unless there is an increase in the nuisance.[23] It is also possible for statute to specifically authorise the activity in question.[24]

(3) STATUTORY NUISANCE

Whilst there is no distinction in Scots law between public and private 8.70 nuisance, which is a feature of the law south of the border, there was a more formal system of nuisance regulation set up under various statutes dating for the most part from the nineteenth century. The statutory control system for general neighbourhood nuisances is now to be found in Part III of the Environmental Protection Act 1990. This was brought into effect in Scotland by the Environment Act 1995 as from April 1996. This extension of English legislation to Scotland means that case law in this area from south of the border will now be relevant in Scotland.

Specific forms of pollution also have their own detailed statutory codes—air pollution is dealt with in the Clean Air Act 1993, Pt I of the Environmental Protection Act 1990 and Part IV of the Environment Act 1995, whilst water pollution is covered by the Control of Pollution Act 1974 and radioactive waste by the Radioactive Substances Act 1993.

(a) Statutory Nuisance in Outline

The following matters constitute statutory nuisances where they 8.71 are prejudicial to health or a nuisance (prejudicial to health means injurious, or likely to cause injury, to health):

    (i) any premises in such a state;
    (ii) smoke emitted from premises;
    (iii) fumes or gases emitted from premises;

---

[20] See the decision of the House of Lords in *RHM Bakeries (Scotland) Ltd v. Strathclyde R.C.*, 1985 S.L.T. 214. The decision in *Kennedy v. Glenbelle Ltd*, 1996 S.L.T. 1186 has clarified the meaning of *culpa*.
[21] *Houldsworth v. Burgh of Wishaw* (1887) 14 R. 920.
[22] Prescription and Limitation (Scotland) Act 1973, s. 8.
[23] *McGavin v. McIntyre and Orles* (1890) 17 R. 818.
[24] *Allen v. Gulf Oil Refining Ltd* [1981] A.C. 1001.

(iv) any dust, steam, smell or other effluvia arising on industrial, trade or business premises;
(v) any accumulation or deposit;
(vi) any animal kept in such a place or manner;
(vii) noise emitted from premises;
(viii) noise emitted from or caused by a vehicle, machinery or
equipment in a road;
(ix) any other matter declared by any enactment to be a
statutory nuisance.

This list covers both specific issues like smoke and noise nuisance as
well as containing general matters. Certain kinds of smoke do not
constitute nuisance—smoke emitted from a chimney of a private
dwelling within a smoke control area; dark smoke emitted from certain
boiler or industrial plant chimneys; smoke emitted from a railway
locomotive steam engine, or dark smoke emitted from industrial or
trade premises. Contaminated land is expressly excluded from the
definition of statutory nuisance.[25] Noise includes vibration. Noise in
streets does not include that caused by traffic generally, the armed
forces or a political demonstration. Noise-generating equipment
specifically includes musical instruments.

(b) Duty of Local Authority to Deal with Statutory Nuisances

(i) Inspection

8.72   It is the duty of every local authority to cause its area to be
inspected from time to time to detect any statutory nuisances.[26] In
addition they must take such steps as are reasonably practicable to
investigate any complaint of a statutory nuisance made to it by a
person living within its area.[27]

(ii) Entry

8.73   If the local authority or a proper officer of the authority have
reasonable grounds for believing that a nuisance exists on any
premises, they may demand entry and, if refused, may obtain a
warrant to do so. They are also entitled to make such tests as are
necessary on condition that, if no nuisance is found, they must
restore the premises to their former condition.

---

[25] 1990 Act, s. 79(1A).
[26] 1990 Act, s. 79(1).
[27] *ibid.*

(iii) Notice

Where a local authority is satisfied that a statutory nuisance exists 8.74
or is likely to occur or recur in the area of the authority, the local
authority must serve a notice called an "abatement notice".[28] This
must be served on the person responsible for the nuisance.[29] If,
however, the nuisance arises from any defect of a structural character, the abatement notice must be served on the owner of the
premises.[30] If the person responsible for the nuisance cannot be
found, the abatement notice must be served on the occupier or
owner of the premises.[31] If a nuisance arises from noise emitted from
an unattended vehicle or unattended machinery or equipment, and
the person responsible for the vehicle, machinery or equipment
cannot be found, the abatement notice may be attached to the
vehicle, machinery or equipment.

The notice imposes all or any of specified requirements:

(i) the abatement of the nuisance or prohibition or restriction
of its occurrence or recurrence;

(ii) the execution of such works and the taking of such other
steps as may be necessary to abate the nuisance and prevent
it occurring or recurring.[32]

The abatement notice must specify the time or times within
which the requirements of the notice are to be complied with,
although it has been held that in the absence of a stated time for
compliance a notice came into effect at midnight following the
day of service.[33]

(iv) Non-compliance with Notice

If a person on whom an abatement notice is served without 8.75
reasonable excuse contravenes, or fails to comply with, any requirement or prohibition imposed by the notice that person is guilty of an
offence. They are liable on summary conviction to a fine not
exceeding level five on the standard scale. If, however, there is a
statutory nuisance committed on industrial, trade or business premises the fine is a figure not exceeding £20,000. "Reasonable
excuse" does not appear to have any specified meaning in the

---

[28] *R. v. Carrick D.C., ex p. Shelley* [1996] Env. L.R. 273.
[29] s. 80(2)(a).
[30] s. 80(2)(b).
[31] s. 80(2)(c).
[32] *R. v. Ferry Strathford Justices, ex p. Watney Mann (Midlands)* [1976] 1 W.L.R.
1101 at 1106.
[33] *Strathclyde R.C. v. Tudhope*, 1983 S.L.T. 22.

legislation. Lack of finance has been held not to amount to a reasonable excuse.[34]

The defence of "best practicable means" is available for certain kinds of nuisance. It covers those committed on industrial, trade or business premises. It applies where the offender is able to prove that the best practicable means were used to prevent, or to counteract the effects of, the nuisance. "Practicable" means reasonably practicable having regard among other things to local conditions and circumstances, to the current state of technical knowledge and to the financial implications.[35] The test is to apply only so far as is compatible with any duty imposed by the law and with safety and safe working conditions and subject to any emergency or unforeseeable circumstances.[36] In the case of noise nuisance, any codes of practice produced under section 71 of the Control of Pollution Act 1974 are relevant.[37]

Where an abatement notice has not been complied with, the local authority may, irrespective of whether there is a prosecution for breach, abate the nuisance and do whatever may be necessary.[38] Any expenses reasonably incurred by the local authority in abating or preventing the recurrence of the nuisance may be recovered from the person by whose act or default the nuisance was caused.[39] Where more than one person is responsible for a statutory nuisance, these costs may be apportioned by the court as it considers fair and reasonable.

(v) Failure to Act by the Local Authority

8.76   If the local authority fails in its duty in regard to nuisances, there are direct means by which individuals may take proceedings. This is less restrictive than the 10 ratepayers or procurator fiscal mechanisms which were available under the Public Health (Scotland) Act 1897. A person who is aggrieved by the existence of a statutory nuisance may bring a summary application before the local sheriff.[40] If the sheriff is satisfied that the alleged nuisance exists or is likely to recur, the sheriff must make an order either of abatement or prohibiting recurrence. Where any works are necessary to secure the abatement or prevent the recurrence these shall be specified.[41]

---

[34] *Saddleworth UDC v. Aggregate and Sand* (1970) 114 S.J. 931.
[35] s. 79(9)(a); see also *Wivenhoe Port v. Colchester B.C.* [1985] J.P.L. 175 (affirmed [1985] J.P.L. 396).
[36] s. 79(9)(d).
[37] *e.g.* Control of Noise (Code of Practice for Construction Sites) (Scotland) Order 1982 (S.I. 1982 No. 601).
[38] s. 81(3).
[39] s. 81(4).
[40] s. 82(1).
[41] s. 82(2).

Where the sheriff is satisfied that the alleged nuisance (renders the premises unfit for human habitation, there m order prohibiting the use of the premises for human habita the premises are rendered fit.[42]

Prior to bringing proceedings before the sheriff against the person responsible for a nuisance, the aggrieved party must give that person a notice in respect of the nuisance giving not less than 21 days' notice in most instances. Only three days' notice is required for noise nuisance.[43]

Contravention of any requirement or prohibition is an offence punishable by a fine not exceeding level five together with a further fine of an amount equal to one-tenth of that level for each day the offence continues after conviction.[44]

The defence of "best practicable means" is available only where industrial, trade or business premises are concerned. The defence is not available where premises are rendered unfit for human habitation.[45]

The sheriff may, after convicting a person for an offence and hearing the local authority, direct the authority to do anything which the convicted person was required by order to do. There is also provision for compensation to the person bringing proceedings to cover their expenses.[46] Where neither the person responsible for the nuisance nor the owner or occupier of the premises can be found, the sheriff may, after giving the local authority an opportunity to be heard, direct the authority to do anything which would have been ordered against the person responsible for the nuisance.[47]

3. REGULATION BY STATUTE

There are three major forms of statutory regulation of landowners and 8.77 property owners which should be noted—building control, planning control and control of disrepair. These supplement restrictions which operate locally and privately, and are a major feature in determining whether or not operations on land or buildings are feasible.

(1) BUILDING CONTROL

The traditional Scottish requirement, as far as control over the 8.78 standard of construction of buildings is concerned, was enforced through the local dean of guild court. This has been superseded by

---

[42] s. 82(3).
[43] s. 82(7).
[44] s. 82(8).
[45] s. 82(10).
[46] s. 82(12).
[47] s. 82(13).

regulations introduced under the Building (Scotland) Acts of 1959 and 1970. These regulations cover such issues as resistance to moisture, fire resistance of material, minimum sizes and external access. Whilst neighbours must receive notice that alterations to buildings are proposed, the building regulations only permit them to object on technical grounds that the building regulations are not being complied with. There is no place in building control for aesthetic or amenity considerations, which are the province of planning control. In addition the local building authority duty of care is limited.

(2) PLANNING CONTROL

8.79 Since 1909 there has been some form of public planning control over new developments to land or buildings. Control is exercised by the elected local politicians on behalf of the community. This discretion is subject to the overriding control of the Secretary of State for Scotland. The major innovation in this area took place in the Town and Country Planning (Scotland) Act 1947 which forms the basis of the current Scottish legislation, the Town and Country Planning (Scotland) Act 1997.[48] The legislation requires any person who has development proposals to obtain planning permission for these proposals. Development broadly covers new buildings, extensions of existing buildings and material change of use of property from, for example, residential to office or commercial purposes. Planning permission is a matter for the discretion of the local planning authority, taking into account such matters as their local development plan and any representations made to them by affected parties. All planning proposals must be made public through appearing on the local authority planning register, although press advertisement is not generally required. The planning register is open for inspection by all members of the public regardless of motive. Planning permission can be granted unconditionally or subject to such conditions as the planning authority chooses to impose.[49]

(3) CONTROL OF DISREPAIR

8.80 Local authorities have wide powers under the Building (Scotland) Act 1959, the Civic Government (Scotland) Act 1982 and the Housing (Scotland) Act 1987 to deal with housing which is in

---

[48] See also the Planning (Listed Buildings and Conservation Areas) (Scotland) Act 1997 and the Planning (Hazardous Substances) (Scotland) Act 1997.
[49] See E. Young and J. Rowan-Robinson, *Scottish Planning Law and Procedure* (Hodge, 1986); A. McAllister and R. McMaster, *Scottish Planning Law* (Butterworths, 1994).

disrepair. The powers cover actions in relation to individual houses as well as whole areas. As far as individual houses are concerned, the 1987 Act provides powers exercisable through the Environmental Health Department ranging from the power to require repairs or improvements to be carried out, to the closure of houses or even their demolition. Dangerous buildings are dealt with by the local authority building control department using powers under the Building (Scotland) Act 1959. Mandatory and discretionary loans are available from the local authority to owners in certain circumstances where either voluntarily or at the behest of the local authority their property is being repaired or improved.

As far as housing in general is concerned, the local authority has an obligation to ensure that the housing in its area meets the "tolerable standard".[50] This allows the local authority to assess the housing needs of its area as required under the 1987 Act. To meet the "tolerable standard" a building requires to be structurally stable, free from rising or penetrating damp, satisfactorily lit, ventilated and have a hot and cold water supply to a sink, an internal w.c. for exclusive use of occupants, an effective drainage system, satisfactory cooking facilities and satisfactory access to all external doors and outbuildings. On the basis of this assessment local authorities will draw up their housing plans including the designation of Housing Action Areas. An authority may designate an area as an HAA for either improvement or demolition or a combination of both. The approval of the Secretary of State is required for such proposals. Local authorities also have powers to control the numbers of individuals who may live in housing under the terms of the Housing (Scotland) Act 1987.[51]

---

[50] Housing (Scotland) Act 1987, Pt IV.
[51] For further details see C. Himsworth, *Housing Law in Scotland* (4th ed., Butterworths, 1995).

Chapter 9

NATURE AND FORMATION OF LEASES

1. Introduction

9.01 A lease involves the hiring of land or heritage for a definite period of time in exchange for the payment of rent. There is a body of law which affects all leases and we will examine this initially. Thereafter there are a number of issues on which the different kinds of leases have distinct provisions. We will look at the major areas of significance and concentrate on conditions, rent levels and security of tenure. There are three major codes of law governing leases in Scotland. First, as far as the renting of dwelling-houses is concerned there are controls over both what condition they must reach to be tenantable as well as restrictions on the rent recoverable by the landlord and limitations on when a landlord can recover possession of the subjects. Similarly, in leases of agricultural property tenants are provided with protections in relation to security of tenure, but in broad terms there is no guarantee as to the viability or suitability of land or fishings rented out. Finally, there are the provisions covering commercial and industrial property. These are regulated by the general rules of the common law of leases and contractual variation is permitted. Minimal protection for commercial tenants exists in Scotland.

(1) Common Features of all Leases

9.02 Where there is a lease, whether it be of agricultural land, commercial premises or a dwelling-house, the rules are the same as to the creation of the lease. The rights and obligations of landlord and tenant are broadly similar at common law. The capacity of the parties to make and take leases is largely covered by the normal rules of contractual capacity.[1] One common feature of leases in Scotland is the concept of tacit relocation. This provides that where an agreement reaches its contractual termination date it is assumed to be continued on the same terms and conditions unless one of the parties formally terminates the agreement with notice. However, there are distinctive and different rules for the fixing of rent, security of tenure and fitness obligations in leases of agricultural land and dwelling-houses.

At common law there were very few limitations on what individuals could agree. Statute has both limited the formal length of leases of dwelling-houses as well as providing that individuals can stay on beyond the term of the agreement. In addition, in some situations members of the family of the occupier may be entitled to stay on in the property on the death of the original occupier.

A lease (formerly known as a "tack") is a contract of hire, 9.03 sometimes termed a "location". Under it, the use of land or some other heritable subject is granted by one party to another for a period of time in return for money, commodities or even services. The grantor is known as the "landlord" or "lessor". The grantee is the "tenant" or "lessee". Formerly, the words "tack" and "tacksman" were used in Scotland and will be encountered in older cases and texts. Where the grantor is a tenant of the subjects under another lease then this is known as the principal or head lease and the second grantee the "sublessee" or "subtenant".

Rankine's classical definition of a lease is as follows:

> "A lease or tack is a contract of location (letting to hire) by which one person grants and another accepts certain uses, current or definitive, or the entire control, of lands or other heritages for a period or periods, definite or indefinite or even in perpetuity, in consideration of the delivery by the grantee of money or commodities or both, periodically or in lump, or in both of these ways. The grantor is known as the lessor, landlord or overlessee, or if he holds immediately under the landlord, the principal lessee. The grantee is known as lessee, tenant, tacksman, sublessee or subtenant. The periodical payment is rent, royalty or lordship: the lump sum is grassum or foregift. The contract is in its essence purely personal: in certain circumstances it gives rise to what is substantially a real right."[2]

---

[1] S. Woolman, *An introduction to the Scots law of Contract* (2nd ed., W. Green, 1994); W. McBryde, *The Law of Contract in Scotland* (Scottish Universities Law Institute Ltd/W. Green, 1987); W. M. Gordon, *Scottish Land Law* (Scottish Universities Law Institute Ltd/W. Green, 1989).

[2] *The Law of Leases in Scotland* (3rd ed., W. Green, 1916), p. 1.

9.04   There are crucial differences between leases and other occupancy rights in land.[3] A grant of a feu, adding a new link in the feudal chain[4] or simple sale of heritage confer rights in perpetuity whilst the rights conferred on the tenant by a lease are generally limited to a specified duration. Compared with a sale of heritage, the property in the case of a lease never becomes that of the tenant—although under modern rent legislation certain tenants may have almost complete security of tenure during their own lifetime and for the lives of other members of the family. The landlord remains the owner and if the conditions of the lease are broken the tenant may be evicted. A purchaser of property, on the other hand, under a valid contract of sale, once title has been recorded in the Land Register for Scotland may do what he wishes with the property (subject, of course, to planning, nuisance, servitude restrictions and any restrictions imposed by his feudal superior, etc.).

The tenant has a right to the limited use of the subjects whilst the owner has full rights to use and dispose. A clear exception is the mineral lease where, by its very nature, the minerals which are the subject of the lease are used up by the tenant.

2. Lease as a Personal Contract

9.05   At common law a lease is a personal contract and is governed by the general rules applicable to contracts. Thus both parties must have legal capacity, and the parties' consent must not be vitiated by fraud or misrepresentation, essential error or force or fear. There must also be *consensus in idem*—in other words the parties must be agreed on the cardinal elements of the contract. In a lease contract there must accordingly be agreement on parties, subjects, rent and duration.

Since a lease (except a lease for one year or less) can be regarded as a contract which creates an interest in land, it must (except for one year or less) be constituted in writing[5] and signed by the parties.[6] A lease does not require to be witnessed in order to be valid; but if the lease is to be registered in the Register of Sasines or Land Register (for the acquisition by the tenant of a real right, see below) or in the Books of Council and Session (in connection primarily with summary diligence, see below) it must be witnessed by one witness for each party's signature.[7]

---

[3] See Chap. 11 on service occupancies and licences.
[4] See paras 5.05 to 5.07.
[5] Requirements of Writing (Scotland) Act 1995, s. 1(2), applicable to all leases for more than one year entered into on or after August 1, 1995.
[6] *ibid.* s. 2(1).
[7] *ibid.* s. 6.

For leases of more than one year entered into before the commencement of the Requirements of Writing (Scotland) Act 1995 a different set of common law rules had to be observed. In particular, written leases had to be either attested or holograph of the granter, or adopted as holograph; and two witnesses were required for each signature.[8]

A contract which creates an interest in land is not to be regarded   9.06 as invalid, despite failing to comply with these statutory formalities, if one of the parties has acted or refrained from acting in reliance on the contract with the knowledge and acquiescence of the other party and the position of the party who has so acted or refrained from acting has been affected to a material extent as a result, and would be adversely affected to a material extent if the other party were entitled to withdraw from the contract on the grounds of failure to comply with the formal requirements of the 1995 Act.[9] Neither party to a lease for more than a year which is never reduced to writing, or is never signed or only improperly signed, can resile if these conditions as to personal bar are satisfied.

This statutory formulation of personal bar replaces the old rules on *rei interventus* and homologation whereby a lease which was defective in form (though not one which had never been reduced to writing at all) was validated if followed by significant actings by one party in reliance on the contract which were known to and permitted by the other party, and those actings were productive of an alteration in the former's circumstances. There are a number of cases dealing with the validation of informal leases under these rules[10] which might prove useful in interpreting the new statutory provisions.

Leases for not more than one year do not require to be in writing,[11] although in practice writing may be adopted (*e.g.* so that the lease can be registered in the Books of Council and Session).

(1) Parties

Both the landlord and the tenant must be clearly identified.   9.07

(2) Subjects

A lease can only operate over heritable property. An analogous   9.08 arrangement over moveable property would be a contract of hire. It

---

[8] See A. McAllister, *Scottish Law of Leases* (2nd ed., 1995), pp. 17–18.
[9] Requirements of Writing (Scotland) Act 1995, s. 1(3) and (4).
[10] See, for example, *Forbes v. Wilson* (1873) 11 M. 454; *Ferryhill Property Investments Ltd v. Technical Video Productions*, 1992 S.C.L.R. 282.
[11] Requirements of Writing (Scotland) Act 1995, s. 1(7).

is also important that there is clear agreement and identification of
the extent of the subjects leased, since this will regulate the limits of
the tenant's right to occupy, as well as the extent of any repairing
obligation which the tenant may have.

(3) RENT

9.09 There must be provision for the payment of rent if a valid lease is to
be created. The rent may be in money or in kind—either in the form
of fruits (grain, minerals or timber) or services. The rent may be
purely nominal or elusory. If the tenant is to pay a grassum or
premium at the start of his lease, but there is no obligation to pay a
periodical rent, there is no lease. Thus, where a garage owner
permitted a person to occupy the garage for 10 years in return
for a lump sum of £200, on the understanding that £20 would be
repaid on termination of the agreement in respect of each unexpired
year of the period, it was held that the absence of a periodic rent
precluded the existence of a lease.[12]

The court will not normally supply a rent where the parties have
failed to agree one,[13] and any agreement in such circumstances will
not constitute a lease under which a tenant might acquire a real right
under the 1449 Act (see below). The court may, however, require an
occupier of property in such circumstances to pay the annual value
of the subjects.[14]

(4) DURATION

9.10 The duration of a lease must be stated or capable of inference from
its terms. It has been held that a lease which was stated to last
"perpetually and continually as long as the grass groweth up and the
water runneth down" was valid,[15] though such a lease might not
satisfy the requirement for a definite ish (termination date) under the
Leases Act 1449. This would prevent the tenant under such a lease
acquiring a real right.

If all other essential aspects of a lease are agreed and the tenant
has entered into possession, the court will normally imply a duration
of one year in the absence of a specified duration in the lease.[16] The

---

[12] *Mann v. Houston,* 1957 S.L.T. 89.
[13] *Shetland Islands Council v. British Petroleum Development Ltd,* 1990 S.L.T. 82.
[14] *Glen v. Roy* (1882) 10 R. 239.
[15] *Carruthers v. Irvine* (1717) Mor. 15195.
[16] *Cinema Bingo Club v. Ward,* 1976 S.L.T. (Sh. Ct.) 90.

implied duration of one year can subsequently be extended by tacit relocation. However a duration will only be implied if there is clearly a lease, and not if the parties had merely conducted protracted negotiations without reaching agreement[17] or if the contract between the parties is only in reality a licence.[18]

3. LEASE AS A REAL RIGHT

If a lease complies with the requirements mentioned then it will be a   9.11
valid lease at common law provided that the requirements as to formality and capacity of the parties are also observed. However, the lease at common law was a personal contract which did not bind singular successors of the lessor. The term singular successors applies to persons who derive a right from the grantor other than through succession either through purchase or in the process of insolvency.

The problem was dealt with by statute in the Leases Act 1449. This provided that a lease should be enforceable against singular successors by the tenant provided that certain conditions were fulfilled. Although this Act was originally designed to protect "the puir pepil that labouris the grunde" it was soon applied to urban property and is the basis of the modern law of leases today. The statute reads (in translation):

"It is ordained for the safety and favour of the poor people that work the land, that they, and all others that have leased or shall lease property in future from any landlord, and have time to run on the lease that if the landlord sells or disposes of that property the tenants shall continue in their leases until their dates of termination on the same terms and conditions."[19]

The requisites under the 1449 Act for a lease to confer a real right as interpreted by the courts are as follows.

---

[17] *Gray v. Edinburgh University*, 1962 S.C. 157.
[18] *Scottish Residential Estates Development Co. Ltd v. Henderson*, 1991 S.L.T. 490.
[19] The original 15th-century version was: "It is ordanit for the sauftie and favour of the puir pepil that labouris the grunde that thai and al utheris that hes takyn or sal tak landis in tym to cum fra lordis and has termes and yeris thereof that suppose the lordis sel or analy thai landis that the takaris sall remayn with thare takis on to the ische of thare termes quhais handis at euir thai landis cum to for sic lik male as thai tuk thaim of befoir" (2nd ed., revised, 1966). The word "tak" or "tack" for lease will still be found in relatively modern documents.

(1) WRITING

9.12 A lease for more than one year must be in writing though if for a lesser period this would be unnecessary. Although a verbal agreement for more than one year may be validated by the actings of the parties,[20] a tenant could not acquire a real right and the lease would not bind singular successors of the landlord.

(2) SUBJECTS

9.13 The subjects must be land. The statute refers to "landes", though this has been interpreted as all adjuncts of land which are capable of separate ownership—mills, minerals, salmon fishing, quarries, ferries, harbours and houses as well as the land itself. Although fishing and shooting are not separate rights in land but incidents of land-ownership, leases of them have been recognised.

(3) DEFINITE ISH OR TERMINATION DATE

9.14 Although at common law a lease may be perpetual, in order to be afforded the protection of the 1449 Act a lease must have a definite ish. This does not mean that it needs to be fixed. A lease may be given for an uncertain period of time provided the date of its ending is bound to happen. Thus a lease may be given for the successive lives of certain persons X, Y and Z. Although it is impossible to say when these three people are finally going to die, it is absolutely certain (in legal terms) that they are all going to die at some date in the future. While it is possible for a lease to be perpetual at common law and, therefore, to be enforceable as between the original parties and their representatives, this will not confer a real right and bind singular successors. It seems possible, though not certain, that a lease for a definite yet extremely long duration may fall under this heading. In one instance a lease of 2,400 years (with an elusory rent) was held to be outwith the 1449 Act though the rent element may well have been conclusive here.[21] However, a lease of 1,140 years has been held to be within the terms of the Act[22] and many leases have been granted for 99 and 999 years.

---

[20] Requirements of Writing (Scotland) Act 1995, s. 1(3).
[21] *Alison v. Ritchie* (1730) Mor. 15196.
[22] *Lord Advocate v. Fraser* (1762) 2 Pat. 66.

(4) Rent

The 1449 Act does not apply if there is no rent. The statute allows 9.15
tenants to remain "at such rent as they took them for" and this
implies there must be a definite rent and that this must not be elusory
or merely nominal. As indicated in *Alison v. Ritchie*[23] the fact that
there was rent which was elusory as well as a duration of 2,400 years
meant that this lease was ineffectual against singular successors. The
problem is that the Act gives no indication of what is satisfactory to
form rent. There is no need for the rent to be fair or reasonable.
There may be a lump sum or grassum in addition to the continuing
rent but a grassum alone will not form a satisfactory rent.[24]

(5) Possession

A tenant must have entered into possession of the subjects of the 9.16
lease in order to acquire a real right under the 1449 Act. Possession
may be exercised either personally, through servants (natural possession) or through another person such as a sub-tenant (civil
possession). The reason for the need for possession is so that a
singular successor or creditor of the landlord or a competing lessee
can learn of the existence of the lease. The need for possession
prevents collusive (*i.e.* fraudulent) agreements. It is the equivalent to
registration of titles to land. Thus if A agreed to buy a house from B
where C was the sitting tenant this would greatly diminish the value
of the property to a purchaser. Unless there is a requirement of
possession for a real right then the purchaser would have no clear
means of knowing about the sitting tenant. Where there are competing leases, the later lease with possession will be preferred to an
earlier lease without possession, although the latter are rare. Where
there is, on the other hand, a singular successor to the landlord the
tenant must have taken possession before the singular successor
becomes infeft, *i.e.* when his written title is registered in the Register
thereby converting the personal right against the seller into a right
against the world. In one case a lease was arranged with entry at
Whitsunday (May 15) but before that date the "landlord" sold the
property. The purchaser recorded his title on April 21. It was here
impossible for the tenant to take possession and convert his own
personal right into a real right against the singular successor, who
was therefore not bound by the lease.[25] Here, also, the fact that the

---

[23] (1730) Mor. 15196.
[24] *Mann v. Houston*, 1957 S.L.T. 89.
[25] *Millar v. McRobbie*, 1949 S.C. 1.

tenant had entered into occupation before the lease came into force to carry out certain farming operations on the subjects could not constitute possession as his rights under the lease did not commence till Whitsunday and these actings could not be referable to the lease, and were only a limited personal licence allowed by the "landlord".

(6) Landlord Infeft

9.17 Where the landlord is heritable proprietor of the subjects of the lease he must be infeft if the tenant is to acquire a real right. Where the landlord is not infeft when the lease is struck the tenant's real right may still be created, by operation of accretion, when the landlord subsequently becomes infeft. This prerequisite for operation of the 1449 Act does not apply if the landlord is not the heritable proprietor where a sub-lease is being granted.

For leases exceeding 20 years the Registration of Leases (Scotland) Act 1857 offers registration of the lease in the Register of Sasines as an alternative to possession under the 1449 Act criteria as a means of acquiring a real right where a property is situated in a non-operational area for the purposes of land registration.

For areas in respect of which the Land Registration (Scotland) Act 1979 has become operational, registration in the Land Register is the only method of acquiring a real right under a lease exceeding 20 years.

4. Restrictions on the Contract of Lease

9.18 A major restriction of note is the prohibition of long leases of residential property. The Land Tenure Reform (Scotland) Act 1974, Pt II, states that any long lease executed after August 31, 1974 may not apply to property used wholly or in part as a dwelling-house. The term "dwelling-house" includes any garden, yard, garage, outhouse or pertinent used along with any dwelling-house. Use as a site for a caravan is not included within the term "use as a dwelling-house". Where use as a dwelling-house is ancillary to the use of the rest of the property leased, and where exclusion of the dwelling-house use would be detrimental to the efficient exercise of the non-dwelling-house use, then this is not struck at in the Act. Examples suggested for this are a caretaker's house in a block of commercial offices or possibly houses for resident staff within an industrial complex. Agricultural holdings, holdings under the Small Landholder (Scotland) Acts and crofts are specifically excluded.

A "long lease" is defined as any lease or right of occupancy granted for payment (other than running costs) which has a duration of more than 20 years (including the option to renew if this takes the period of the lease beyond 20 years). For leases created before 1974 which contain a provision for renewal in excess of 20 years the Law Reform (Miscellaneous Provisions) (Scotland) Act 1985 indicates that such renewals may still be granted. Houses under the Rents Acts are not struck at in any way here so that a tenant may exercise security of tenure rights to remain in the house as long as the Rent Acts provide.

5. CONSTITUTION OF A LEASE

As a contract for the creation of an interest in land[26] a lease requires 9.19 to be in writing and signed by the parties. However, where a lease is for not more than a year, this will not be required (see below). No particular form of writing is required provided that the intention of the parties can readily be ascertained from the writing used, nor does it matter what the contract is called. Simply calling an agreement a "licence" does not mean it cannot in fact be a lease. The fact that a more formal form of agreement was envisaged by the parties which does not materialise, does not have the effect of a condition preventing a valid lease coming into being. Typically it may be agreed to lease a property "subject to lease drawn out in due form". What this does is to require a formal lease to be prepared to give effect to binding missives.[27]

6. GENERAL RULES APPLICABLE IN LEASES

(1) TENANT'S OBLIGATIONS

Tenants must take and retain possession. The landlord will want the 9.20 subjects to be possessed as this will prevent the condition of the subjects' deterioration through want of occupation. If there is no possession the landlord may bring the lease to an end, sue for resumption of possession in an action of implement, or alternatively bring an action of damages for loss occasioned by the tenant's failure. The obligation to possess does not require the tenant to reside personally on the subjects although this may be specifically agreed between the landlord and tenant in the contract of lease. The

---

[26] Requirements of Writing (Scotland) Act 1995, s. 1(2).
[27] *Erskine v. Glendinning* (1871) 9 M. 656.

obligation to retain possession will not in the case of a shop extend to carry on business at the premises let though the premises must be kept furnished sufficiently for the purposes of hypothec (to make the rent secure), kept heated and aired.[28] This stems from the need to prevent damp from non-use and can be seen in a case involving a dwelling-house. The tenant was sued for damages in respect of deterioration of the subjects from exposure to damp, frost and dirt, damage from burst waterpipes and the breakage of windows from outside as a result of the deserted appearance of the house.[29] A tenant of an inn was also successfully sued when there was loss of goodwill after the premises were shut for months.[30]

Tenants must not "invert possession". Subjects are let for a particular purpose and the tenant may only use the subjects for that purpose. The purpose may be expressly stated in the contract, in which case it is easy to discover whether there has been a breach or not. Alternatively it may be inferred from the subjects—a dwelling-house for residence; a garden for horticulture; or a shop for trading etc. Where the tenant uses the subjects for purposes outwith those either expressed or implied, this amounts to inversion of possession. This is, in effect, a course of conduct inconsistent with the objects of the lease. The landlord may lose the right to complain of inversion either by express renunciation or through acquiescence, as where a tenant used a paper mill as an oil mill for six years and then his assignee used it as a grist mill for one year with the knowledge of the landlord. Here the landlord could not have the original use restored.[31]

9.21   The tenant must use reasonable care in the management of the subjects and will be liable to make good any damage caused by negligence such as burst pipes resulting from non-occupation of premises. The duty to exercise reasonable care might extend beyond the end of the lease, particularly if the tenant still has effective control of the premises.[32] In addition, the tenant must abide by any specific rules as to management. There may be a restriction on building on the subjects let, or a prohibition of any trade or business on the premises. Such a typical restriction limiting premises to use as "residential dwelling-house only" will be breached by use of such subjects as a school or even a charitable institution where no money is taken such as a hospital.

Rent may take various forms and may be payable at either the

---

[28] *Whitelaw v. Fulton* (1871) 10 M. 27.
[29] *Smith v. Henderson* (1899) 24 R. 1102.
[30] *Graham v. Stevenson* (1792) Hume 781.
[31] *Young and Co. v. Ramsey* (1824) 2 S. 793.
[32] *Fry's Metals Ltd v. Durastic Ltd*, 1991 S.L.T. 689.

legal or conventional term, *i.e.* either on the traditional Scottish quarter days[33] or on some other dates specified in the lease.

In leases where the landlord has a right of hypothec, the tenant must stock the premises to such an extent as will cover one year's rent (that being the extent of the rent secured by hypothec).

The tenant must not assign or sublet unless there is an express or 9.22 implied power to do so. An assignation of a lease is a transfer by the tenant of his interest in the lease to another person called the assignee, who becomes the new tenant in place of the assignor. The assignor (sometimes known as the grantor or cedent) ceases to have any further interest in the lease. A sub-lease is a lease granted by a tenant of all or part of the subjects leased so that the original tenant becomes the landlord of the sub-tenant whilst still remaining the tenant of the original landlord. Where in a lease the tenant is given a clear and right to assign or sub-let (as where the contract is granted to the tenant "his assignees and sub-lessees whomsoever") then this will displace any common law presumption against either assignation or sub-letting. Where the lease is not express then the tenant may sub-let or assign only as far as the particular kind of lease gives the power and this is determined by the common law as well as statute.

In urban unfurnished premises there is a common law presumption in favour of assignation and sub-letting. The basis of the rule is the lack of "solidarity" between landlord and tenant in such leases as compared with agricultural leases where the element of personal choice of the tenant (*"delectus personae"*) is strong. The common law position has been altered since the introduction of secure tenancies and assured tenancies in the 1980s for certain kinds of dwelling-house lease. For secure tenancies in the public sector[34] it is an implied term in every such tenancy that the tenant shall not assign, sub-let or otherwise give up to another person possession of the house or any part of it or take in a lodger without the consent in writing of the landlord. This consent must not be unreasonably withheld. In private sector assured tenancies (*i.e.* those entered into after January 2, 1989) under section 23 of the Housing (Scotland) Act 1988 it is an implied term of every such tenancy that the tenant must not assign the tenancy, or sub-let or part with possession of the whole or any part of the premises let.[35] There is no condition as to unreasonable withholding of consent modifying the assured tenancy prohibition.

---

[33] In terms of the Term and Quarter Days (Scotland) Act 1990 these are now Candlemas (February 28), Whitsunday (May 28), Lammas (August 28) and Martinmas (November 28).

[34] Housing (Scotland) Act 1987, s. 55.

[35] Housing (Scotland) Act 1988, s. 23.

9.23   Furnished lets have no implied power as the "rent" consists of two distinct parts—the rent for the premises and the sum for hire of the furniture. This latter contract of hire is purely personal and does not carry the power to assign or sub-let the furniture. As the two contracts of hire of premises and furniture are so closely bound together as to be inseparable, it follows from this that the personal nature of the furniture hire prevents assignation or sub-letting of the subjects without express consent. Leases for the tenant's life and leases for the duration of the tenant's term of office implicitly include the powers to assign or sublet as being deemed of unusual duration, as do agricultural leases of extraordinary duration.

Such subjects as furnished urban leases and agricultural leases of ordinary duration do not carry an implied right to assign or sub-let as indicated above. In addition, in mineral leases the significant factor is the duration of the lease. Where the lease of minerals is for an extraordinary duration then this will carry power to assign and sub-let. Sporting leases more than any other kind of lease are subject to the limiting effects of *delectus personae* and are accordingly not capable of assignation or sub-let without express approval. The reason is that much depends on the way these rights of fishing and shooting are exercised as this affects the comfort of the landlord, his relations with his farm tenants and the preservation of sufficient stock. Thus, these leases have strong elements of the agricultural lease about them and so may not be assigned and sub-let without approval. Where there is no implied power to assign and sub-let then, unless the landlord consents, there can be no such alienation. Even where the power is implied at common law the right may be excluded by a clause in the lease. One reason is to keep out impecunious "tenants" who may not be able to meet their debts.

9.24   Where relevant, the landlord may modify the clause's wording by adding that there may not be assignation without "consent in writing" or "unless specifically approved of by the Landlord". This still gives the landlord an arbitrary power of veto and it is not thought that the landlord would be required to give reasons. There must, however, not be oppression in the landlord's exercise of his right. This is a familiar notion in English landlord and tenant law and was considered, in another context, in *Dorchester Studios (Glasgow) Ltd v. Stone*.[36]

The court will not permit any covert assignation or sub-lease which is cloaked by another name but, in fact, is a breach of the prohibition on assignation or sub-letting. Thus, an arrangement where the tenant of a shop removed his goods and gave occupation

---

[36] 1975 S.C. (H.L.) 56.

to a person alleged to be his "shopman" who in fact carried on a different trade, was held to be a mere transparent device to evade the operation of the restriction.[37]

(2) LANDLORD'S OBLIGATIONS

The primary right of the tenant is to be put into possession of the 9.25 subjects let and to be maintained in such possession, and it is obligatory on the landlord to fulfil this obligation. This right to possession means that the landlord transfers to the tenant his own rights in law to remove and eject third parties or the tenant may alternatively demand that the landlord exercise this right on the tenant's behalf. Possession must be given timeously; if the landlord is unable to give possession on the agreed date the tenant cannot be expected to wait indefinitely, although the precise timing will depend on the circumstances of the case (including the character and duration of the lease).[38] Although in most cases possession will be given of the whole of the subjects, failure to give full possession of the entire subjects may not always be fatal.[39] This will be a matter of degree.

Although in the case of land and houses generally the very nature of the grant implies full possession, in other leases the rights granted are of a more limited character. Thus a lease of fishings does not prevent the landlord using the water where this does not interfere with the fishing, and a letting of woods gives no right to interfere with the surface of the subjects except in so far as necessary for the profitable exercise of the right.

The tenant's right to possession is of limited value unless it is a continuing right. Thus, the landlord guarantees to do nothing to adversely affect the tenant's possession throughout the lease or any part of it. This "guarantee" is called a warrandice and is often, though not always, expressly included in the terms of the contract. It is always implied. This guarantee on the continuing possession of the tenant is the basis of any action by the tenant against the landlord for total or partial eviction. Before the tenant can establish breach of the obligation of maintenance in possession there must be either total or partial eviction. If there is partial eviction then an action for damages usually in the form of a reduction of rent (referred to as an abatement of rent) is appropriate. Where there is total eviction the tenant will normally be entitled to restitution or to damages.

Where the tenant is unable to occupy the premises as a result of 9.26 their total destruction, the lease automatically comes to an end

---

[37] *Hatton v. Clay and McLuckie* (1865) 4 M. 263.
[38] *Drummond v. Hunter* (1869) 7 M. 347.
[39] *Webster v. Lyell* (1860) 22 D. 1423.

under the doctrine of *rei interitus* (destruction of the thing)[40] unless the lease states that it is nevertheless to continue in effect. A similar result arises where supervening legislation makes it impossible for the tenant to possess the lease on the agreed terms.[41]

A tenant is not entitled to abandon a lease merely because the purpose for which the lease was entered into becomes impossible, as where the tenant's licence of a wine and spirit merchants' shop was revoked.[42] Equally, a tenant cannot claim to have been evicted from possession where the tenant knew of the risk of eviction, or the tenant is himself the author of his eviction.

A landlord may incur liability for damages for derogation from grant in circumstances (*e.g.* the carrying out of building operations) which would not give rise to liability for third parties (such as neighbours) in the same circumstances.[43]

The obligation of the landlord not to derogate from his grant by acting in breach of the implied duty of peaceable possession does not extend to omissions as well as acts. Thus, the landlord is not liable for damage caused by water from a defective drain on neighbouring property, even if owned by him.[44]

9.27 At common law landlords renting out land or commercial premises are not obliged to guarantee the quality of the crops or the profitability of commercial locations. As to buildings, commercial leases normally impose obligations on the tenant as far as repair of the premises is concerned. The position in dwelling-houses is markedly different. At common law there is an obligation that premises must be tenantable and habitable. In case landlords should opt to exclude the common law obligation, legislation imposes two distinct obligations on landlords of dwelling-houses. In any residential lease contract there is an implied condition that the house is at the commencement of the tenancy and during the tenancy kept by the landlord in all respects reasonably fit for human habitation.[45] In addition, in leases for periods of less than seven years there is an implied obligation that the landlord will keep in repair the structure and exterior of the house (including drains, gutters and external pipes) as well as keep in repair and working order the installations in the house for the supply of water, gas and electricity and for

---

[40] *Cantors Properties (Scotland) Ltd v. Swears and Wells Ltd*, 1980 S.L.T. 165.
[41] *Tay Salmon Fisheries v. Speedie*, 1929 S.C. 593.
[42] *Hart's Trs v. Arrol* (1903) 6 F. 36.
[43] *Huber v. Ross*, 1912 S.C. 898.
[44] *Golden Casket (Greenock) Ltd v. BRS (Pickfords) Ltd*, 1972 S.L.T. 146.
[45] Housing (Scotland) Act 1987, Sched. 10, para. 1; however, the condition is not implied in leases of not less than 3 years where the tenant undertakes to put the property into a habitable condition.

sanitation and for space heating or heating water. Landlords are expressly prohibited from putting a provision in the lease that the tenant will repair the premises including painting, pointing or rendering the premises or paying money in lieu of repairs.[46]

(3) REMEDIES OF LANDLORD AND TENANT

Where one party breaches the implied or express obligations of the lease, then the remedies available to the other party are as follows. 9.28

(a) Landlord's Remedies

(i) Rent

The landlord has all the normal remedies of a creditor such as an action in the sheriff court for the sum due. A decree in the landlord's favour can be enforced by diligence such as an arrestment (where the property is in the hands of a third party), poinding (where the property is in the hands of a debtor) or adjudication (where there is attachment of heritable property for debts preventing voluntary alienation by the debtor). If there is a cautioner (guarantor) then the landlord may proceed against that person in the ordinary way and take the above action if there is no response to requests for payments of the guaranteed rent. 9.29

Although it is normally necessary for a creditor to obtain a decree before doing any form of diligence against his debtor, it may be possible for a landlord to do diligence on an extract registered lease, which is treated for this purpose as equivalent to a decree for sums due under the lease. For this remedy to be available the tenant must have consented (usually *in gremio*) to registration of the lease for execution (*i.e.* the doing of diligence), and the lease must have been registered in the Books of Council and Session and an extract obtained. This process is known as summary diligence.

In addition to the normal remedies as a creditor for rent, the landlord of certain premises has the special remedy of hypothec available by implication. This is a right in security, without possession of the subjects over which it extends, in favour of the landlord to ensure he gets the rent.[47] Hypothec is enforced by raising a court action of sequestration for rent. The right was an implied term of all leases but legislation has now taken most non-urban subjects outside the operation of hypothec. 9.30

The right operates over subjects known as *invecta et illata* (things

---

[46] Housing (Scotland) Act 1987, Sched. 10, para. 3.
[47] G. Maher and D. Cusine, *The Law and Practice of Diligence* (Butterworths, 1990).

brought in and carried into the property). They include furniture, books, pictures, plates and other moveable property brought onto the property by the tenant, stock-in-trade in shop premises and trade equipment and machinery.

In *Scottish and Newcastle Breweries Ltd v. Edinburgh District Council*[48] the landlord sought to exercise its right of hypothec to recover rent due. One of the items which the landlord sought to sell was a collection of beer kegs which were on the premises but which were the property of a brewery company. The brewery company sought interdict to prevent the sale of the kegs. It claimed that the kegs were excluded from the landlord's hypothec. The judge held, however, that the kegs were part of the *invecta et illata* of the tenant. He considered that the kegs were part of the ordinary equipment and stock-in-trade of someone leasing a public house.

Certain articles are excluded, such as cash, bonds, bills and other documents of debt as well as clothing and tools of the trade which are absolutely necessary to enable the tenant to gain a living. There are special rules covering business premises, mines and quarries, fisheries, agricultural and pastoral subjects and horticultural subjects.[49]

9.31   Possession of articles by the tenant raises a presumption of ownership. Thus a tenant is presumed to own everything on the premises for the purposes of hypothec, except where goods are (clearly) in other persons' possession—there are problems when the articles belong to others.[50] Goods owned by the tenant's children, guests, servants and lodgers are excluded as people cannot pledge property which does not belong to them. There are, however, exceptions where property not belonging to the tenant comes under the landlord's right of hypothec.[51] As for goods on hire it is presumed that the hirer was aware of the risk that the subjects might form part of the landlord's hypothec and that had the landlord realised that the plenishings were not available to him for hypothec he would have demanded more furnishing of the premises. Single articles on hire-purchase are also included—the owners of a juke box hired to a café owner claimed that even without intimation to the landlord single articles were not covered by hypothec, but this argument was rejected and the view expressed that the hirers accepted the possibility of the goods being sequestrated by the landlord and made allowances in the rent charged.[52] However,

---

[48] 1979 S.L.T. (Notes) 11.
[49] See G. Maher and D. Cusine, *The Law and Practice of Diligence* (Butterworths, 1990).
[50] *Rossleigh Ltd v. Leader Cars Ltd*, 1987 S.L.T. 355.
[51] *D. H. Industries v. R. E. Spence and Co. Ltd*, 1973 S.L.T. (Sh. Ct.) 26.
[52] *Ditchburn Organisation (Sales) v. Dundee Corporation*, 1971 S.C. 96.

where the hiring is occasional and transient (as where china was hired for a dinner party) then these do not come within the landlord's rights.[53] Goods deposited or gratuitously lent are the same as hired articles, namely that in these circumstances there may still be hypothec over such goods even if it is only a single article. Goods for repair in the custody of the tenant for this purpose are exempt, but not where the buyer of goods merely leaves them with the tenant for convenience.

Hypothec covers not only rent under the lease but also any capital sum or interest on a capital sum laid out by the landlord. One year's rent due or current is covered. Each year's rent is secured successively and arrears are not included. Sequestration must be within three months from the last term of payment, otherwise the hypothec falls. If this is done the landlord will get full preference. The sale may take place after the three months but provided that there is no undue delay that amounts to abandonment this does not matter. Thus it has been said to be wise to apply the sequestration to the rent actually due and in security of the rent to become due at the next term where this is possible (*i.e.* not for crops).[54]

Certain rights are preferred to the landlord's hypothec—Crown 9.32 rights such as taxes and duties (though not exactions of a public nature, merely declared to be preferable to private debts), superior's hypothec, wages of employees, deathbed and funeral expenses. The landlord's right of hypothec is preferable to the rights of other creditors.

(ii) Other Obligations

The landlord may raise an action of implement to compel per- 9.33 formance of an obligation, or of an interdict to prevent the tenant committing some breach of the lease's conditions as by failing to occupy the subjects or by, say, selling goods which are outwith the goods permitted in the lease. The landlord may alternatively bring the lease to an end and claim damages.[55]

(b) Tenant's Remedies

(i) General

Again the equitable remedies of interdict and implement are 9.34 available to a tenant to prevent a landlord from acting outwith the provisions of the lease or compel performance. Where there has

---

[53] *Adam v. Sutherland* (1863) 2 M. 6.
[54] G. C. Paton and J. G. S. Cameron, *Leases* (1967), pp. 215 *et seq.*
[55] See para. 9.41.

been a breach then the tenant may seek damages or an abatement of rent where possession is given of only part of the subjects in the lease or where the landlord fails to keep the subjects in a fit state of repair. Where the breach by the landlord is sufficiently material then the tenant may abandon the lease as where defective drains resulted in the death of the tenant's daughter.[56] Lesser failures by the landlord may lead only to the right of the abatement of rent rather than abandonment as where a landlord failed to provide gas fittings in a shop as promised at his own expense.[57] In these cases, of course, each situation is judged on its own merits as to whether in a particular set of circumstances the breach is material enough to permit the tenant to throw up the lease (resile). As indicated, the effect of destruction of the subjects (*rei interitus*) is to allow such abandonment of the lease, though the fact of *damnum fatale* will preclude an action of damages by the tenant.

(ii) Retention of Rent

9.35   Retention of rent is a device permitted to tenants whose landlords fail to comply with their tenancy obligations. This right allows the tenant to withhold rent to force the landlord to carry out the obligations in question. When that purpose is achieved the withheld rent is due in full. If the tenant seeks damages or an abatement of rent a separate action must be raised.

(4) TERMINATION OF LEASES

(a) Tacit Relocation

9.36   Strictly this is, in fact, an exception to the rule that contracts for a certain period of time cease upon the expiry of that time, *i.e.* at the end of a year, a one-year agreement to supply fruit to a grocer would lapse and neither party could complain when the other party treated the contract as ended. However, in certain contracts (lease; partnership; service), there requires to be notice to end a contract even though the contract is continued either for the length of the previous contractual period or a year (whichever is the shorter). This constructive renewal of the contract operates under the doctrine of tacit relocation (literally "implied rehiring"). This means that by not giving notice of termination of the contract the parties tacitly or impliedly agree to continue the contract. The lease will continue on the same terms and conditions as before, except the maximum

---

[56] *Scottish Heritable Security Co. v. Granger* (1881) 8 R. 459.
[57] *Davie v. Stark* (1876) 3 R. 1114.

duration of a lease continued under tacit relocation is one year. If at the end of this further year there is again no notice of termination from either party then the lease is tacitly continued for yet a further year and so on until finally there is notice or some other form of termination.

The doctrine can operate for shorter leases too and the majority of tenement flats were traditionally let on either a monthly or weekly basis and they continued by tacit relocation (theoretically every month or week), often for many years. In effect there is a fresh contract every time the doctrine operates although the period of let is looked upon as one whole. From the tenant's point of view the requisite notice to terminate must still be given even if the tenant does not continue in possession of the subjects, as the new contract is equally binding as regards such notice.

(i) Subjects

Tacit relocation applies to all kinds of leases, though there are 9.37 minor exceptions dictated for the most part by common sense—leases for less than one year for grazing or mowing (uses here being seasonal), fishings and shootings merely for a season, holiday house lettings for a season or less and service occupancies.[58] It is no bar to tacit relocation that the party having an interest to prevent it is incapacitated by insanity, minority or death. On the other hand, the right to plead tacit relocation is not lost by the death of the person entitled to claim, as the successor takes over such a right.

(ii) Notice

Due notice must be given to exclude the operation of tacit 9.38 relocation even where the lease provides that the tenant is to remove at the date of termination without warning or process of removing. Houses with or without land not exceeding two acres, let for more than a year, are covered by the Sheriff Courts (Scotland) Act 1907 as to notice—"notice of termination of tenancy shall be given in writing to the tenant".

(iii) Formality of Notice

It seems that a technically invalid notice could equally well 9.39 exclude the operation of tacit relocation, as the essence of the doctrine is consent. There are problems where there are joint landlords or tenants and the notice to exclude comes from one or more of

---

[58] See para. 11.15.

such a group but not all. Here, though, it appears that notice given by such person or persons would be equally effective to exclude tacit relocation as if it had come from all the tenants/landlords.[59] In some situations it may well be that continued possession by the tenant is not a result of tacit relocation but on an entirely new lease. Thus, where a landlord intimated an increase in rent and the tenant replied he would not pay it but did not give notice to terminate the lease and remained in possession, it was held that he had consented to the new terms and was in the position of a tenant under the new lease and its new terms, not on tacit relocation of the old lease.[60]

Tacit relocation will operate where the parties seeking to exclude it bar themselves, as where the landlord gives notice to quit but takes no further steps and allows the tenant to remain in possession, and similarly with a tenant who gives notice to quit and remains. Mere delay in taking steps to remove the tenant will not itself set up tacit relocation but it will be inferred where this delay is beyond a reasonable time.

(b) Termination During the Lease

9.40   A lease may be brought to an end before the stipulated date of termination in several ways where the parties agree to this. In a renunciation the tenant gives up the lease where there is agreement or acquiescence by the landlord. Renunciation may be express and may be in either a bilateral form or unilateral with an acceptance by the landlord, though apart from the need for the renunciation to be clear and explicit there are no formal requirements. Rescission applies where there is some failure by the landlord (or, in theory, by the tenant) to adhere to the implied or express obligations of the lease, and may be accompanied by an action for damages. Also the lease may make provision for breaks. This means that at some specified time during its currency the lease may be terminated. The break may be in favour of either party or both and it will give a landlord the power of total resumption of the subjects and a tenant the option to renounce the lease. Unlike an irritancy there need be no reason such as a breach of conditions. Usually breaks occur at one or more specified times although power may be given to break the lease at any time with suitable notice. Notice of intention to exercise the right to break the lease must be given in the manner and within the period of notice laid down in the lease. If no time is stated and the right is exercised by the landlord, then a reasonable time must

[59] *City of Glasgow v. Brown*, 1989 S.C.L.R. 439 and 679.
[60] *McFarlane v. Mitchell* (1900) 2 F. 901.

be given to the tenant. If a tenant fails to leave then the landlord has a right to an action of removing.

(c) Irritancies

The lease may be brought to an end by the landlord if the tenant 9.41 fails to comply with the terms of the contract. Such a provision is termed an irritancy. Irritancies may be either legal or conventional. Normally this will prevent the landlord also claiming damages for premature termination of the lease unless this right is expressly reserved. The right of irritating the lease rests solely with the landlord and a tenant who is contravening the lease's conditions subject to irritancy does not have the right to abandon the lease—where in a 19-year lease there was a conventional irritancy in the case of the tenant's bankruptcy it was held that this gave the landlord the option to put an end to the lease when the tenant became bankrupt but did not allow the tenant the privilege of ending his obligations when this occurred.[61]

Legal irritancies exist both at common law and under statute. At common law the irritancy covers non-payment of rent for a period of two years. When the rent has not been paid for at least two years then the landlord could have the irritancy declared by the sheriff and insist on a summary removing.

As far as legal irritancies for agricultural subjects are concerned these are now dealt with under the Agricultural Holdings (Scotland) Act 1991, which provides that if six months' rent is due and unpaid the landlord may raise an action in the sheriff court for removal of the tenant at the next term of Martinmas or Whitsunday unless the arrears are paid or caution found for the arrears and a further year's rent. A legal irritancy may be purged (*i.e.* satisfied) by payment of the arrears before decree is extracted in an action to enforce payment.

Conventional irritancies cover such matters as non-payment of rent. Typically, the period of irritancy may be changed either by shortening or even lengthening the permitted time for arrears. Also the procedure may be simplified and purging may be excluded. Hypothec gives urban landlords strong rights and the 1949 Act provides remedies for the agricultural landlord, though the irritancy clause will still be included. It is very important where there is no hypothec as in sporting leases.

Irritancies also frequently centre on the prohibition of assignation or sub-letting. Where permitted at common law, this right may be

---

[61] *Bidoulac v. Sinclair's Tr.* (1889) 17 R. 144.

excluded and fenced with an irritancy so that not only is the right of the assignee null but also the original tenants lose the rights they had under the lease in effect as a punishment for attempting to assign the lease against the wishes of the landlord. Similarly for unauthorised sub-tenants. Any breach of the conditions of the lease may under an irritancy result in the tenant receiving notice to quit, for example failure to possess or stock the subjects, or even where the tenant commits a breach of any other term or condition of the lease such as using the subjects as a shop or public house.

9.42   There must be a court action unless the tenants quit voluntarily. Landlords must exercise their rights within a reasonable time, but these will be regarded as kept in reserve during negotiations with the tenant on the breach.[62] The breach must be proved, unless admitted by the tenant, generally by means of an action of declarator of irritancy. Once incurred, unlike a legal irritancy, a conventional irritancy could not be purged. The principle was strictly applied. A tenant was due to pay rent at Whitsunday and failed to do so. There was a conventional irritancy if the rent remained unpaid for three months and the landlord, after giving notice of his intention, raised an action for declarator of irritancy and an order ordering him to remove. The tenant paid the arrears before the court case was heard. It was held that this was not good enough and the landlord was entitled to decree.[63] The court has prevented the oppressive use of the irritancy as where several tenants were owing parts of rent for subjects and one tenant offered to pay the whole and the landlord had refused and insisted on irritancy. However, the strictness of irritancy can be seen where an irritancy on a tenant's insolvency was still held enforceable where the tenant settled with his creditors[64] and where the landlord was able to evict a tenant who was 11 days' late in proffering the rent.[65]

There has been a change introduced following concern at the harsh way in which the conventional irritancy was being used by some commercial landlords whose tenants did not enjoy the rights of security of tenure of dwelling-house tenants[66] (see below). As far as dwelling-house leases are concerned there is usually the need for the court to be satisfied that it is reasonable to allow the landlord to repossess the property.[67]

---

[62] *Penman v. Mackay*, 1922 S.C. 385.
[63] *McDouall's Trs v. MacLeod*, 1949 S.C. 593.
[64] *Tennent v. Macdonald* (1836) 14 S. 976.
[65] *Dorchester Studios (Glasgow) Ltd v. Stone*, 1975 S.C. (H.L.) 56.
[66] Law Reform (Miscellaneous Provisions) (Scotland) Act 1985, ss. 5 and 6.
[67] Rent (Scotland) Act 1984, Sched. 2 (protected tenancies); Housing (Scotland) Act 1987, Sched. 3 (secure tenancies); Housing (Scotland) Act 1988, Sched. 5 (assured tenancies).

(d) Termination at the End of the Lease (ish)

At the normal end of a lease the tenant is required to remove from 9.43
the subjects let. Under Scots law, as indicated, unless there is notice
given to a tenant by the landlord or vice versa then tacit relocation will
have the effect of continuing the lease. Thus there must be a notice of
removing. The process of the tenant relinquishing the lease is known
as "removing". Where this takes place at the normal ish of the
contract this is termed "ordinary removing", whilst where this is
premature to the date of ish it is known as "extraordinary removing".

7. STATUTORY RESTRICTIONS ON THE LEASE CONTRACT

Over the past century various special rules have been introduced in 9.44
relation to a wide range of leases covering residential property and
agricultural land, as well as to a limited extent commercial subjects.
These cover both the terms of the tenancy on such matters as rent
and payment for improvements as well as the right of tenants to
continue in their property beyond the term of their contract.

(1) RESIDENTIAL PROPERTY

(a) Private Rented Housing

Traditionally the lease was a contract where the rent as fixed by the 9.45
parties was conclusive and there was no body to whom one could
appeal. Similarly, when the tenancy came to an end the tenant had no
right to remain provided that notice to quit had been served preventing tacit relocation operating. Throughout Europe from 1914
onwards protection was given to residential tenants against arbitrary
eviction and rent rises. These protections were broadly retained until
the attempt to end rent control and security of tenure in the Rent Act
1957. This controversial legislation was abused by landlords who
sought to persuade their tenants to leave by a variety of unsavoury
methods. The response of the Labour administration, the Rent Act
1965, provided a new means of dealing with the question of rents for
private rented housing. In place of the policy of "freezing" rents the
1965 legislation provided for fixing rents in accordance with specified
criteria as well as reviewing these. The Rent Act 1974 provided that
leases of furnished property should be treated the same as unfurnished as to both rent fixing and security of tenure.

The subsequent apparent disappearance of many properties from
the letting market led to concern from some quarters that the
amalgamation of the two codes, giving full protection to furnished

tenants, had dried up the supply of furnished property. However, at the same time there was an extension of renting by landlords using arrangements which avoided the protection of the Rent Acts. There was an attempt by the Conservative government to stimulate the traditional private rented sector in the Tenants' Rights etc. (Scotland) Act 1980 with the introduction of the short tenancy. In order to qualify as a short tenancy a tenancy had to be for not less than one year and not more than five years as well as have a fair rent registered and notification to the tenant that the tenancy was a security-free shorthold. They were not a success and the final stealthy return to market principles occurred in the Housing (Scotland) Act 1988. Henceforth tenants entering contracts on or after January 2, 1989 would have restricted rights as to rent levels and security of tenure. However, learning from the unfortunate post-1957 experience those with rights under the older legislation retained those rights. It is therefore necessary to decide which of the private sector codes apply to any particular tenancy. This will normally be decided by the date of the contract.[68]

(b) Regulated Tenancies under the Rent (Scotland) Act 1984

9.46   For privately owned housing rented prior to January 2, 1989, the 1984 Act applies provided that there is no specific exclusion. Such tenancies are termed protected or regulated. Tenancies entered into prior to January 2, 1984 are excluded from the coverage of the 1984 Act. In order to qualify for the benefits of the legislation it is necessary that the tenancy satisfy both the positive requirements laid down for a protected tenancy as well as not come within the category of excluded tenancies. It must satisfy the statutory conditions laid down in the Rent (Scotland) Act 1984.[69] It must be let as a dwelling-house (which may be a house or part of a house); let as a separate dwelling; the rateable value on the appropriate day must not exceed a specified sum; a rent must be payable under the tenancy and it must be not less than two-thirds of the rateable value on the appropriate day; and the rent must not include bona fide payments in respect of board or attendance.

Part I of the Rent (Scotland) Act 1984 specifically excludes certain tenancies from coverage of the protected tenancy regime. Certain types of property do not receive the full measure of protection enjoyed by most unfurnished and furnished leases of housing (although some of them are afforded a degree of security). Some of the excluded areas have their own codes of protection, such as

---

[68] s. 42 deals with transitional situations.
[69] s. 1.

local authority housing, whilst others are less contentious because full protection is obviously less appropriate—licensed premises—or totally inappropriate—like holiday homes. These exclusions are stated in the 1984 Act,[70] and cover agricultural land exceeding two acres; public sector tenancies—where the landlord is a local authority, New Town Development Corporation, the Housing Corporation, the Scottish Special Housing Association or any housing trust, housing association or housing co-operative; licensed premises; Crown tenancies; student tenancies granted by specified educational institutions; holiday lets; tenancies granted by resident landlords; and properties released by the Secretary of State from rent regulation.

(i) The Impact of the Protected Tenancy Regime

Two central rights emerge from a tenancy covered by the Rent (Scotland) Act 1984. The first relates to the level of rent payable and the second the right to remain in the property after the formal termination of the tenancy.   9.47

(1) Rents. The system of fair rents set up in the original 1965 reforms did not apply automatically. Even where a tenant lived in a property below the appropriate rateable value level, and paid sufficient rent for the Acts to apply, and where the landlord was not exempted for some reason (like a local authority), then there was still no obligation on either landlord or tenant to apply to have a fair rent fixed. There was nothing to prevent the landlord asking any rent and the tenant paying it. Ignorance of rights, fear or satisfaction with the level of rent meant that there was no automatic guarantee that property which came within the jurisdiction of the Rent Acts would ever have a fair rent registered. This was to some extent consistent with the original aims of Richard Crossman in setting up the "fair rent" system as a long stop to prevent blatant exploitation.   9.48

A rent could be registered voluntarily at the behest of landlord or tenant, or both. This involved applying to the machinery for rent-fixing set up under the 1965 Act. This comprised two tiers—Rent Officers, who dealt with initial rent fixing; and Rent Assessment Committees (RACs), which were available to reconsider any rents where either or both parties were not happy with the Rent Officer's decision. Rent Officers were (and are) full-time officials, whilst those who deal with the querying of their decisions are part-time professionals and lay persons drawn by the Secretary of State for Scotland

---

[70] s. 2.

from a panel of lawyers, valuers and lay people. There is also a President of the Rent Assessment Committees who, along with a Vice-President, exercises overall supervision of RACs. Rent Assessment Committees sit in panels of three, and deliver their decisions without dissenting notes. The procedure involves visiting the property as well as oral and written representations.[71]

9.49   The formula for determining rents introduced in the Rent Act 1965 remains almost unchanged in the current legislation.[72] Rent Officers and RACs must have regard to certain factors and ignore others in coming to a fair rent figure as well as making one crucial assumption. In determining a fair rent, the rent fixers—the Rent Officer or Rent Assessment Committees—must specifically have regard to all the circumstances and, in particular, they must apply their knowledge and experience of current rents of comparable property in the area. In addition, they are required to have regard to the age, character and locality of the dwelling-house and its state of repair. Where there is furniture involved, the state of this furniture as regards its quantity, quality and condition must be looked at. They must disregard the personal circumstances of the parties, any disrepair which stems from the tenant failing to abide by the terms of the lease, tenants' improvements and any deterioration in the condition of furniture. There are certain assumptions that supply and demand are in balance. This involves in practice making a "scarcity deduction". A percentage of the rent is deducted from the market rent as representing the impact of scarcity on the level of rents. Two main methods have dominated the rent fixing process—use of comparables[73] or return on capital investment.[74]

9.50   **(2) Security of tenure and proctection from eviction**. The security of tenure provisions attempt to ensure that the landlord is barred from evicting arbitrarily or merely on whim. The principle which is incorporated in the legislation is that a landlord can rid himself of a tenant only for an approved reason. Again, as in the rent-fixing process, these protections are voluntary. There is no obligation on a landlord to obtain a court order for possession if the tenant is compliant. Similarly, there is no compulsion on the tenant to exercise his rights of security. The provisions will only come into play if the tenant is unwilling to leave when the landlord purports to put the contract of lease to an end.

---

[71] J. A. M. Inglis, "*The Fair Rents System*" in *A Scots Conveyancing Miscellany* (1990).
[72] Rent (Scotland) Act 1984, s. 48.
[73] *Tormes Property Co. v. Landau* [1971] 1 Q.B. 261.
[74] *Learmonth Property Investment Co. v. Aitken*, 1970 S.C. 223.

The Scottish rule in the law of leases of tacit relocation means that, even where a contract of lease reaches its end, it is automatically continued until one of the parties gives notice of termination. If tenants give notice of termination they cannot be compelled to continue in the tenancy. If, however, one were to attempt to leave before the term of the lease there would be liability for the contractual obligations. Normally landlords cover themselves for this eventuality by taking both rent in advance and a deposit—although this is often actually taken to cover breakages, it is typically applied to cover other forms of loss to the landlord.

Where the landlord gives the appropriate notice to quit then, despite the compulsive wording of such notices, the tenant in a protected tenancy does not need to leave. He can stay on in the property, relying on the Rent Acts. His occupancy is known as a statutory tenancy. The onus is on the landlord to show that the tenant should leave for one of the approved reasons. Such reasons may be of two kinds—discretionary or mandatory—depending on whether the sheriff may or must terminate the tenancy.[75]

The sheriff has discretionary powers in many of the eviction situations which come up before the court. This means that the sheriff must normally be satisfied not only that the situation falls within the terms of the specific ground of possession, but also that to grant the order for possession would be reasonable. The specific approved reasons are that the landlord is ending the tenancy but offering suitable alternative accommodation[76]; or that there is a recognised reason for terminating—rent arrears or the tenant is in breach of the tenancy; nuisance or annoyance; condition of dwelling-house deteriorated; condition of furniture deteriorated; tenant withdraws a notice to quit; assignation/sub-let of whole house; house reasonably required by the landlord for occupation by a full-time employee; house reasonably required by landlord for occupation as a residence for self or close family member[77]; excessive rent charged for sub-let; overcrowded house.

9.51

In addition, there are a number of reasons where the sheriff must make an order for repossession—owner-occupier who gave tenant notice when renting; retirement home; off-season holiday let; educational body student let; short tenancy; minister/lay missionary property; ex-agricultural worker; amalgamation of

---

[75] Rent (Scotland) Act 1984, Sched. 2.
[76] *Redspring v. Francis* [1973] 1 All E.R. 640; *Siddiqui v. Rashid* [1980] 3 All E.R. 184.
[77] There is an additional requirement for this specific head that the court must not make an order for possession if it is satisfied that greater hardship would be caused by granting the order than refusing it.

farms; farm occupation; adapted for special needs; Armed Forces personnel.

9.52 After 1965 and the introduction of the Rent Act into unfurnished property, there was a shift of investment by landlords into providing furnished accommodation with its limited rights of security. Similarly, after the amalgamation of the furnished and unfurnished codes in 1974, there were a number of moves by landlords to avoid allowing their tenants rights.[78] Some of the avoidance devices were quite transparent such as holiday lettings which were not really for such a purpose. Others offended against the prohibition on contracting out of the Rent Acts rather less obviously—bed and breakfast where some food was made available, or the deferred purchase agreement which could be both a genuine and a fake transaction. The simplest avoidance mechanism was the licence—all the signs of a lease but the name changed. In England the licence gave rise to extensive litigation between 1978 and 1988 and the position is still far from clear.[79] While the Housing (Scotland) Act 1988 provides a mechanism which provides landlords with market rents and provides no security of tenure beyond the term, some landlords may still choose to use these mechanisms in certain circumstances. The most obvious will be where they wish to rent out for a very short period—the short assured tenancy has a minimum initial term of six months.

Apart from allowing civil action to enforce a contract, the Rent Acts have provided a criminal sanction against landlords who attempt to deprive tenants of their rights. Protection against this was given in the original Rent Act 1965. This was retained in the Rent (Scotland) Act 1984 and has been strengthened by the Housing (Scotland) Act 1988. It is a criminal offence under Part III of the Rent (Scotland) Act 1984 for any person unlawfully to deprive the residential occupier of any premises or attempt to do so, unless he proves he believed, or had reasonable cause to believe, that the residential occupier had ceased to reside in the premises.

If any person, with intent to cause the residential occupier to give up occupation of the premises or to refrain from exercising any right or pursuing any remedy in respect of the premises, commits acts calculated to interfere with the peace or comfort of the residential occupier or members of his household or persistently withdraws or withholds services reasonably required for the occupation of the premises as a residence, he shall be guilty of an offence. The person guilty is liable to a fine or imprisonment or both.

---

[78] See Angus McAllister, *Scottish Law of Leases* (Butterworths, 1989), p. 208.
[79] *Street v. Mountford* [1985] A.C. 809; *Antoniades v. Villiers* [1988] 3 W.L.R 1205; *A.G. Securities v. Vaughan* [1988] 3 All E.R. 1058.

In order to avoid tenancies having their rents restricted but these 9.53
rents being inflated by "hidden" charges, the Rent Acts have always
prohibited premiums. The interpretation of when a payment is a
premium has been the scene of quite extensive litigation, mainly in
England. The statutory control is found in Part VIII of the Rent
(Scotland) Act 1984.

(b) Assured Tenancies under the Housing (Scotland) Act 1988

Any contracts entered into after the commencement of Part II of 9.54
the Housing (Scotland) Act 1988, January 2, 1989, can no longer be
regulated tenancies. Most private sector tenancies are likely to be
assured tenancies. The key features of the Scottish assured tenancy
are that it lessens the degree of security of tenure whilst also
abolishing any direct method of regulating the rents landlords
charge other than the operation of supply and demand.

The definition of an "assured tenancy" requires that there be four
elements as well as requiring that it does not come within the
category of one of the excluded tenancies laid down in the Act.
The specified elements are that there should be a tenancy; the
property must be let as a separate dwelling; the tenant or at least
one of the tenants must be an individual; and the property must be
the tenant's only or principal home.

Certain kinds of tenancies are excluded from coming within the
assured tenancy framework—tenancies entered into before January
2, 1989, low rent premises, shops, licensed premises, agricultural
land, agricultural holdings, student lettings by specified educational
institutions, holiday lettings, resident landlords, Crown tenancies,
public sector landlords, shared ownership agreements, protected
tenancies, housing association tenancies, secure tenancies and temporary accommodation for homeless persons.[80]

(i) Rents and Other Conditions

There are more limited rights for tenants of assured tenancies as to 9.55
rent fixing and security of tenure than with protected tenancies.
Although there is no equivalent for a tenant applying to have fair
rent fixed, there is a procedure where the Rent Assessment Committee can be involved where no provision has been made for rent
increases in the tenancy agreement.

Where the negotiated rent period comes to an end and the landlord
seeks to increase the rent the tenant may apply to the Rent Assessment
Committee for a determination of the rent.[81] A landlord seeking an

---

[80] Detailed in Sched. 4.
[81] s. 24.

increase of rent at this time must serve a notice on the tenant in the form prescribed by the Secretary of State. Tenants cannot initiate the referral procedures themselves as with the fair rent system. It is assumed that they find the initial rent level acceptable. The fact that the rent level may not be accepted by the local authority for housing benefit purposes was drawn to the Government's attention. As alternatives to the proposed increase, the landlord and tenant can agree to a change in the rent different from that in the notice or they may agree that there should be no change in the rent.

9.56   Landlords in assured tenancies can avoid the Rent Assessment Committee having a role by providing for a rent increase either by a specified sum or by a percentage of the rent. There appears to be no reason why the specified sum cannot be related to some external method of measurement such as changes in the Retail Price Index or a similar factor, provided that such a mechanism is ascertainable by the tenant without undue difficulty.[82]

Where a tenant refers a notice of increase to an RAC they must fix a rent which they consider the house would let for in the open market by a willing landlord. There are no detailed criteria as found in the fair rent formula. Relevant issues could include the capital value of the property, the extent of past and likely capital appreciation, levels of alternative investments and their capital growth potential. In addition the state of repair of the property and its age, character and locality should provide guidance as to what rent it is reasonable to ask for the property in question. Once a body of rents exists these will also be available as "comparables" as under the Rent (Scotland) Act 1984.

The RAC are also to disregard the effect of certain factors such as the fact that the tenancy was granted to an individual who was already a sitting tenant. In addition, tenants' "voluntary" improvements are not to be counted against them in their rent although repairs would not be relevant. If tenants have expended money on improving the landlord's property they are not expected to pay for the privilege. On the same lines, the RAC must disregard tenants' damage or harm to the landlord's property. Just as tenants do not have to pay for their improvements so it is reasonable that they should not benefit from their misdeeds. If tenants have caused the property to deteriorate they cannot expect to obtain a lower rent as a result of their failing to abide by the conditions of the tenancy.[83]

---

[82] s. 24 as amended by Sched. 11 to the Local Government and Housing Act 1989.

[83] See also s. 48(3)(a) of the Rent (Scotland) Act 1984 for equivalent ground in regulated tenancies.

In addition, there is provision for the fixing of rental and non-rental 9.57
terms in statutory assured tenancy, *i.e.* where an assured tenant takes
advantage of the rights of security of tenure[84] and remains in the
property after the termination date of the original contract, then
provision is made for the adjustment of the terms of rent and terms
other than rent. The variation does not affect specific rights given in
the Act covering the prohibition on assignation without consent and
the requirement that there be access for repairs.

Where a notice of proposed changes is duly served then the
recipient, whether landlord or tenant, has three months from the
date of service to refer this proposal to the RAC. If there is no
referral then the terms proposed become the terms of the agreement.[85] Where there is a reference to the RAC then their task is to
assess the terms with reference to what terms might reasonably be
expected to be found in a contractual assured tenancy granted by a
willing landlord to a willing tenant. The RAC have discretion to
adjust the rent where they approve proposals to change the tenancy
conditions. This includes changes proposed by the committee themselves.[86]

(ii) Security of Tenure

Often a rental agreement contains a clause or clauses purporting 9.58
to take away the rights of the assured tenant in relation to security of
tenure and requiring the tenant to quit the premises without any
further order at the end of the contract. Such statements are of no
effect and are overridden by the express requirement in the legislation that a tenancy cannot be brought to an end except through an
order by the sheriff.[87]

The current statute retains the concept of security of tenure but
extends those situations where landlords can have tenants evicted.
Under the assured tenancy regime, as with regulated tenancies under
the Rent (Scotland) Act 1984 and secure tenancies under the
Housing (Scotland) Act 1987, there is a requirement that possession
orders only be given on one or more of the grounds specified in the
legislation. The grounds for repossession must be established as well
as proper notice given.

The sheriff has no power to make an assured tenancy possession
order except in specified circumstances.[88] One or more of the

---

[84] s. 16.
[85] s. 24.
[86] s. 17.
[87] s. 18 and Sched. 5.
[88] Specified in Sched. 5.

grounds for possession must be established. There are two situations which can exist when a possession order is sought—in certain instances the sheriff has discretion and must be satisfied not only that the conditions in the ground are satisfied but also that it is reasonable to grant the order for possession. In other situations, if the ground is satisfied, there is no element of discretion and the order must be granted. As well as giving a notice to quit, proper notice of proceedings must be observed before there can be an order for possession.[89]

9.59   Where a mandatory ground is established[90] then the sheriff must grant a possession order. In addition some of the grounds may only be available after the specified time laid down in the contract—off-season holiday lets and lettings to students by specified educational institutions.[91] There are also grounds which are within the discretion of the sheriff.[92] These cover suitable alternative accommodation being offered; the tenant withdrawing a notice to quit; persistent delay in rent payment; rent arrears; breach of tenancy obligations; condition of house or furniture deteriorated; nuisance, annoyance and illegal/immoral use of premises and property occupied by an ex-employee. The sheriff must be satisfied as to the overall reasonableness of making the order. It involves taking into account every relevant circumstance affecting the interests of the parties such as their conduct and any possible hardship which might result if the order were to be made, as well as the interests of the public. The question of the possibility of the tenant obtaining other accommodation as well as any rights under statute such as legislation for homeless persons is relevant.

The Housing (Scotland) Act 1988 makes provision for the sheriff to adjourn, sist (temporarily halt), suspend or postpone possession.[93] Where the landlord is seeking possession under one of the discretionary grounds the action can be postponed or sisted. Even where a possession order is granted it is possible for the sheriff to postpone the date when the eviction is to take place. Alternatively conditions can be set concerning payment of rent arrears or about any other conditions. The sheriff may adjourn an action unless it is a

---

[89] s. 19, which lays down the time-limits as two months for i. landlord's former home (ground 1); ii. mortgage repossession (ground 2); iii. minister/lay missionary (ground 5); iv. H.A. demolition/reconstruction (ground 6); v. inherited tenancy (ground 7); vi. suitable alternative accommodation (ground 9); vii. ex-employee tenancy (ground 17)—and two weeks in any other case.
[90] Sched. 5, Pt I.
[91] Sched. 5, Pt I.
[92] Sched. 5, Pt II.
[93] s. 20.

situation where the landlord is using one of the mandatory grounds of possession or if it is a "short assured tenancy".

The sheriff may not exercise these provisions in relation to halting or postponing possession actions for short assured tenancies and tenancies where the mandatory grounds are used. The mandatory grounds cover situations where the landlord wants the property for his own home or if it was formerly his own home; mortgage default; off-season holiday lets; student tenancies; property tenanted by a minister/lay missionary; demolition or reconstruction work is to go ahead and needs vacant possession; tenancies inherited under a will or on intestacy; or where there are three months rent arrears.

The criteria for landlords regaining their property when they provide the sitting tenant with suitable alternative accommodation is on the same lines as those provided in the Rent (Scotland) Act 1984 and the Housing (Scotland) Act 1987. This can stem from either a local authority certificate of suitability or from being deemed by the sheriff to be suited looking to whether the accommodation is reasonably suited to the needs of the tenant and his family. This is determined by looking to proximity to work and whether the property is similar as regards rental to equivalent public sector housing or reasonably suitable to means and needs of the tenant. 9.60

(c) Short Assured Tenancies

This is a quite distinct form of assured tenancy whose main distinction is that there is no provision for a right to a continuation of the term of the tenancy beyond the term of the original minimum of six months. A short assured tenancy requires that there be a minimum period of six months and notice must be served to the effect that the tenancy is a short assured tenancy.[94] The landlord can regain possession of a short assured tenancy either automatically on giving notice or on any of the assured tenancy repossession grounds.[95] This notice establishing that the tenancy is a short assured tenancy must be served on the prospective tenant before the creation of the tenancy. The notice indicates to a prospective tenant that the landlord will be allowed to evict provided that the proper notice is given as well as that there is a right to apply to the Rent Assessment Committee for a rent determination. There can be no valid short assured tenancy unless this notice is served and in such cases a tenancy would be an assured tenancy. Where at the end of the short assured tenancy it continues by tacit relocation or there is a 9.61

---

[94] s. 32.
[95] Sched. 5, Pt I.

new contractual tenancy of the same or substantially the same premises then such a tenancy is a short assured tenancy. This applies whether or not the requirements as to length of time of the tenancy and notice apply to the renewed tenancy.

(i) Rent Determination

9.62   There is a limited role for the RAC provided that certain criteria are satisfied.[96] The tenant can have the rent decided by the RAC. The criterion they must apply is what rent the landlord might reasonably be expected to obtain under a short assured tenancy. There is an element of circularity in this except that it is expected that those occupying under less secure shorthold assured tenancies will have to pay lower rents than the market assured tenancy rents. Before they can make a determination they must be satisfied that there is a sufficient number of similar houses in the district let on either kind of assured tenancy. In addition they are not to fix a rent even where there are sufficient comparables unless the rent paid by the tenant is significantly higher than the rent which the landlord might reasonably expect to be able to obtain judging by rents charged locally. The rent determination lasts for one year from the date when it comes into operation. The previous private sector rents fixed under the Rent (Scotland) Act 1984 lasted for three years although the English legislation since 1980 provided for two-year intervals.

(ii) Security of Tenure

9.63   The tenant of a short assured tenancy has no defence to a properly based possession action.[97] As mentioned the landlord has this ground as an addition to those mandatory and discretionary grounds available.[98] Where there is a short assured tenancy the sheriff must grant an order for possession if he is satisfied the tenancy has reached its termination date, that tacit relocation is not operating, that no further contractual tenancy is in existence and that the landlord has given notice that he requires possession of the house. This is rather different from the question of whether the landlord "reasonably requires" the house "for occupation as a residence" as occurs under the Rent (Scotland) Act 1984.[99] Here the requirement is formal and does not involve the landlord satisfying any test of necessity. It is for the landlord to decide if possession is required of the property and does not seem to be open to the

---

[96] s. 34.
[97] s. 33.
[98] Sched. 5.
[99] Grounds 7 and 8, Sched. 2.

sheriff to consider whether the landlord has an objective need for the property. In addition to a notice to quit, the legislation requires that a notice of proceedings for possession be served on the tenant. The period of the notice that the landlord requires possession must be either two weeks, two months or such period in excess of two months as the tenancy agreement provides.

(d) Public Sector Rented Housing

Proposals for introducing tenants' security were well under way 9.64 before the General Election of 1979 under the Labour Government and these were adopted by the incoming Conservative Government. These rights were introduced in the Tenants' Rights Etc. (Scotland) Act 1980 (for Scotland) and the very similar English equivalent, the Housing Act 1980. Both the public sector codes have been consolidated and the law for Scotland is contained in the Housing (Scotland) Act 1987.

(i) Secure Tenancies

Part III of the Housing (Scotland) Act 1987 makes provision for 9.65 security of tenure for public sector tenants. These are termed secure tenancies and exist if the dwelling-house is let as a separate dwelling; the tenant is an individual and the dwelling-house is his only or principal home; and the landlord is a public body.[1] Housing association tenancies entered into prior to January 2, 1989 are also covered but where these landlords enter tenancies after the introduction of the Housing (Scotland) Act 1988 assured tenancies are created.[2]

Certain tenancies are specifically excluded from the ambit of secure tenancies under Schedule 2 of the Housing (Scotland) Act 1987—premises occupied under contract of employment where the contract of employment requires the tenant to occupy the house for the better performance of duties; temporary letting to persons taking up employment in the area and seeking accommodation; temporary letting pending development; decant property let temporarily; homeless persons' temporary accommodation; agricultural and business premises.

(ii) Rents for Local Authority Accommodation

These are a matter for the discretion of the local authority. They 9.66 may "charge such reasonable rents as they may determine for the tenancy or occupation houses provided by them". The local

---

[1] 1. A local authority or water or sewerage authority; 2. New Town Development Corporation; 3. Scottish Homes; 4. a police authority; 5. a fire authority.
[2] See paras 9.54–9.60.

authority must review its rents from time to time and make such charges as circumstances may require. When deciding the standard rents to which their housing revenue account relates they must take no account of the personal circumstances of the tenants.

In relation to the operation of the general discretion there is the overall restriction of *ultra vires*. One local authority tried to avoid the impact of the Housing Finance Act 1972. The Act imposed mandatory rent increases which one authority attempted to avoid by raising the rent of one house from £7.71 a week to £18,000 a week (the property was empty, so that the figure was notional rather than actual). In this case, *Backhouse v. Lambeth Borough Council*,[3] the court said that the figure was one which no reasonable authority could have arrived at, and was not a valid exercise of the authority's powers under the English obligation corresponding to the Scottish 1987 Act.

Apart from this, it is up to the local authority whether they operate rent pooling or differential rents, provided they do not offend the unreasonableness test, which would make the decision *ultra vires* the local authority's power.

(iii) Security of Tenure

9.67   A secure tenancy may not be brought to an end except in the following circumstances which may not be varied by the tenancy agreement—death of the tenant where there is no person qualified person to succeed[4]; declining of tenancy by qualified person; death of succeeding qualified person; written agreement between the landlord and tenant; abandonment of the tenancy; possession order from the sheriff court; and four weeks' notice by tenant to the landlord.

(iv) Abandonment of Tenancy

9.68   If a landlord considers that the tenant may have ceased to be resident in the house tenanted the authority may repossess. The landlord must have reasonable grounds for believing that the dwelling is unoccupied and the tenant does not intend to occupy it as his home. Apart from entering to secure the dwelling against vandalism the landlord may take possession of the house with notice stating that the landlord has reasons to believe that the house is unoccupied and that the tenant does not intend to occupy it as his home; requiring the tenant to inform the landlord within four weeks of service of the notice if he intends to occupy the house as his home;

---

[3] (1972) 116 S.J. 802.
[4] s. 46.

and informing the tenant that if it appears to the landlord at the end of the four-week period that the tenant does not intend so to occupy the house that the tenancy will be terminated forthwith. When the notice has been served and when the landlord has made such enquiries as may be necessary to be satisfied that the dwelling is unoccupied and that the tenant does not intend to occupy it as his home then at the end of the four-week period a further notice is served bringing the tenancy to an end. Where these requirements have been complied with there may be repossession without further proceedings.[5]

(v) Possession Order from Sheriff

The landlord must serve a notice on the tenant of proceedings for possession.[6] This notice must be served in prescribed form. This is provided by the Secretary of State in statutory instrument and includes the ground on which the action is being raised. In addition to the notice of proceedings, the landlord must serve a notice to quit bringing the tenancy to an end. In the ensuing summary cause the sheriff may adjourn proceedings for repossession for a period or periods with or without imposing conditions as to payment of outstanding rent or other conditions. There is no precise equivalent to the private sector split between discretionary and mandatory grounds except that under certain grounds an order must be made where other suitable accommodation will be made available for the tenant when the order takes effect.[7] 9.69

The grounds or heads for possession resemble those grounds available in the private sector where the tenant's conduct makes it appropriate that there be eviction—rent unpaid or any other obligation broken; using the house or allowing it to be so used for immoral or illegal purposes; deterioration of the house or common parts owing to acts of waste or neglect or default by the tenant or any resident or lodger; condition of furniture has deteriorated due to ill-treatment by tenant or lodger or sub-tenant; absence from the dwelling-house by tenant and spouse without reasonable cause for a continuous period exceeding six months or ceasing to occupy house as principal home; and conduct which is a nuisance or annoyance in or in the vicinity of the house and it is not reasonable in all the circumstances that the landlord should be required to make other accommodation available to the tenant. For these grounds the sheriff must be satisfied that it is reasonable to make an order.

---

[5] s. 49.
[6] s. 47.
[7] s. 48 2(b) and grounds 8 to 15 of Sched. 3.

9.70   The remaining grounds cover situations where by and large the
house is inappropriate and hence the court must be satisfied that
suitable accommodation is available for the tenant; conduct which is
a nuisance or annoyance in or in the vicinity of the house and in the
opinion of the landlord it is appropriate in the circumstances to
require the tenant to move to other accommodation; overcrowding
in terms of the Housing (Scotland) Act 1987; demolition or substantial work on the building intended by the landlord within a
reasonable time and this work cannot reasonably be done without
obtaining possession of the house; house designed or adapted for
occupation by a person with special needs and there is no longer
such a person occupying the house and the landlord requires the
house for occupation by another person with special needs; house
part of group designed or provided with or located near facilities for
persons in need of special social support and there is no longer a
person with such a need occupying the house and landlord requires
it for another person with such needs; housing association landlord
whose objects are or include housing persons who are in a special
category by reason of age, infirmity, disability or social circumstances and tenant no longer in such circumstances or house no
longer suitable for tenant's needs and accommodation required for
someone who is in a special category; landlord's rights have either
ended or will do within six months from raising of possession action.

9.71   Where the landlord is repossessing property and providing alternative accommodation its suitability is determined according to
whether the security is equivalent, as well as whether it is reasonably
suitable. In deciding whether a house is reasonably suitable to the
needs of the tenant and the family the sheriff must have regard to
specific factors.[8] These are proximity to the place of work of the
tenant and other members of the family compared with the existing
dwelling-house (this also includes attendance at an educational
establishment); the extent of the accommodation required by the
tenant and his family; the character of the accommodation offered
compared with the existing house; the terms on which the accommodation is offered compared with the existing house; where furniture is provided, how it compares with previously provided furniture;
and any special needs of the tenant or his family.

(2) AGRICULTURAL LAND

9.72   From the first legislation on agricultural holdings in 1883 there has
been legislation to ensure that tenants are not deprived of their

---

[8] Sched. 3, Pt II of the Housing (Scotland) Act 1987.

improvements on leaving the land. The freedom of contract of the parties has been modified considerably over the years and the legislation confers on tenants substantial rights of security, an arbitrated rent, as well as compensation for improvements and disturbance.

The Agricultural Holdings legislation[9] applies to leases of "land used for agriculture which is so used for the purpose of a trade or business". Agriculture covers every sort of farming activity including horticulture, fruit growing and market gardening.

(a) Rent and Other Conditions

Tenants of agricultural holdings have statutory rights which 9.73 include the right to a written lease of at least a year and the right to have the question of their rent referred to arbitration. This is to be fixed at the rent which the holding might reasonably be expected to let in the open market by a willing landlord to a willing tenant disregarding the tenant's right to security. The landlord has the right to automatic rent increases for certain improvements provided that the tenant is given timeous notice.

Apart from rent, the tenant has the right of freedom of cropping, subject to the obligation to exercise good husbandry, the right to remove fixtures and to have a record of the holding and its fixed equipment.[10-11] This record is required for any claims for continuous good farming and claims for deterioration or dilapidation. The parties are expressly prohibited from contracting out of the obligations like freedom of cropping and compensation whilst some rights in the legislation are subject to contractual variation.[12] Compensation is available for disturbance and improvements. Game damage is covered by the common law. The question of improvements is based on the value to an incoming tenant and in the event of failure to agree there is provision for arbitration.

(b) Security of Tenure

The tenancy can be terminated for non-payment of rent but this 9.74 does not affect the compensation rights available for improvements. Apart from this, where a landlord serves a notice to quit the tenant may serve a written counter-notice and require the matter to be dealt with by the Land Court. Their consent must be given before there can be termination. They must be satisfied on one or more of the

---

[9] Agricultural Holdings (Scotland) Act 1991.
[10-11] Specified in ss. 5 and 8 of the 1991 Act and including buildings, fences, ditches, drains, farm roads and water and sewerage systems.
[12] See Gill, *Law of Agricultural Holdings in Scotland* (2nd ed., W. Green, 1990).

following grounds—that the landlord's purpose in seeking recovery is in the interests of good husbandry, in the interests of sound estate management, and desirable for the purposes of agricultural research, education, experiment, demonstration, smallholdings, allotments; that greater hardship would be caused by refusal than consenting; and that the landlord proposes to terminate the tenancy for the purpose of the land being used for a non-agricultural use. In addition, the Land Court must withhold consent to the operation of the notice to quit if it appears to them that a fair and reasonable landlord would not insist on possession.[13-14]

Recourse to the Land Court is excluded in certain circumstances and the landlord will be able to recover possession—for instance when the tenant is bankrupt, where within the last nine months a Certificate of Bad Husbandry has been issued by the Land Court or where the tenant is guilty of a breach which is not capable of being remedied in reasonable time and at economic cost.

(3) CROFTERS AND COTTARS

9.75 Statutory control over the position of crofts was introduced in 1886 to cover those holding from year to year who lacked security of tenure, suffered high rents and had no rights as to compensation for improvement.[15] The code was introduced in the crofting counties—Argyll, Caithness, Inverness, Orkney, Ross and Cromarty, Shetland and Sutherland. In 1911 the protections were extended to those in the rest of Scotland and landholders were classified as either small landholders or statutory small tenants.

A distinct crofting code was re-introduced by the Crofters (Scotland) Act 1955 to cover holdings within the crofting region and that code, as amended, has now been consolidated in the Crofters (Scotland) Act 1993. The code covers the holdings occupied by small landholders and statutory small tenants prior to the introduction of the 1955 legislation.[16] The legislation provided for the application of the legislation to new crofts provided they did not exceed a certain size or rental[17-18] to be determined by the Secretary

---

[13-14] *Altyre Estate Trs v. McLay*, 1975 S.L.T. (Land Ct.) 12, where a unit was not viable on its own and the landlord sought to recover it for amalgamation. The tenant had farmed it along with a holding one mile away for 30 years.

[15] Donald MacCuish and Derek Flyn, *Crofting Law* (Butterworths, 1990).

[16] As to the very limited compensation rights of cottars, see MacCuish and Flyn, *op. cit.*, Chap. 11. Cottars are those paying no rent for a dwelling-house or tenants from year to year paying rent not exceeding £6, in the crofting counties, but whose presence and status is recognised by the landowner.

[17-18] Under the 1955 legislation this was either 50 acres or £50 annual rental. The Crofters (Scotland) Act 1961 increased the acreage limit to 75 acres.

of State. There is provision for enlargement of existing crofts by the addition of non-crofting land provided that the total extent and rental do not exceed the specified limits. The Crofters Commission has a duty to maintain a Register of Crofts although this is not conclusive as to any holding being a croft.[19] In 1976 the crofting code was significantly amended to introduce the right to acquire ownership of the croft house as well as croft land.[20]

The crofting code lays down statutory conditions which must be complied with, including the requirement of the crofter to pay rent, to cultivate the croft, not to subdivide it, not to sell intoxicating liquors and to permit the landlord access to take minerals, timber and fishing.

The rent payable may be altered by agreement in writing between landlord and crofter. There is a specific right for crofters to apply for a fair rent.[21–22] Either the crofter or the landlord can apply to the Land Court for such a determination. The parties must be heard and the Land Court must take into consideration all the circumstances of the case, of the croft and of the district and in particular must take into consideration any permanent or unexhausted improvements on the croft, suitable thereto, which have been executed or paid for by the crofter or any predecessors in the tenancy. 9.76

As far as security of tenure is concerned, a crofter must not be removed from the croft unless one year's rent is unpaid or there is breach of one or more of the statutory conditions. No contracting out is permitted. If there is a breach of conditions the landlord can apply to the Land Court. They must consider any objections raised by the crofter and may make an order for removal. In addition, there is a procedure for resumption of the whole or part of the croft by the landlord "for some reasonable purpose[23] having relation to the good of the croft or the estate or to the public interest". The Land Court may, if satisfied as to these matters, authorise the resumption and require the crofter to surrender the whole or part of the croft. Adequate compensation either by letting other land of equivalent value or money or rent adjustment is provided for. Provision is also made for termination of crofting tenancies where there are "absentee" crofters. This involves the Crofter's Commission taking action 9.77

---

[19] Crofters (Scotland) Act 1993, s. 41.

[20] Crofting Reform (Scotland) Act 1976.

[21–22] Crofters (Scotland) Act 1993, s. 6(3).

[23] *ibid.* s. 20—reasonable purpose includes use of land for building houses, small allotments, harbours, piers, boat shelters, churches, schools, halls or community centres, planting, roads for vehicular access from croft to public road or seashore or any other purpose likely to provide employment for crofters and others in the locality or protection of any object of historical or archaeological interest.

where it is in the general interest of the crofting community in the district that the tenancy of the croft be terminated and let to some other person.[24] Where there is termination, whether voluntary or involuntary there is entitlement to compensation for improvements based on the amount which the landlord might reasonably be expected to receive from an incoming tenant if the croft were offered for letting on a crofting tenancy on the open market.[25]

(4) COMMERCIAL PREMISES

9.78 In Scotland there is no developed body of law providing rent control or security of tenure for the tenants of commercial premises. In the event that a tenant of commercial premises finds the terms offered by a landlord unacceptable there is no body of law which provides for such a disagreement to be arbitrated to which the tenant may have recourse. Rents in all commercial premises—offices, shops or industrial premises—are determined by the market. Inability to pay or exorbitance of the rent is not a concern of any forum of appeal or adjudication. There may be provision for arbitration in the tenancy agreement.[26]

There is provision for a limited right to renew a tenancy of a shop covered by the Tenancy of Shops (Scotland) Act 1949. This applies to any premises where any retail trade or business is carried on. The statute specifically covers "the business of a barber or hairdresser, the sale of refreshments or intoxicating liquors, the business of lending books or periodicals when carried on for the purpose of gain, and retail sales, but does not include the sale of programmes and catalogues and other similar sales at theatres and places of amusement". The legislation has been held to cover a garage selling second-hand cars and selling accessories, a sub-post office selling stamps and an optician's where dispensing and sale of spectacles was the sole business. Where a tenant is unable to obtain a renewal of the tenancy from the landlord on satisfactory terms there may be application to the sheriff. The sheriff may decide that there should be a renewal but is limited to the period of one year on such terms as the sheriff thinks in all the circumstances reasonable. There may be refusal to renew if the sheriff considers it reasonable to do so. The sheriff must refuse to renew if there has been a material breach of the tenancy conditions, or the tenant is bankrupt, or if the landlord has offered to sell to the tenant at an arbitrated price, or if alternative

---

[24] Crofters (Scotland) Act 1993, s. 22—currently a crofter is absent if not ordinarily resident on or within 16 kilometres of the croft measured in a straight line.

[25] Crofters (Scotland) Act 1993, s. 32.

[26] See *McAllister, op. cit.*, Chap. 10.

accommodation has been offered, or if the tenant has given notice to terminate on the strength of which the landlord has contracted to sell or lease the premises and there would be serious prejudice if possession could not be obtained, or if in all the circumstances of the case greater hardship would be caused by renewing the tenancy than by refusing to renew. The sheriff's decision is not subject to appeal.

Commercial tenancies of subjects other than shops are covered by 9.79 the normal rules as to termination of the tenancy. There is no guarantee that a tenant will be provided with a renewal. It will depend on the contract. The protection that does exist for commercial tenants is to be found in the Law Reform (Miscellaneous Provisions) (Scotland) Act 1986 which introduced a formal requirement when a landlord was seeking to enforce a conventional irritancy. To prevent what was seen as the harshness of tenants being evicted for trivial lateness in rent payment[27] it is now provided that after monetary irritancies have been incurred the tenant must be given a further 14 days' written notice to pay the arrears. Only after the lapse of this period without payment may the landlord go ahead and enforce the irritancy.[28] At the same time, statutory protection was provided for tenants where landlords are seeking to enforce other irritancies. The court may only enforce the irritancy in cases where it considers that a fair and reasonable landlord would do so.[29] There may be no contracting out of this provision.

[27] *Dorchester Studios (Glasgow) Ltd v. Stone,* 1975 S.C. (H.L.) 56; *HMV Fields Properties Ltd v. Tandem Shoes Ltd,* 1983 S.L.T. 114.
[28] Law Reform (Miscellaneous Provisions) (Scotland) Act 1985, s. 4; *C.I.N. Properties Ltd v. Dollar Land (Cumbernauld) Ltd,* 1992 S.L.T. 669.
[29] s. 5; see *Blythswood Investments (Scotland) Ltd v. Clydesdale Electrical Stores (in receivership),* 1995 S.L.T. 150.

CHAPTER 10

RIGHTS IN SECURITY

1. INTRODUCTION

10.01 The most familiar symbols of rights in security are the pawnshop on the one hand and the building society on the other. These signify the most common forms of security in respect of moveable and heritable property respectively. The essence of a security is that it is a property right in a specific item of property. This property acts as security for a debt and, in the event of the debtor becoming insolvent, the holder of the security has a preferential right in the secured property before other unsecured creditors. Typically a building society lends the purchase price to the buyer and takes out a security right over the house being purchased.

Rights in security may arise by operation of law (such as hypothec and lien, discussed below) or by agreement. Some security rights are governed by the common law, whilst others (including all securities over heritable property) are governed by statute and must take a prescribed statutory form.

10.02 Distinctions exist depending on whether the property involved is moveable or heritable. The difference noted in Roman law was between pledge and mortgage.[1] The former involves delivery whilst this is not available in the latter. Since possession is the badge of ownership as far as moveables are concerned, it is important that potential purchasers or lenders be made aware of the prior debtor's rights. This is effected through delivery. As far as heritable rights are concerned, the existence of a public property register protects a purchaser or subsequent lender from undisclosed security rights over the property concerned. Any security over the property would emerge on consultation of the Register of Sasines or Land Register.[2] Finally there are special arrangements in existence for securities over

---

[1] Just., *Inst.*, iii. 4 and iv. 6, 7.
[2] See Chap. 6.

ships. A ship may be mortgaged in a statutory form which must be registered by the registrar in the prescribed manner. This gives the creditor a real right of security without possession.[3] The order of registration determines preference between creditors[4] but a mortgage is secondary to a bond of bottomry, a maritime lien[5] or a lien for repairs.[6] Because the holder of a mortgage is not in possession, he has a variety of powers including interdict to prevent the mortgagor dealing with the ship in such a way as to materially prejudice the security[7] as well as the power of sale.[8] This latter includes the taking of possession.[9]

2. SECURITIES OVER MOVEABLES

The basic principle which underlies Scots law on security rights over moveables is the requirement for delivery. Although there are now significant exceptions to this notion, it is a useful baseline from which to start consideration of the nature and operation of security rights. The doctrine derives from Roman law that it is by delivery that the ownership of things passes, not by mere agreement.[10]   10.03

The traditional pawnshop transaction typifies securities rights in relation to moveables. Here the borrower pledges the goods and delivers them to the lender. The pledge may be redeemed by repayment of the capital and interest. If goods are not subject to the security rights of the creditor, then in a bankruptcy the creditor has no preferred position and stands alongside other creditors. Delivery may be satisfied not only by the physical transfer of the goods in question but also where there is symbolic delivery or constructive delivery. Physical delivery has included enclosure of goods within a fence and the delivery of the key to the lender[11] and is not required in situations where delivery is impossible.[12] Symbolic delivery is acceptable for goods which are shipped and for which a bill of lading is issued. The bill of lading is regarded as a symbol of

---

[3] Merchant Shipping Act 1995, Sched. 1, para. 7.
[4] *ibid.*, Sched. 1, para. 8.
[5] See below.
[6] *Tyne Dock Engineering Co. v. Royal Bank of Scotland*, 1974 S.L.T. 57.
[7] *Laming and Co. v. Seater* (1889) 16 R. 828.
[8] Merchant Shipping Act 1995, Sched. 1, para. 9.
[9] Bell, *Prin.*, §1382A.
[10] *Traditionibus non nudis pactis dominia rerum transferuntur.*
[11] *Liquidator of West Lothian Oil Co. Ltd v. Mair* (1892) 20 R. 64 (although that case concerned a contract of sale, not of loan or security).
[12] *Darling v. Wilson's Tr.* (1887) 15 R. 180.

the goods and its transfer has the same effect as the physical delivery of the goods themselves.[13] Other forms of symbolic delivery have not found favour in the courts.[14] Where, however, goods are in a store there may be effective delivery (known as constructive delivery) where the delivery order is addressed to the storekeeper or by the indorsation of the storekeeper's warrant. Before constructive delivery operates, there must be intimation of the transfer and the goods must be ascertained. In addition, the store must be neutral and outwith the borrower's control, and intimation must be to the storekeeper, not to a third party who has access to the store for other purposes.[15]

10.04   It is not always easy or convenient to deliver goods which are alleged to be the security for the transaction. To avoid the inconvenience of delivery, a variety of mechanisms have been used with a varying degree of success. A genuine sale even where the aim is to provide security has been accepted[16] but not a sale which is truly intended to operate as a security without delivery,[17] nor a sham lease[18] nor the labelling of goods by the lender as "owner". Furthermore, delivery is not required where the goods are already in the transferee's possession, provided the good faith of the transaction is not in doubt.[19]

These problems of delivery were particularly felt by commercial concerns and the floating charge was introduced into Scots law in 1961 to allow a security over both moveables and heritage without the need for delivery. It can be granted by an incorporated company[20] or by an industrial or provident society.[21] To be operative it must be registered with the registrar of companies. There is no need for transfer of possession or intimation, in the case of moveable property, nor for recording or registration in the appropriate property register in the case of heritable property.[22] The charge crystallises or attaches only when a company goes into liquidation[23]

---

[13] Bell, *Prin.*, §417.
[14] *Paul v. Cuthbertson* (1840) 2 D. 1286 (part cutting of standing trees); *Stiven v. Cowan* (1878) 15 S.L.R. 422 (sasine ceremony aimed to affect machinery as well as heritage).
[15] *Rhind's Tr. v. Robertson and Baxter* (1891) 18 R. 623; *Anderson v. McCall* (1866) 4 M. 765; *Hayman v. McLintock*, 1907 S.C. 936.
[16] *Duncanson v. Jefferis' Tr.* (1881) 8 R. 563.
[17] See for example *Balcraig House's Tr. v. Roosevelt Property Services Ltd*, 1994 S.L.T. 1133.
[18] *Heritable Securities Investment Ass. v. Wingate and Cos. Tr.* (1880) 7 R. 1094.
[19] *Orr's Tr. v. Tullis* (1870) 8 M. 936; *Milligan v. Ross*, 1994 S.C.L.R. 430 (though both these cases relate to rights of ownership rather than security).
[20] Companies Act 1985, Part XVIII, ss. 462–466).
[21] Industrial and Provident Societies Act 1967, s. 3(1).
[22] Companies Act 1985, s. 462(5).
[23] Companies Act 1985, s. 463(1).

or upon appointment of a receiver by the holder of the floating charge.[24] It does not attach to any particular item of property but usually (subject to the terms of the charge) to the company's whole property and undertaking. It has been held that the word "property" in this context has a non-technical meaning, so that when a floating charge crystallises it does not attach to property in respect of which the debtor company remains the registered proprietor but in respect of which it has granted a disposition (as yet unrecorded) in favour of purchasers.[25] In the absence of a ranking provision in the floating charge, a crystallised charge ranks behind any fixed charge which has been constituted as a real right before the floating charge crystallised, any other floating charge registered at an earlier date, and any fixed securities arising by operation of law (such as landlord's hypothec). In addition a receivership is subject to any arrestment dated prior to the date of registration of the floating charge.[26]

3. HERITABLE SECURITIES

There are statutory limitations on the kinds of securities which may 10.05 be created over heritage. The older pre-1970 forms of fixed security[27] will continue to be found but since the introduction of the Conveyancing and Feudal Reform (Scotland) Act 1970 the only competent form of fixed security over heritable property in Scotland is the standard security.[28] Heritable property may also be secured by way of a floating charge[29] but, as indicated above, that method is only available to an incorporated company or an industrial or provident society.[30] By contrast, any person or corporation having right to an interest in land may grant a standard security.

There are two prescribed forms in which a standard security may be granted. In order to create a real right of security it must be recorded in the Register.[31] Recording vests the interest over which the security is granted in the creditor as security for performance of the debtor's obligations—normally this would involve making mortgage payments

---

[24] Insolvency Act 1986, s. 53(7).
[25] *Sharp v. Thompson*, 1997 S.L.T. 636.
[26] *Iona Hotels Ltd (in receivership), Petrs*, 1991 S.L.T. 11.
[27] Bond and disposition in security; cash credit bond and disposition in security; *ex facie* absolute disposition—discussed at some length in W. M. Gordon, *Scottish Land Law*, Chap. 20.
[28] In terms of the Conveyancing and Feudal Reform (Scotland) Act 1970.
[29] See above.
[30] Industrial and Provident Societies Act 1967.
[31] Formerly Register of Sasines and now, under Land Registration (Scotland) Act 1979, the Land Register.

promptly.[32] The conditions which attach to standard securities are specified in the 1970 Act.[33] Some, though not all, of these standard conditions may be varied by agreement. The ranking of competing creditors is determined by the date of recording or registration of any properly executed standard security, although this may be altered by agreement.[34] However the preference in ranking of a prior security is restricted, upon the giving to the creditor of notice of the creation of a postponed security, to present advances, future advances which he is bound to make and present and future interest thereon.[35] The debtor may redeem the debt by giving two months' notice.[36] Where the debtor defaults in repayments or otherwise breaches the terms of the security the creditor may serve a default notice, or a calling up notice, or both.[37] If the debtor fails to comply with a default notice or a calling up notice, the creditor may exercise various statutory rights which include the right to take possession of and sell the subjects.[38] The debtor's right of redemption is unqualified, however, and may be exercised notwithstanding that the debtor is in default.[39] The creditor has a statutory duty to take all reasonable steps to ensure that the best price reasonably obtainable is secured for the property.[40] If the creditor is unable to sell the subjects or any part of them, a decree of foreclosure may be sought in respect of the unsold portion of the property.[41] A decree of foreclosure extinguishes the debtor's right of redemption, and will be in terms capable of being recorded in the Register of Sasines or registered in the Land Register, as appropriate, thus vesting the property in the creditor.

10.06   When one creditor has a heritable security over two subjects belonging to the debtor and another creditor has a postponed security over one of these subjects the first creditor is termed the catholic creditor and the other the secondary creditor. The catholic creditor must use his securities so as to maximise the value of the secondary creditor's security, but need not thereby do anything

---

[32] Conveyancing and Feudal Reform (Scotland) Act 1970, s. 11(1).
[33] See Sched. 3.
[34] s. 13(3)(b) and Sched. 2, Note 5.
[35] s. 13(1).
[36] s. 18.
[37] ss. 21 and 19 respectively.
[38] s. 20.
[39] *G. Dunlop and Son's J.F. v. Armstrong*, 1994 S.L.T. 199; but although the court accepted that the creditor's right of sale and the debtor's right to serve a notice of redemption could co-exist, the opinion was expressed that the position would differ once the creditor had concluded an enforceable contract to sell the security subjects.
[40] s. 25.
[41] s. 28.

which adversely affects his own legitimate interests in securing full payment. Thus the secondary creditor cannot prevent the catholic creditor choosing to obtain payment by realising the security subjects over which the secondary creditor also has a security. The catholic creditor in such circumstances must, however, assign to the secondary creditor his security over the remaining security subjects.

In cases where separate secondary creditors each have a postponed security over security subjects in respect of which a catholic creditor has a prior security, the secondary creditors must bear the burden of the catholic security rateably in proportion to the respective values of each property regardless of the respective dates of creation of the secondary securities.[42]

4. SECURITIES OVER INCORPOREAL PROPERTY

It is not possible to effect delivery of incorporeal property by its very nature. It may be transferred in security by a written assignation followed by intimation to the debtor. Both these elements must be included. Thus, there would be no security created if the policy were merely deposited with the creditor without assignation[43] and no preferential right would be created by the transfer of a policy of insurance without intimation to the insurance company.[44] The position as regards shares in a company is a little more complex. Whilst these may be used as a security through transferring them to the creditor subject to an obligation to retransfer, this is a cumbersome and expensive process. Simply depositing the share certificates effects no security.[45] A duly executed transfer of the shares may be given to the creditor with the certificates. In such a case the date of grant of the security is the date of delivery of the share transfers, not the date on which the transfers are registered with the company.[46] The right in security thus created is not prejudiced by the debtor's bankruptcy, even if registration of the transfer occurs within 60 days of the debtor's sequestration. Where a loan is secured against a promise to transfer shares at a future time when requested to do so by the creditor, however, the debtor will not give a valid right

10.07

---

[42] *Ferrier v. Cowan* (1896) 23 R. 703.
[43] *Wylie's Exrx v. McJannet* (1901) 4 F. 195.
[44] *Strachan v. McDougle* (1835) 13 S. 954.
[45] *Gourlay v. Mackie* (1887) 14 R. 403.
[46] *Guild v. Young* (1884) 22 S.L.R. 520.
[47] Bankruptcy (Scotland) Act 1985, s. 36; *Gourlay v. Mackie* (1887) 14 R. 403.

in security if the transfer is ultimately requested and registered within 60 days of bankruptcy.[47] However, the transfer would be effectual even where it was registered after the petition for sequestration of the debtor had been presented, provided registration occurred before the trustee had taken steps to register as owner of the shares.[48–49]

5. HYPOTHEC

10.08 Hypothec provides a security without transfer of possession. Hypothecs may be legal or conventional. A legal hypothec is available to superiors, landlords, solicitors and in certain maritime forms. Superiors have rights of hypothec for feu duty over the goods brought onto the property by their vassals. The landlord's hypothec applies in the same way over tenants' property for rent. Certain leases of rural subjects are excluded from the operation of hypothec.[50] Solicitors have, both at common law and under statute rights to have the expenses of an action met out of any expenses the client may be entitled to as well as out of most property recovered in the action.[51] There are certain maritime hypothecs which give creditors the right in security over the ship without possession on a variety of questions including to seamen for wages, to salvors for any sum due for salvage, to anyone for damages caused directly by the ship and for repairers to cover repairs executed or necessaries supplied in a foreign port. These rights may be enforced by sale and they rank before mortgage holders. The only recognised conventional hypothecs relate to bonds available in maritime dealings. Bottomry is available to creditors over a ship without possession whilst *respondentia* is available for the cargo. Their role has been displaced by the introduction of the floating charge.[52]

6. LIEN

10.09 Unlike hypothec, lien operates on the basis of possession. This provides a right to retain goods in settlement of a debt. Here perhaps the best known is that of the innkeeper for unpaid bills. The lien gives a right to remain in possession of property which belongs to

---

[48–49] *Morrison v. Harrison* (1876) 3 R. 406.
[50] Hypothec Abolition (Scotland) Act 1880 on leases of rural subjects.
[51] Solicitors (Scotland) Act 1980.
[52] See above.

another party who is failing to meet some obligation. The creditor has a limited title only, and must transfer the property to the debtor when the debt has been satisfied. There is a general lien which is a right to retain until some balance arising on a contract is discharged. No lien founded on possession can be asserted if it would conflict with the express or implied terms of the contract under which possession is obtained. The courts exercise an equitable control over liens.[53]

Special liens exists in a variety of situations, most notably in the employer/employee relationship and in certain relationships of agency like bankers, factors and solicitors. Since there is a mutual relationship in contracts of employment, employees who are in possession of articles belonging to the employer, are entitled to retain them until they have been paid for their work on that contract. Proof of a particular custom of trade is not required. It is not material that no work has been done on the article in question if the article is placed with the creditor to enable some task to be carried out.[54] Bankers have a general lien over all bills, notes and negotiable securities lodged in their capacity as a monetary agent rather than merely for safe keeping. The lien covers any balance due by the customer.[55] Express notice or previous knowledge of the true ownership of negotiable instruments lodged by stockbrokers alters the reasonable assumption that these belonged to the stockbroker.[56] Factors or mercantile agents[57] have a general lien over all goods, bills, money or documents belonging to the employer which have come into their possession in the course of their employment.[58] It covers all advances made to the principal, the factor's salary or commission, and any liabilities incurred on the principal's behalf.[59] It does not cover debts due to the factor on another account, in the event of the bankruptcy of the principal.[60]

Solicitors have a general lien over all papers placed by clients in their hands. This includes title deeds and wills. Solicitors may not

10.10

---

[53] See, for example, *Garscadden v. Ardrossan Dry Dock Co.*, 1910 S.C. 178.

[54] *Meikle and Wilson v. Pollard* (1880) 8 R. 69; it has been held that, on the basis of a special lien, goods belonging to a manufacturer but held by another company contracted to install the goods for the manufacturer, could be retained by the installers pending payment of a sum of money due under the agreement between them: *National Homecare Ltd v. Belling and Co. Ltd*, 1994 S.L.T. 50.

[55] Bell, *Prin.*, §1451.

[56] *National Bank of Scotland v. Dickie's Tr.* (1895) 22 R. 740.

[57] See Factors Act 1889, s. 1(1) for a definition, but note that the term has been held to extend, as far as lien is concerned, to auctioneers and stockbrokers.

[58] Bell, *Prin.*, §1445.

[59] *Glendinning v. Hope and Co.*, 1911 S.C. (H.L.) 73.

[60] *Miller v. McNair* (1852) 14 D. 955.

obstruct the course of justice by refusing to produce papers for an action,[61] but otherwise are entitled to withhold a client's file until their business account is settled or otherwise secured (*e.g.* by consignation of the taxed account) even where the client seeks the papers to sue the solicitor for professional negligence.[62] The lien covers business accounts and advances made in the ordinary course of business, such as to counsel or witnesses.[63] A similar general lien is not enjoyed by parallel professionals like accountants, whose lien over papers only relates to work done in connection with those particular papers rather than the whole professional account.[64] The lien operates against clients rather than against third parties. The solicitor must give up all papers to a company liquidator or trustee in sequestration, subject to an implied reservation of the lien. The solicitor's expenses will be postponed to those of the liquidation or sequestration.[65] The lien only gives a right of retention and does not permit disposal and is of limited value when there is no estate from which the expenses can be taken.[66]

Innkeepers have a lien over the ordinary items of luggage of their guests for the amount of the bill[67] but this does not cover the clothes of the guest.[68] It does not cover articles not brought as luggage but hired during the stay,[69] nor items delivered by a third party for the use of the guest,[70] but it will extend to goods brought by the guest but belonging to a third party.[71] The Hotel Proprietors Act 1956 makes certain modifications to the common law excluding vehicles or property therein as well as horse, harness and other equipment.[72] The fact that an item belonged to another person and the hotel proprietor knew of this does not prevent the sale of the item.[73] An innkeeper is entitled by statute, after advertisement, to sell by auction goods brought to or left in the inn in satisfaction of a debt for board and lodging, provided that the goods have been held for at least six weeks. Any surplus is to be accounted for to the guest.[74]

---

[61] *Callmen v. Bell* (1793) Mor. 6255.
[62] *Yau v. Ogilvie and Co.*, 1985 S.L.T. 91.
[63] *Richardson v. Merry* (1863) 1 M. 940.
[64] *Findlay v. Waddell*, 1910 S.C. 670.
[65] *Miln's J.F. v. Spence's Trs*, 1927 S.L.T. 425.
[66] *Garden, Haig Scott and Wallace v. Stevenson's Tr.*, 1962 S.C. 51.
[67] Bell, *Prin.*, §1428.
[68] *Sunbolf v. Alford* (1838) 3 Mees. & W. 248.
[69] *Broadwood v. Granara* (1854) 10 Ex. 417.
[70] *Bermans and Nathans Ltd v. Weibye*, 1983 S.L.T. 299.
[71] *Bermans and Nathans Ltd, supra.*
[72] s. 2(2).
[73] *Bermans and Nathans Ltd, supra.*
[74] Innkeepers Act 1878, s. 1.

Chapter 11

SUBSIDIARY PROPERTY RIGHTS

There are certain categories of property rights which provide 11.01 benefits to those who enjoy them but are more restricted than full ownership. Liferents are a creature of Scots common law. The status of licenses, especially where residential accommodation is concerned, is less well-defined. Occupancy rights can be created by wills and trusts as well as existing in a slightly different form as the creation of statute. There is extensive case law on liferents although the other two categories have been discussed much less in the courts.

1. LIFERENTS

Property may be enjoyed by an individual during their lifetime 11.02 only. Their status is similar to that of a tenant. They may enjoy the fruits of the property as well as being responsible for the annual costs which an owner would have to meet, such as property taxes. The rights of the liferenter are determined by the document creating the liferent. However, the common law has established various rules which are to operate where the document is silent. A liferent has been defined as "the right to enjoy the use or the fruits of a subject without destroying or encroaching upon the substance".[1]

The liferenter receives the fruits and income yielded up during the occupancy. The fiar receives the capital or the property itself (the fee). This arrangement generally operates where a person wishes to pass ownership of some item of property into the hands of another but reserve the use of the property to a third person during that third person's lifetime. Thus a regular arrangement in Scots law has been for a father to leave the family home in fee to the children but to reserve a liferent over the property to his wife. The widow is given occupancy and use of the house during her lifetime. The children are, however, left the ownership of the house. Their rights of occupancy only attach on the death of their mother. A different example of a liferent and fee

---

[1] W. Dobie, *Manual of the Law of Liferent and Fee in Scotland* (1941), p. 1.

relationship is that of the mother receiving the right to use the property or receive the income in the case of a liferent over investments, and the offspring receiving the property or the capital invested.

Liferents can be created in favour of any person and the right to the fee can go to any person or organisation. As its name suggests, a liferent comes to an end at the death of the liferenter or liferentrix. Other dates, however, can be set for the dissolution of the liferent such as the liferenter attaining the age of majority or upon his or her marriage. A liferent must be distinguished from other types of limited property rights.

Right of occupancy

11.03   A liferent is more extensive than a right of occupancy since liferenters are entitled to use the rents from the relevant properties for their own purposes. There is, however, an obligation to pay the burdens of the property such as feu duty which does not apply to those with only a right of occupancy.[2]

Annuity

11.04   An annuity can be defined as a limited right to a periodical payment of money which is paid each year. Since an annuitant is entitled to receive a fixed sum each year, it may be that in times of recession some of the capital will have to be realised in order to pay annuitants their income. This is the single most important distinguishing feature between an annuity and a liferent, the fact that an annuity may encroach upon the capital.[3] In the event that the capital sum is exhausted, the rights of the annuitant will depend on the original document constituting the annuity. If it stems from a contract with an insurance company, then the annuity is payable irrespective that the annuitant has taken out more than was put in. Where the fund is set up under a will, the annuity will cease.

(1) CLASSIFICATION OF LIFERENTS

The law recognises three distinctive groups of liferents.

(a) Legal Liferents and Conventional Liferents

11.05   The legal liferents of terce and courtesy[4] were implied by the common law until 1964 and provided rights for widows and widowers in the intestate estates of their late spouses. They may also be

---

[2] *Clark's Trs* (1871) 9 M. 435.
[3] *Colquhoun's Trs v. Colquhoun*, 1922 S.C. 32.
[4] W. M. Gordon, *Scottish Land Law* (W. Green, 1989), p. 474.

created through statute or a decision of the court. A conventional liferent is one created by some person's express wish. An example of this type would be a testator creating a liferent and fee situation in a will.

(b) Liferents by Constitution and by Reservation

The former, often called simple liferent, is created where the 11.06 owner of property grants to someone else a liferent over it. In such a case the fee can either be retained by the granter or sold to a third party. The latter occurs where owners of property sell the fee but retain the liferent for themselves.

(c) Proper Liferents and Beneficiary Liferents

The former is created by direct grant (*e.g.* in a will). In the latter 11.07 the relationship of liferenter and fiar is created through the operation of a trust. In such a case the property is actually vested in trustees with the liferenter receiving a right to benefit termed a *jus crediti*.

Since a liferent is supposed to exist in a way which means that the property or the capital itself cannot be destroyed, a liferent cannot be created over a fungible—*i.e.* something destroyed in its use such as the contents of a wine cellar.

(2) THE RIGHTS OF THE LIFERENTER

The liferenter is entitled to the fruits of the property, but not to 11.08 anything which is part of the *corpus* of the property or the capital. The costs of repair over the property will be borne by either liferenter or fiar depending on whether the repair is payable out of interest or out of capital. Whether the cost of repair is payable out of capital or interest depends on the test as to whether the repair is a once-and-for-all-payment or something which is likely to recur annually. Routine maintenance would come out of the liferenter's share whilst a major reconstruction would fall to the fiar. As for the benefits of an estate, the liferenter is entitled to ordinary windfalls of timber on the property. The fiar, on the other hand, is entitled to the wood growing on the estate and to any trees blown down in an exceptional storm. The liferenter is permitted to cut wood which has reached maturity.[5]

---

[5] Dobie, *op. cit.*, Pt III, Chap. 4.

(3) ALIMENTARY LIFERENTS

11.09   An alimentary liferent is one which is intended for the support of
the liferenter and has been declared to be so by its creator. It
cannot, as a result, be assigned by the liferenter nor can it be
attached by that person's creditors nor, once accepted, can it be
renounced.[6]

(4) EXTINCTION OF LIFERENTS

11.10   A liferent is extinguished generally upon the death of the liferenter.
It can also be discharged because of some other event, or upon the
liferenter renouncing it, or upon the liferent and fee becoming vested
in the same person.[7]

(5) APPORTIONMENT OF INCOME

11.11   At common law, income accrues on a daily basis. The apportion-
ment of income can create problems:

   (i) Where during the lifetime of the liferenter stocks and shares
        are actually sold off. In this case, the liferenter is entitled to a
        compensatory payment of a sum equivalent to the dividend
        which is likely to have been paid on the shares at the next
        date a dividend was payable.
   (ii) Where the liferenter dies during the financial year. In this,
        case apportionment will be necessary in order to determine
        how much of the dividend will go to the representatives of
        the liferenter and how much will go to the fiar. This
        apportionment is done on a time basis and under the
        provisions of the Apportionment Act 1870 dividends accrue
        day to day and must be paid on that basis.

2. LICENCES

11.12   Provided certain requirements are satisfied, a lease confers rights
against the whole world rather than simply providing personal
rights enforceable against the original landlord.[8] These
requirements are that there must be agreement, heritable subjects,

---

[6] *Dewar's Trs v. Dewar*, 1910 S.C. 730.
[7] *Martin v. Bannatyne* (1861) 23 D. 705.
[8] See paras 9.11–9.12.

rent, a termination date and possession. In England and Wales the law has recognised since the seventeenth century a lesser form of right called a licence. This involves the landlord providing less than the full range of rights to the occupier. This has occurred where the relationship between the parties is close and the intention is assumed not to be to create a landlord and tenant contract. This has occurred typically where the parties are related or are friends.

Where a person is allowed to occupy property rent free and where there is no rent and none contemplated then this will not amount to a lease. There has in the past been a willingness of the courts to say that parties in the relationship of landlord and tenant, without any rent agreed, intend that the annual value or market rent of the premises shall be taken as the rent.[9] This does not apply where there is clearly lack of consensus as to whether there is to be a lease.[10] There may, however, be sufficient for there to be a lesser right of licence. In one instance a company occupied subjects for a proposed oil terminal from July 1974 whilst negotiations on the terms of the lease were conducted. The oil terminal became operational in September 1978 but no lease had been agreed. The Court of Session rejected the suggestion that there was a lease here.[11] There is, however, scepticism as to the concept of the licence where the only reason behind labelling an agreement is to avoid restrictions on the occupier's rights. Hence, in one case the occupier was forbidden in their lease agreement from sub-letting out the premises in question. To avoid this restriction the property was rented out using "licence" agreements which were stated not to be leases. The Court of Session rejected this device.[12]

(1) COMMERCIAL PREMISES, RATES AND LICENCES

The case law relied on to discuss licences stems from disputes about whether rates are payable by the occupiers. In situations where a contract does not consist of a grant of heritage but rather the right to use a particular part of it or to put a particular part of it to some use, this question of the payment of rates has been discussed. Rates were payable by tenants but not if it could be argued that the occupiers did not enjoy full tenancy rights. 11.13

---

[9] *Glen v. Roy* (1882) 10 R. 239.
[10] *Gray v. Edinburgh University*, 1962 S.C. 157.
[11] *Shetland Islands Council v. British Petroleum Development Ltd*, 1990 S.L.T. 83.
[12] *Brador Properties Ltd v. British Telecommunications plc*, 1992 S.L.T. 490.

An important factor used by the courts in determining if the users under these commercial contracts were to be charged occupiers' rates was the issue of exclusivity of the possession. Where possession was exclusive, then the agreement was a lease. If, however, possession was only partial, then it would not be a lease. This distinction can be seen in two cases involving garages. In *Broomhill Motor Co. v. Assessor for Glasgow*[13] a number of lock-ups were let for rents which included water, heating, light and washing facilities, and each occupant had a key. The garage company, though, had a right of access to the lock-ups to inspect and clean and the occupants were expected to, and in most cases did, obtain supplies from the garage. It was held that, as there was no independent occupation by the occupants, this contract was only a right to use defined portions of the premises for a limited purpose and hence rates were not payable by those who parked their cars in the lock-ups. By contrast, in *Chaplin v. Assessor for Perth*[14] the proprietor of a piece of ground erected a number of wooden lock-ups, each with its own key, which were occupied by car owners under verbal agreements. The proprietor received a weekly or daily payment and either party could terminate the agreement at a week's notice. Although no services were given the occupiers were entitled to use free of charge a wash bed and a wooden shed. The agreements here gave the occupier exclusive possession during his period of occupation and so they were held to be leases and rents were payable by the garage occupiers.

(2) RESIDENTIAL PROPERTY AND LESSER RIGHTS OF OCCUPANCY

11.14 The difficulty is that the limited case law in Scotland which is cited has been concerned essentially with what the status of an agreement is for the purposes of valuation and rating. None of the Scottish valuation cases actually mention the English concept of the lesser right of "licence".[15] The distinct issues of abuse and avoidance of statutory protection raised by licences in the context of residential property have never been fully discussed in Scotland. The nearest which the courts have come to discussing this issue is in a case concerning an agreement to occupy a cottage for an unspecified period of time in exchange for certain estate management duties. In *Scottish Residential Estates Development Co. Ltd v. Henderson*[16] the approach adopted by the Inner House was that their task was to

---

[13] 1927 S.C. 447.
[14] 1947 S.C. 373.
[15] Robson and Halliday, *Residential Tenancies* (1998), Chap. 1.
[16] Court of Session, May 17, 1990.

construe the intention of the parties. Since the agreement of the parties specifically indicated that no relationship of landlord and tenant was to be entered into by the parties and since there was no ish, their Lordships felt that with this crucial feature of the agreement missing there was no lease. However, such an approach contrasts with that taken by the House of Lords in looking at evasions of the Rent Acts.[17]

Whilst the valuation cases are cited as examples of how the distinction between leases and licences would be treated by the Scottish courts, there is no traditional recognition of such a second-class tenancy right in residential property prior to the introduction of the right of security of tenure for tenants in 1915. This shifted the burden onto landlords to establish that they needed a reason to regain possession of their property beyond the fact that the tenancy had been formally terminated.[18] It would be strange if landlords were able simply to avoid the impact of security of tenure as it applies to tenancies by simply renaming their contracts licences. The fact that in reality full possession is given would even in England qualify for the agreement to operate as a tenancy, where the courts have indicated that they will not entertain such methods of depriving citizens of statutory protection.[19]

3. Service Occupancy

As far as occupancy by employees is concerned this may, in certain 11.15 circumstances, involve a full lease. A separate express agreement for occupancy will confer tenancy rights which are not dependent on the employment contract. This tends to be the exception. If there are no express provisions a more limited right, ceasing on the termination of the employment, may be inferred. Each case will be judged on its particular circumstances. A service occupancy (*i.e.* the limited right of occupancy during employment) will be inferred only if the occupation of the house is necessary for the performance of the employee's duties. It is not enough that one is only eligible for the house if one is employed in certain jobs. Thus, for example, a company employee living in a company-owned house, where there was nothing expressly stated about the occupancy, would, on ceasing to work for the company, be able to live in the particular house as it was not necessary for the performance of company

---

[17] *Antoniades v. Villiers* [1989] 3 W.L.R. 1205.
[18] See paras 9.45–9.71.
[19] *Street v. Mountford* [1985] A.C. 809.

duties. In such circumstances, the occupancy would in fact be a lease rather than a service occupancy.

The test as to the distinction between a lease and a service occupancy is whether the occupation itself is that of an employee. A baker occupied one of three houses in Dingwall which his employer found for him and to whom he paid a small rent. He was told this "went with the job" but not that the occupation would cease with his employment. This was held to be a lease as it in no way related to his efficiency as a baker where he lived.[20] Where, however, a sum was deducted from a teacher's salary equal to the annual value of the Education Authority's house occupied by him, it was held that the contract was one of the service not of lease.[21]

4. RIGHTS OF OCCUPANCY

11.16 These occur in both a common law and a statutory form. Under Scots succession law it has been possible for individuals to provide that another individual shall have the right to occupy property in accordance with the wishes of the testator. The courts have recognised these wishes along with the various different restrictions which have accompanied such testamentary documents. These rights and the distinction between them and liferents were discussed in a series of cases in the nineteenth and early twentieth century.[22] The beneficiary who enjoys a mere right of occupancy thus may not let the premises. He is only liable for a tenant's burdens, such as occupier's taxes, but not feu duty or building repairs.

In addition, the 1980s saw the introduction of statutory rights for spouses and cohabitees to prevent them being evicted from the matrimonial home and allowing them to prevent the sale or disposition of said home. These rights are found in the Matrimonial Homes (Family Protection) (Scotland) Act 1981. This legislation provides rights and remedies which are largely temporary. They are usually employed pending a divorce settlement but can, nonetheless, provide valuable protection against oppression by a richer partner.

(1) THE NATURE OF STATUTORY OCCUPANCY RIGHTS

11.17 Where the spouse who is owner or tenant refuses to allow the other partner the right to enter and occupy then this right may only be exercised with the leave of either the sheriff court or Court of

---

[20] *MacGregor v. Dunnett*, 1949 S.C. 510.
[21] *Pollock v. Assessor for Inverness-shire*, 1923 S.C. 693.
[22] Discussed by Dobie, *op cit.*, Pt III, Chap. 7.

Session, *i.e.* there should be no "self-help".[23] There is no time limit as to the grant of rights of occupancy to spouses.

These rights are exercisable not only by spouses but also where a man and woman are living with each other as if they were man and wife, and allows periods of up to six months to be granted.[24] In addition the law also allows such a partner to bring in any child of the family.[25] Where parties have been cohabiting it is not necessary for them to be actually cohabiting when the action of regulation is raised as this would defeat the purpose of the legislation.[26] The test is whether the parties were living together at the time when the conduct giving rise to the application arises. There is, however, no power to grant interim occupancy rights pending the determination of an application for occupancy rights.[27]

(2) The Property Covered by Occupancy Rights

Occupancy rights can be exercised over the matrimonial home. 11.18 This is defined as: "any house, caravan, houseboat or other structure which has been provided or has been made available by one or both of the spouses, or has become a family residence."[28] Garden ground and other ground normally occupied with or required for the amenity and convenience of the dwelling in question is also included. In general terms, where a property is tenanted or owned by one of the partners prior to marriage/cohabitation then this would become the matrimonial home upon marriage or when the couple can be said to be a cohabiting couple. The relevant factors in deciding when a couple are cohabiting in terms of the 1981 Act are the length of time for which they have been living together and whether there are any children of the relationship.[29]

---

[23] *Nimmo v. Nimmo*, Glasgow Sh. Ct., Aug. 12, 1983 (noted in 29 J.L.S. 4; see also D. I. Nichols and M. C. Meston, *The Matrimonial Homes (Family Protection) (Scotland) Act 1981* (W. Green, 1986) and A. Jackson, M. Robertson and P. Robson, *The Operation of the Matrimonial Homes (Family Protection) (Scotland) Act 1981* (1988).

[24] s. 18

[25] Since the Law Reform (Miscellaneous Provisions) (Scotland) Act 1985, s. 13(3) amended the 1981 Act.

[26] *Armour v. Anderson*, 1994 S.L.T. 1127.

[27] *Smith-Milne v. Gammack*, 1995 S.C.L.R. 1058.

[28] s. 22.

[29] s. 18(2).

(a) Property Excluded from being a "Matrimonial Home"

11.19   Where a residence is provided or made available by one spouse
for that spouse to reside in separately from the other spouse then
this does not amount to a matrimonial home.[30] By the same token
there is authority which indicates that where a property is provided for the other spouse to live in this is not a matrimonial
home either. This interpretation of the 1981 Act was made by
Lord Mayfield in the Outer House in *McRobbie v. McRobbie*.[31]
Here the husband had purchased a house for the wife and child to
live in after separation and never lived in the property himself. His
Lordship was not satisfied that this was a matrimonial home in
terms of the Act.

(3) REGULATION OF OCCUPANCY RIGHTS

11.20   Apart from providing a guarantee that one spouse cannot simply
turn the other one out into the street, there is provision that the
courts may not only declare and order the enforcement of occupancy
but also restrict, regulate and protect such rights.[32] The criteria for
such restriction, regulation and protection, etc., are whether it is just
and reasonable having regard to all the circumstances of the case,
including:

   (i) the conduct of the spouses in relation to each other and
       otherwise;
  (ii) the respective needs and financial resources of the spouses;
 (iii) the needs of any child of the family;
  (iv) the extent to which the matrimonial home is used in con-
       nection with a trade, business or profession of either spouse;
       and
   (v) whether there has been an offer of suitable alternative
       accommodation by the other spouse.[33]

In *Fyfe v. Fyfe*[34] Lord Mayfield dealt with a case involving a wife
who had been hospitalised and who was suffering from multiple
sclerosis and who was initially successful in the sheriff court[35] at
preventing her husband selling the matrimonial home. She then

---

[30] Amendment introduced by the Law Reform (Miscellaneous Provisions) (Scotland) Act 1985, s. 13 (10).
[31] O.H., August 3, 1983 (noted in (1984) 29 J.L.S.S. 5).
[32] s. 3 (1).
[33] s. 3 (3).
[34] O.H., Dec. 12, 1985 (noted in *Scottish Housing Law News* (1987) 2/29).
[35] See para. 12.37.

sought to have her occupancy rights declared as she hoped to be able to return to the house. However, she was unsuccessful and in due course the sale was allowed to go ahead.[36]

The issue of suspension of occupancy rights is dealt with elsewhere.[37] The question of the regulation of occupancy rights through restrictions on use of parts of the matrimonial home is not one which has been raised before the courts except on the rarest of occasions.

---

[36] See para. 12.31 *et seq.*
[37] See paras 12.38–12.45.

CHAPTER 12

RIGHTS RELATED TO
PROPERTY OCCUPATION

12.01 There are a number of rights which relate to the occupation of
property which are the product of statutes. These are for the most
part of recent origin and include rights to be housed, the right to be
rehoused, the right to purchase rented housing and the right to
dispossess co-occupiers.

1. RIGHTS TO BE HOUSED

12.02 There are two kinds of statutory obligation on local authorities to
provide housing for individuals in their district. In the first place,
since 1919 there has been a general obligation on local authorities to
assess the need for accommodation in their area and the need for
further accommodation.

However, this is of benefit to the general public and is not directly
enforceable by individuals through the courts. The view is taken that
the authority has the discretion vested in them.[1] Under statute, every
local authority must consider the housing conditions in their area
and the needs for further housing accommodation.[2] Local authorities, in selecting their own tenants, must ensure that a reasonable
preference is given to persons occupying houses which do not meet
the tolerable standard, who are occupying overcrowded houses, who
have large families or are living under unsatisfactory housing conditions, and homeless persons.[3]

Until 1919 there was no general requirement to assess housing
need, and what local authority housing existed came from local
initiatives aimed at clearing away city-centre slums in such towns as
Glasgow, Edinburgh and Greenock. In 1917 a Royal Commission

---

[1] *Cameron v. Inverness C.C.*, 1935 S.L.T. 281.
[2] Housing (Scotland) Act, 1987, s. 1.
[3] s. 20(1).

set up to look into the housing conditions of the industrial and agricultural workforce (after disturbances over housing conditions in the Lanarkshire coalfield in 1912) found that investment in building housing for the working classes below the level of the prosperous artisan had all but dried up. This structural failure of the traditional means of supply of rented housing provided the impetus for supplementing the power to build.

Each local housing authority (*i.e.* the council) must consider the housing conditions in their district and the needs of the district with respect to the provision of further housing accommodation.[4] In considering the needs of their area for further housing the local authority must have regard to the special needs of chronically sick or disabled persons.[5] The authority may carry out its duty, after assessing the local need, by erecting, converting, acquiring or altering, enlarging, repairing or improving houses or other buildings such as hostels (with the limitation that, where a garden is provided, it must not exceed one acre).[6] Having provided such accommodation, the authority may lease it or sell it.[7]

(1) SELECTION OF TENANTS

There are various restrictions on how the local authority may go 12.03 about the process of selecting tenants. The authority, in addition to complying with the requirements of the Sex Discrimination Act 1975, the Race Relations Act 1976 and the Disability Discrimination Act 1995, must follow certain rules as laid down in the Housing (Scotland) Act 1987. Part 1 of the 1987 Act vests the general management, regulation and control of houses held for housing purposes in and to be exercised by the authority.[8]

(2) ADMISSION TO THE HOUSING LIST

In considering whether an applicant is entitled to be admitted to a 12.04 housing list, a local housing authority must take no account of the age of the applicant provided that person has attained the age of 16 years; or the income of the applicant and his family; or whether, or to what value, the applicant or any of the family owns or has owned heritable or moveable property or any outstanding liability

---

[4] Pt I, s. 1.
[5] s. 1(4).
[6] s. 2.
[7] s. 12.
[8] s. 17.

(for payment of rent or otherwise) related to the tenancy of any house of which the applicant is not a tenant; or whether the applicant is living with, or in the same house as, his spouse or cohabitee.[9] In addition, admission to the waiting list must not depend on residence in the area where an applicant is employed in the area of the local authority, or has been offered employment in the area of the local authority, or wishes to move into the area of the local authority and the local authority is satisfied that his purpose in doing so is to seek employment, or has attained the age of 60 years and wishes to move into the area of the local authority to be nearer a younger relative, or has special social or medical reasons for requiring to be housed within the area of the local housing authority.[10]

Where the rules of the authority give priority to applicants on its waiting list it shall apply these no less favourably to those incoming groups noted above than it applies them to any tenant living in the area with similar housing needs who is seeking a transfer to another house belonging to the local authority.[11] The rules adopted by the authority covering admission to the house waiting list, priority in allocation of houses and tenant transfer must be published and be available for perusal, be on sale at a reasonable price and be available in summary form on request to members of the public.[12]

(a) Priority on the Housing List

12.05   A local authority must secure, in relation to all houses held by them for housing purposes, that in the selection of their tenants a reasonable preference is given to various groups[13]—persons occupying housing which does not meet the tolerable standard; those in overcrowded houses; those with large families; those living under unsatisfactory housing conditions; and homeless persons to whom they have a statutory duty.[14]

(b) Prohibitions in Allocation

12.06   No account must be taken, in allocating local authority housing, to the following matters—the length of time the applicant has resided in the area, any outstanding liability (for payment of rent or otherwise) attributable to the tenancy of any house of which the

---

   [9] s. 19.
   [10] *ibid.*
   [11] *ibid.*
   [12] s. 21.
   [13] s. 20.
   [14] See paras 12.07–12.19.

applicant is not (and was not when the liability was incurred) a tenant, age, income or value of any heritage/moveables. This is particularly important where there is relationship breakdown. In addition, there must be no requirement that an application must have been in force for a minimum period or that a divorce or separation be obtained or that the applicant is no longer living with or in the same house as some other person, before the applicant is eligible for the allocation of housing.

Specific enforceable obligations are also imposed by statute in respect of homeless persons and are of a positive kind. These involve the local authority securing that accommodation be made available to those homeless applicants who satisfy the local authority that they meet the tests imposed under the legislation.[15] This accommodation will normally be from their own stock but may be in the private rented sector.

(c) Homeless Individuals and Families

The legislation is unequivocal as to the existence of housing duties 12.07 towards qualifying homeless applicants.[16] There is also a *Code of Guidance on Homelessness*[17] which explains the effect of the legislation, provides guidance and offers suggestions of good practice. The code does not have statutory force but must be taken into consideration when an authority is exercising its duties under the legislation.[18] Authorities do not, however, have to follow its advice.[19] In order to qualify for direct assistance a person must be homeless or threatened with homelessness. In addition to those who have no right to occupy accommodation, anyone occupying unsatisfactory accommodation may be entitled to be provided with accommodation. It includes those who have no accommodation in Scotland or England and Wales[20] as well as someone living in temporary refuge accommodation such as night shelters[21] and women's refuges[22] or who had accommodation outside Great Britain. Applicants are treated as having no accommodation where they do not have accommodation which they have the right or permission to occupy along with the members of the family unit.[23] The right or

---

[15] ss. 28, 31 and 32.
[16] s. 31(2).
[17] Scottish Office, September 1997 (3rd ed.).
[18] *Kelly v. Monklands D.C.*, 1986 S.L.T. 169.
[19] *Mazzaccherini v. Argyll and Bute D.C.*, 1987 S.C.L.R. 475.
[20] s. 24.
[21] *R. v. Waveney B.C., ex p. Bowers, The Times*, May 25, 1982.
[22] *R. v. Ealing LBC, ex p. Sidhu* (1982) 2 H.L.R. 45.
[23] s. 24(2).

permission can be expressed or implied. It may stem from a rule of law or enactment such as the rights of occupancy of a non-entitled spouse or cohabitee under the Matrimonial Homes (Family Protection) (Scotland) Act 1981.[24]

In addition, a person who actually has accommodation is still regarded as homeless[25] where they cannot secure entry to the property such as after forcible eviction by a landlord. The fact that one has a housing right which may not be put into effect is recognised as amounting to homelessness. It also covers housing which has been made the subject of a closing order thus rendering the right of ownership or tenancy inoperable. Accommodation is also unacceptable if it is probable that occupation will lead to violence from some other person residing in the property[26] or if there are threats from another resident and that person is likely to carry out the threats. In addition, the legislation since 1991 covers the situation of those who previously resided with the applicant, whether in that accommodation or elsewhere, where it is probable that occupation will lead to violence or threats of violence which are likely to be carried out. The changes introduced in 1990[27] provide that a person is homeless if they have accommodation which it would not be reasonable to continue to occupy. This would cover violence or threats of violence from neighbours as well as accommodation which is in poor physical condition but does not meet the specific tests as to overcrowding and being a threat to health. Applicants are also homeless if they have accommodation but it is statutorily overcrowded and may endanger the health of the occupants.

People are also entitled to assistance if they are threatened with homelessness if it is likely that they will become homeless within 28 days.[28] This covers those who have tenancy rights which are likely to be lost through a successful possession action in the courts. It also covers situations where permission to stay is withdrawn, as by a parent from a child.

(i) Priority Need

12.08   There are two further hurdles which must be satisfied before the applicant is entitled to full assistance from a local authority. The applicants for assistance as homeless persons must have a priority

---

[24] s. 1 (spouses) and s. 18 (cohabitees).
[25] s. 24(3).
[26] *R. v. Broxbourne B.C., ex p. Willmoth (No. 2)* (1989) 21 H.L.R. 415.
[27] Law Reform (Miscellaneous Provisions) (Scotland) Act 1990, s. 65, amending s. 24 of the Housing (Scotland) Act 1987.
[28] s. 24(4).

need. The following have a statutory priority need for accommodation—women who are pregnant, people with dependent children or who are vulnerable or are homeless as a result of an emergency. Within the category of vulnerability the legislation indicates five specific conditions—old age; mental illness; mental handicap; physical disability; and children leaving care. In addition, a person may be vulnerable as a result of any other special reason.[29] The general test of vulnerability according to the Court of Appeal depends on whether a person is "less able to fend [for himself] so that injury or detriment will result when a less vulnerable man will be able to cope without harmful effects".[30]

(ii) INTENTIONAL HOMELESSNESS

Local authorities' obligations to provide accommodation to home- 12.09
less applicants in priority need are restricted to providing temporary accommodation where the homelessness is deemed to be intentional. Applicants become homeless intentionally if they deliberately do or fail to do anything in consequence of which they cease to occupy accommodation which is available for their occupation and which it would have been reasonable for them to continue to occupy.[31] In such instances the obligation is restricted to providing accommodation for such period as the authority considers will give a reasonable opportunity to secure accommodation available for occupation by the applicant.[32]

(a) Is Accommodation Available?

When looking at whether the applicant is intentionally homeless, 12.10
the authority must consider whether the applicant has given up accommodation which is sufficient for both the applicant and any other person who might reasonably be expected to live with him.[33] The fact that accommodation was previously available cannot displace the requirement to make enquiries at the time of application.[34] Accommodation offered but never accepted by the applicant is not available for occupation.[35]

---

[29] s. 25(1)(c).
[30] *R. v. Waveney D.C., ex p. Bowers* [1982] 3 All E.R. 727, CA.
[31] s. 26(1).
[32] s. 31(3).
[33] s. 41.
[34] *R. v. Westminster C.C., ex p. Ali* (1983) 11 H.L.R. 83.
[35] *R. v. Westminster C.C., ex p. Chambers* (1982) 81 L.G.R. 401; *R. v. Ealing LBC, ex p. McBain* [1986] 1 All E.R. 13, CA.

(b) Is it Reasonable to Continue to Live in Accommodation?

12.11   The authority must have regard to the housing conditions which
led the applicant to give up the accommodation.[36] Overcrowding or
damp, unhealthy[37] or dangerous conditions[38] may lead to a finding
that it would not have been reasonable to continue to live in that
accommodation. The cost of the accommodation[39] and lack of
employment prospects[40] have also featured as reasons why accommodation could not continue to be occupied. In deciding whether or
not it would have been reasonable to continue to occupy the
available accommodation, the authority may look at the general
circumstances prevailing in relation to housing in the district of the
local authority.[41] In addition to looking at the housing suitability,
factors personal to the circumstances of the applicant are relevant.[42]
These have included violence from a partner,[43] threats of violence
from outwith the household,[44] medical problems of the applicant,[45]
and the unavailability of welfare benefits.[46]

(c) Is Homelessness a Result of Action/Non-action?

12.12   There must be a direct link between the actions of the applicant
and the loss of accommodation, and the homelessness must be a
consequence of these actions.[47] Authorities are entitled to look back
to events in the past which triggered off the current state of homelessness.[48] The authority must look at the question of causation at
the date the applicant became homeless rather than the date of
application.[49] Where someone gave up permanent accommodation
and was later evicted from temporary accommodation, the authority
would still be entitled to look back and examine why the applicant
had ceased to occupy the permanent accommodation in the first
place. The disadvantages of intentional homelessness, then, will not

---

[36] *R. v. Eastleigh B.C., ex p. Beattie (No. 1)* (1983) 10 H.L.R. 134.
[37] *R. v. Westminster C.C., ex p. Ali* (1983) 11 H.L.R. 83.
[38] *R. v. Westminster C.C., ex p. Bishop* (1993) 25 H.L.R. 459, CA.
[39] *R. v. Hillingdon LBC, ex p. Tinn* (1988) 20 H.L.R. 305.
[40] *R. v. Kensington and Chelsea LBC, ex p. Cunha* (1989) 21 H.L.R. 16.
[41] s. 26(4).
[42] *R. v. Hammersmith and Fulham LBC, ex p. Duro-Rama* (1983) 81 L.G.R. 702.
[43] *R. v. Tynedale D.C., ex p. McCabe* (1991) 24 H.L.R. 384.
[44] *R. v. Peterborough B.C., ex p. H* (*supra*).
[45] *R. v. Wycombe D.C., ex p. Homes* (1988) 22 H.L.R. 150, QBD.
[46] *R. v. Hammersmith and Fulham LBC, ex p. Duro-Rama* (1983) 81 L.G.R. 702.
[47] s. 26(1).
[48] *Hynds v. Midlothian D.C.*, 1986 S.L.T. 54; *Mazzaccherini v. Argyll and Bute
D.C.*, 1987 S.C.L.R. 475.
[49] *Din v. Wandsworth L.B.C.* [1983] 1 A.C. 657.

be avoided by an applicant giving up accommodation and obtaining other temporary accommodation.[50] Accommodation which has been treated as merely temporary and which has failed to break this chain of causation includes off-season holiday lets,[51] holiday lets,[52] staying with friends or relatives,[53] lodgings without security of tenure[54] and bed and breakfast accommodation.[55] Although the effect of obtaining one of the modern post-1988 tenancies without security of tenure has not been settled in the courts,[56] the *Code of Guidance* suggests that where a short assured tenancy has expired and not been renewed the tenant should not be regarded as intentionally homeless.[57] If, however, another cause intervenes to result in the loss of accommodation where, but for this occurrence, the applicant probably would have been intentionally homeless, the same principle applies as where a flat which the applicant gave up was subsequently rendered uninhabitable by an ex-partner. The applicant could not in such circumstances be deemed intentionally homeless.[58]

(d) Deliberate Actions or Omissions

There is a difference between actions which are deliberate and those which are involuntary or largely attributable to external factors. Typical of deliberate actions are wilful non-payment of rent, anti-social actions by members of the family resulting in eviction, and choosing to sell one's house where there is no risk of losing it. The Government's *Code of Guidance* suggests that the following would not normally amount to deliberate actions—failure to keep up mortgage or rent payments because of real personal or financial difficulties, arrears of a partner, victims fleeing domestic violence, pregnant women deemed intentionally homeless on account of their pregnancy, people no longer able to afford rent or mortgage payments, and living conditions which have degenerated to a point where they cannot reasonably be expected to live. Actions and omissions accepted as non-deliberate by the courts have included failing to pay rent or mortgage payments through financial

12.13

---

[50] *Dyson v. Kerrier D.C.* [1980] 1 W.L.R. 1205.
[51] *Dyson v. Kerrier D.C.* [1980] 1 W.L.R. 1205.
[52] *Lambert v. Ealing LBC* [1982] 2 All E.R. 394.
[53] *De Falco v. Crawley B.C.* [1980] QB 460.
[54] *Mazzaccherini v. Argyll and Bute D.C.*, 1987 S.C.L.R. 475; *R. v. Merton LBC, ex p. Ruffle* (1989) 21 H.L.R. 361.
[55] *R. v. Harrow LBC, ex p. Holland* (1982) 4 H.L.R. 108.
[56] *R. v. Christchurch B.C., ex p. Conway* (1987) 19 H.L.R. 238.
[57] *Code of Guidance*, para. 8.5.
[58] *Gloucester C.C. v. Miles* (1985) 83 L.G.R. 607; 17 H.L.R. 292, CA.

hardship,[59] leaving accommodation early where there is no effective defence to a possession action[60] and fleeing violence and threats of violence from political opponents.[61]

(e) Acts or Omissions in Good Faith

12.14   Where acts or omissions are made in good faith by a person who was unaware of any relevant fact, they are not to be treated as deliberate.[62] The test is whether the individual concerned would have thought rather than whether a reasonable person would have known. For instance, a person with learning difficulties might be regarded as being unaware of a relevant fact. Similarly, a person who is confused or demented should not be regarded as having acted deliberately.[63] The fact that there has been anti-social behaviour should take account of the reasons for this, such as mental illness.[64] The courts have accepted as unaware of a relevant fact a young woman coming from abroad who assumed that availability of accommodation for her brothers meant that she would be treated the same by her father on her entry into Britain,[65] a tenant who failed to appreciate the need as indicated in correspondence to respond promptly in order to secure a tenancy renewal[66] and a young woman who did not believe her father's threats to refuse her re-entry to the family home if she stayed with her mother while pursuing a higher education course away from home.[67] The acceptance of a mistaken belief is subject to the proviso that the belief must be intrinsically reasonable.[68]

(f) Acquiescence/Non-acquiescence

12.15   In order to be caught by the intentionality section, an applicant must have been responsible for the action or omission. Where families are concerned, all members of the family unit are initially assumed to be party to the acts of one member. Accordingly, if these acts lead to a finding of intentionality then this covers all the family unit.[69] There are some situations where it would be unreasonable to

---

[59] *R. v. Wyre B.C., ex p. Joyce* (1983) 11 H.L.R. 72.
[60] *R. v. Portsmouth C. C., ex p. Knight* (1984) 82 L.G.R. 184 (tied accommodation and dismissal); *R. v. Surrey Heath B.C., ex p. Li* (1984) 16 H.L.R. 79 (licensees).
[61] *R. v. Westminster C.C., ex p. Iqbal* (1990) 22 H.L.R. 215, QBD.
[62] s. 26(3).
[63] *Code of Guidance*, September 1997, para. 8.6.
[64] *ibid.*
[65] *R. v. Wandsworth LBC, ex p. Rose* (1984) 11 H.L.R. 105.
[66] *R. v. Christchurch B.C., ex p. Conway* (1987) 19 H.L.R. 287.
[67] *Wincentzen v. Monklands D.C.*, 1987 S.C.L.R. 712; 1988 S.L.T. 847.
[68] *ibid.* per I.H.
[69] *R. v. Swansea C.C., ex p. John* (1982) 9 H.L.R. 58.

assume that, for example, one partner acquiesced in the actions or omissions amounting to intentionality.[70] The courts have recognised non-acquiescence in such situations as when the husband failed to heed the wife's urgings to pay the rent[71] or mortgage,[72] and the surrender of the tenancy by the wife when leaving her husband where there was later reconciliation.[73] It is not enough to simply assert non-acquiescence.[74] However, this will be much easier to establish where there is some tangible evidence of non-acquiescence such as making payments towards paying off rent arrears.[75]

(g) Different Assessments of Intentionality by Authorities

Local authorities must accept a different assessment by another 12.16 authority on intentionality[76] where the applicant is referred back under the local connection provisions[77] unless there is no sound basis for the rejection of the original decision.[78] This involves the second authority making full investigations including getting the relevant information on which the first authority made its decision.[79] By the same token, where one authority makes a negative decision on intentionality and the unsuccessful homeless person applies elsewhere, the second authority normally must make its own investigations into the question of intentionality. It cannot simply assume the first authority's decision is correct without having grounds for such a belief.[80]

(h) Examples of Intentionality

Actions which have resulted in the loss of accommodation and a 12.17 finding of intentionality include wilful non-payment of rent[81]; voluntarily terminating a tenancy[82]; giving up a job with "tied

---

[70] *Lewis, loc. cit.* at 31.
[71] *R. v. West Dorset D.C., ex p. Phillips* (1985) 17 H.L.R. 168; *R. v. East Northamptonshire D.C., ex p. Spruce* (1988) 20 H.L.R. 508.
[72] *R. v. Eastleigh B.C., ex p. Beattie* (1983) 10 H.L.R. 134.
[73] *R. v. Penwith D.C., ex p. Trevena* (1984) 17 H.L.R. 526.
[74] *Stewart v. Monklands D.C.,* 1987 S.L.T. 630; *R. v. East Hertfordshire D.C., ex p. Bannon* (1986) 18 H.L.R. 515.
[75] *R. v. Thanet D.C., ex p. Groves* (1990) 22 H.L.R. 223.
[76] *R. v. Slough B.C., ex p. Ealing L.B.C.* [1981] Q.B. 801.
[77] s. 33(2); see paras 12.18–12.19.
[78] *R. v. Tower Hamlets LBC, ex p. Camden LBC* (1988) 21 H.L.R. 197.
[79] *R. v. Newham LBC, ex p. Tower Hamlets LBC* [1992] 2 All E.R. 767; 23 H.L.R. 62, CA.
[80] *R. v. South Herefordshire D.C., ex p. Miles* (1983) 17 H.L.R. 82.
[81] *Robinson v. Torbay B.C.* [1982] 1 All E.R. 726; *Hynds v. Midlothian D.C.,* 1986 S.L.T. 54.
[82] *Dyson v. Kerrier D.C.* [1980] 1 W.L.R. 1205; *Mazzaccherini v. Argyll and Bute D.C.,* 1987 S.C.L.R. 475.

accommodation"[83]; failing to maintain a satisfactory tenancy[84]; moving from abroad without ensuring that there is accommodation available in Great Britain[85]; moving from another part of the United Kingdom without ensuring permanent accommodation is available[86]; as well as arguing with relatives.[87]

(iii) LOCAL CONNECTION

12.18 In exercising their obligations towards homeless applicants local authorities have a power to investigate whether an applicant has a local connection with the district of another local authority in Scotland, England or Wales.[88] In determining what having a local connection with a district means there are four issues to be considered[89]: past normal voluntary residence, employment, family associations, or any special circumstances. Residence is not deemed to be of a person's choice where that person was serving in the regular armed forces of the Crown or was in prison or was detained under the mental health legislation.[90] The courts, including the House of Lords, have accepted decisions taken in strict conformity with the guidelines laid down in the *Agreement on Procedures for Referrals of the Homeless*[91] as lawful.[92] These are reflected in the *Code of Guidance*.[93] In addition, the House of Lords has suggested that, whilst a local connection not founded upon one of the four grounds is irrelevant, an applicant does not have a local connection simply through satisfying one or more of the grounds. Local connection is established through either one or more of these factors being present. It is these which spell out a local connection in real terms.[94] It must be built up and established and this is done through

---

[83] *R. v. North Devon D.C., ex p. Lewis* [1981] 1 All E.R. 27; but *cf. R. v. Kensington and Chelsea LBC, ex p. Minton* (1988) 20 H.L.R. 648.

[84] *Mackenzie v. West Lothian D.C.*, 1979 S.C. 433; *R. v. Salford C.C., ex p. Devenport* (1983) 82 L.G.R. 89.

[85] *R. v. Tower Hamlets LBC, ex p. Monaf* (1988) 20 H.L.R. 529.

[86] *R. v. Peterborough D.C., ex p. McKernan*, QBD, July 17, 1987; *R. v. Vale of White Horse D.C., ex p. Preen*, QBD, April 18, 1983.

[87] *R. v. Dacorum Borough Council, ex p. Brown* (1989) 21 H.L.R. 405, QBD.

[88] s. 28(2).

[89] s. 27.

[90] s. 27(2).

[91] Association of District Councils, Association of Metropolitan Associations and the London Boroughs Association, June 6, 1979, reproduced in A. Arden, *Housing Act 1985 Part III* (4th ed., 1996).

[92] *R. v. Eastleigh B.C., ex p. Betts* [1984] 2 A.C. 613, HL.

[93] para. 9.9.

[94] *R. v. Eastleigh B.C., ex p. Betts* [1984] 2 A.C. 613.

either residence, employment, family connection or other special circumstances.[95]

Normal residence has been interpreted following strictly the guidelines in the agreement[96] which equate this phrase with six months' residence during the past 12 months or three years during the previous five years. Longer periods of residence have not been recognised where the character of the residence did not denote permanence.[97] The general category of special circumstances has not been accepted as covering the tenant's desire to stay in a particular area[98] nor membership of local institutions or organisations.[99]

If the authority establishes in its inquiries that there is a local 12.19 connection elsewhere and none in its own area, the question of referral arises.[1] Pending agreement or referral elsewhere, the responsibility for housing the applicant remains with the original authority.[2] The conditions of referral affect both the applicant and any person who might reasonably be expected to reside with them.[3] The referral can operate in respect of another local authority where the original authority is satisfied that there is no local connection with it and there is one with the other authority.[4] This is subject to the overall test that the applicant will not run the risk of domestic violence in the other authority's district.[5] A person runs the risk of domestic violence if she runs the risk of violence from a person with whom, but for the risk of violence, she might reasonably be expected to reside.[6] This includes a person with whom she formerly resided.[7] Alternatively a woman runs the risk of violence if she runs the risk of threats of violence from a partner or ex-partner and these threats are likely to be carried out.[8] It is lawful for an authority to refer an applicant to an authority with whom the applicant has no local connection, provided all parties find such an arrangement to be acceptable.[9] Where applicants are entering

---

[95] *ibid.* p. 627.
[96] *R. v. Eastleigh B.C., ex p. Betts* [1983] 2 A.C. 613.
[97] *Brooks v. Midlothian D.C.,* O.H., December 12, 1985.
[98] *R. v. Islington LBC, ex p. Adigun* (1986) 20 H.L.R. 600.
[99] *R. v. Vale of White Horse D.C., ex p. Smith and Hay* (1984) 17 H.L.R. 160.
[1] s. 33.
[2] *R. v. Beverley B.C., ex p. McPhee, The Times,* October 27, 1978.
[3] s. 33(2).
[4] s. 33(2)(a) and (b).
[5] s. 33(2)(c).
[6] s. 33(3)(a).
[7] *ibid.*
[8] s. 33(*b*); *R. v. Islington LBC, ex p. Adigun* (1988) 20 H.L.R. 600.
[9] *R. v. Wyre B.C., ex p. Parr* (1982) 2 H.L.R. 71.

Britain from abroad they are to be treated as having a local connection with the authority to which they apply.[10] If there is a local connection outwith Great Britain the local authority may refer the applicant back, exercising its power of securing accommodation from some other person.[11] The local authority must be satisfied that such a reference would not cause the applicant to run the risk of domestic violence.[12]

Since local authorities are given discretion to operate the homeless persons legislation the appropriate method of challenge is through the medium of judicial review. The standard rules for judicial review apply under Rule of Court 260(B) which came into effect on April 30, 1985. Damages may also be sought as part of the review process.[13] Provided an authority accept that they are under a duty it is also possible to seek damages in the sheriff court.[14]

2. RIGHTS TO BE REHOUSED

12.20 Where occupiers of property affected by public works lose their current housing they are entitled to be rehoused in certain circumstances. Where a person is displaced from residential accommodation on any land in consequence of compulsory purchase, redevelopment or notices affecting sub-standard housing then, if suitable alternative accommodation on reasonable terms is not otherwise available to that person, the local authority must secure that suitable alternative accommodation will be provided.[15] There can be displacement where the dwelling is being improved and the original dwelling loses its identity.[16] Where there is different accommodation, it must be within a reasonable distance from the locality of the house from which the person is to be displaced.[17] There is limited case authority that this does not entail the provision of permanent accommodation and can be limited to securing temporary bed and breakfast accommodation pending discussion on permanent accommodation.[18]

---

[10] *R. v. Hillingdon LBC, ex p. Streeting* [1980] 1 W.L.R. 430.
[11] s. 35(1)(b).
[12] *R. v. Bristol C.C., ex p. Browne* [1979] 1 W.L.R. 1437.
[13] *Mallon v. Monklands D.C.*, 1986 S.L.T. 347.
[14] *Purves v. Midlothian D.C.*, 1986 SCOLAG 144.
[15] Land Compensation (Scotland) Act 1973, s. 36; Housing (Scotland) Act 1987, s. 98.
[16] *Casale v. Islington LBC* (1985) 18 H.L.R. 146.
[17] Housing (Scotland) Act 1987, s. 98.
[18] *R. v. Bristol Corporation, ex p. Hendy* [1974] 1 All E.R. 1047; *R. v. Hertfortshire D.C., ex p. Smith, The Times*, January 25, 1990, on the equivalent English legislation; *Glasgow D.C. v. Douglas*, unreported, discussed in 1979 SCOLAG 76.

3. RIGHT TO BUY RENTED HOUSING

There are two groups of individuals entitled to buy certain kinds of 12.21
rented housing. Broadly this does not apply in the private rented
sector. Sitting tenants who have secure tenancies may exercise the
right to buy whether or not the landlord wishes to sell or not. In
addition, approved bodies may buy public sector housing whether
the landlord wishes to sell or not, provided that the tenant is willing
for the transfer to go ahead.

(1) TENANT'S RIGHT TO BUY

From 1980, public sector tenants were given the right to purchase the 12.22
properties they were renting in certain circumstances. The coverage
was extended in 1986 to tenancies granted by regional councils and
housing associations. The law was consolidated in the Housing
(Scotland) Act 1987. In terms of the Housing (Scotland) Act 1988
housing association tenancies granted on or after January 2, 1989 are
assured tenancies and these do not carry the right to purchase.[19]

(a) Entitlement to Buy

Immediately prior to the date of service of the application to 12.23
purchase, the tenant must have been resident for not less than two
years in occupation of a house or a series of houses rented out by a
public sector landlord. The right is also available to other relatives
of the tenant—spouses, children (over the age of 16), or spouse of a
child.[20] The property must be occupied as the tenant's only or
principal home.[21] This has been interpreted to allow purchase by
a prisoner[22] but not by someone permanently hospitalised.[23] The
tenant must remain entitled until the offer to sell has been accepted.[24] In computing what amounts to occupation the legislation
provides that this includes occupation as a child. This covers
children over 16 living in the property of a tenant to whose rights
the applicant subsequently succeeds.[25]

---

[19] s. 43; for the position on the rights of those offered new tenancies, see *Milnbank Housing Ass. v. Murdoch*, 1994 S.C.L.R. 684.
[20] See s. 61(10)(v)—*McDonald v. Renfrew D.C.*, 1982 S.L.T. (Lands Tr.) 30; *Robb v. Kyle and Carrick D.C.*, 1989 S.L.T. (Lands Tr.) 78.
[21] s. 44(1)(a).
[22] *Beggs v. Kilmarnock and Loudoun D.C.*, 1996 S.L.T. 461.
[23] *McLoughlin's C.B. v. Motherwell D.C.*, 1994 S.L.T. (Lands Tr.) 31.
[24] *McKay v. City of Dundee D.C.*, 1996 S.L.T. (Lands Tr.) 9.
[25] *Hamilton v. City of Dundee D.C.*, 1996 S.L.T. (Lands Tr.) 14.

(b) Property Subject to the Right to Buy

12.24   The full list of landlords whose property qualifies for the right to buy is specified in the Housing (Scotland) Act 1987[26] and covers public sector bodies. The most significant are councils (formerly district and regional councils) and Scottish Homes (formerly Scottish Special Housing Association).

The basic rule is that secure tenancies are covered. A secure tenancy involves three requirements.[27] The property must be let as a separate dwelling.[28] The tenant must be an individual and the property must be the applicant's only or principal home.[29] The landlord must be one of a specific list of public sector tenancies noted.

Some of the properties of these landlords are exempted as they are specifically declared not to be secure tenancies.[30] These cover premises occupied under a contract of employment; temporary letting to person seeking accommodation; temporary letting pending development; temporary accommodation during works; accommodation for homeless person; agricultural and business premises; police and fire authorities; and houses part of, or within curtilage of, certain other buildings used for non-housing purposes.

Most of the case law in relation to the right to buy stems from disputes about whether or not property that a public authority has been renting out falls within these exemptions.[31] The question as to whether accommodation is occupied for the better performance of the employee's tasks has yielded extensive case law. The Lands Tribunal has looked at the reality of tasks actually done rather than at the formal contractual position.[32] The question of whether a building is part of or within the curtilage of non-housing property has generally been concerned with former schoolhouses[33] or related properties.[34] As indicated, housing association tenancies were

---

[26] s. 61(11).

[27] Housing (Scotland) Act 1987, s. 44.

[28] *Thomson v. City of Glasgow D.C.*, 1986 S.L.T. (Lands Tr.) 6; *Hannan v. Falkirk D.C.*, 1987 S.L.T. (Lands Tr.) 18.

[29] *Jenkins v. Renfrew D.C.*, 1989 S.L.T. (Lands Tr.) 41.

[30] Housing (Scotland) Act 1987, Sched. 2.

[31] *Fernie v. Strathclyde R.C.*, 1994 S.L.T. (Lands Tr.) 11—on adding further reasons at the Tribunal stage.

[32] *McKay v. Livingston Dev. Corpn.*, 1990 S.L.T. (Lands Tr.) 54; *MacDonald v. Strathclyde R.C.*, 1990 S.L.T. (Lands Tr.) 10; *Gilmour v. City of Glasgow D.C.*, 1989 S.L.T. (Lands Tr.) 74; but see *De Fontenay v. Strathclyde R.C.*, Lands Tr., July 24, 1989.

[33] *Walker v. Strathclyde R.C.*, 1990 S.L.T. (Lands Tr.) 17.

[34] *Fisher v. Fife R.C.*, 1989 S.L.T. (Lands Tr.) 26; *Shipman v. Lothian R.C.*, 1989 S.L.T. (Lands Tr.) 82.

briefly covered by the right to buy provisions after 1986 and until January 2, 1989 under the Housing (Scotland) Act 1988 and for those tenants with a right to buy, these rights continue. A subsequent grant of an assured tenancy has been deemed not to end a secure tenancy and the related right to buy.[35] Those housing association tenancies which are covered are also subject to certain exceptions for specialist housing provision and other housing associations where sale would be particularly inappropriate.[36]

The Secretary of State may authorise refusal to sell certain houses   12.25 provided for persons of pensionable age where these have facilities[37] which are substantially different from those of an ordinary house and which have been designed or adapted for occupation by a person of pensionable age whose special needs require accommodation of the kind provided by the house.[38] The fact that the facilities are installed after the commencement of the tenancy does not remove the property from the exempt category.[39] Exempt status has, however, been denied where alarm call facilities to a warden exist but have not been connected,[40] and a warden's house itself to which alarm systems were connected could be sold off.[41] Where the landlord's application for exempt status is refused then the landlord must make an offer to the tenant in accordance with the standard sale procedure.

(c) The Price for Sales

The price is to be the market value of the house less any discount   12.26 for years of occupancy.[42] The market value of the house is to be decided by the district valuer or a qualified valuer nominated by the landlord and accepted by the tenant. It is up to the landlord which of these individuals is selected. In fixing the market value the assumption must be made that the house is available for sale on the open market with vacant possession at the date of service of the application to purchase. The discount varies as between flats and houses and depends on the extent of the occupation by the tenant. For houses the discount is 32 per cent of the market value together with an additional one per cent of the market value for every year beyond

---

[35] *Milnbank Housing Ass. v. Murdoch*, 1994 S.C.L.R. 684.
[36] s. 61(4).
[37] s. 69.
[38] See SDD Circular 38/1980 for guidance on how the Secretary of State would operate this exemption.
[39] *Kennedy v. Hamilton D.C.*, 1996 S.L.T. 1276.
[40] *City of Dundee D.C. v. Anderson* 1994 S.L.T. 46.
[41] *Houston v. East Kilbride Dev. Corp.*, 1995 S.L.T. (Lands Tr.) 12.
[42] s. 62.

two of continuous occupation by the appropriate person immediately preceding the date of service of the application to purchase the house. The period for continuous occupation includes a succession of houses provided by any of the public sector bodies indicated[43] as well as any armed services accommodation provided by the Crown. The maximum discount is 60 per cent. This would be reached after 30 years. The discount for flats starts at 44 per cent of the market value together with an additional two per cent of the market value for every year beyond two of continuous occupation by the appropriate person immediately preceding the date of service of the application to purchase the flat. Again succession of occupation is permitted. The maximum discount for flats is 70 per cent of the market value—this would be reached after 15 years. For discount purposes the tenant is the appropriate person unless there would be a higher discount by looking to the spouse—provided that they are cohabiting at the time of service of the application to purchase.

Where there is outstanding debt on a property incurred by a local authority in making improvements there is provision for the price to be adjusted to take account of this work. Where a debt is incurred by the local authority after a certain date on improvement work on a property, the price to be fixed in a right to buy must not be less than that outstanding debt or the market value of the house, whichever is the lesser.[44] The term "outstanding debt" is defined as meaning "any undischarged debt arising from the cost of works of improvement . . . together with the administrative costs attributable to these works".[45]

12.27   In the event of the tenant selling the property before the expiry of three years from the date of service of a notice of acceptance by the tenant, the landlord may recover a proportion of the difference between the market value of the house and the discounted price at which the tenant purchased the property.[46] This does not apply where part only of the property is sold and the remainder continues to be the only or principal home of the purchasing tenant. It only applies on the first disposal during the period. The proportion of the difference varies from 100 per cent where the disposal occurs in the first year to 66 per cent during the second year and 33 per cent during the third year.

There is no recovery of discount where the disposal is by the executor of the deceased owner[47] or as a result of a compulsory

---

[43] s. 61(11).
[44] s. 62(8).
[45] *Wingate v. Clydebank D.C.*, Lands Tr., November 2, 1989.
[46] s. 72.
[47] *Clydebank D.C. v. Keeper of the Registers of Scotland*, 1994 S.L.T. (Lands Tr.) 2.

purchase order or the disposal is to a member of the owner's family who has lived with him for a period of 12 months before the disposal and there is no payment involved. If, however, the tenant dies before completion of the purchase, and the executor goes ahead with a sale within three years of the missives being concluded then the relevant proportion of the discount is recoverable.[48]

(d) The Sale Procedure

A specific procedure is laid down for the purchase of public sector 12.28 housing under the Housing (Scotland) Act 1987.[49] A tenant who seeks to exercise a right to purchase a public sector house must serve an "application to purchase" notice on the landlord. This notice must contain a notice that the tenant seeks to exercise the right to purchase, a statement of any period of qualifying occupancy and the name of any joint purchaser.[50] The landlord must, unless disputing the application, within two months of receipt of the application to purchase serve an "offer to sell".[51] This must contain the market value of the house, the discount and the resulting price of the house along with any conditions the landlord intends to impose and an actual offer to sell the house at the price and under the conditions mentioned. Where the tenant wishes to exercise the right to purchase and does not dispute the terms of the offer then a "notice of acceptance" must be served on the landlord within two months of the offer to sell or of any date resolving a dispute on any aspect of the sale.[52] Reasonable conditions of sale may be included in the offer to sell, provided that the conditions allow the tenant to have as full enjoyment and use of the house as owner as were enjoyed as tenant.[53] In addition, they must secure the tenant such additional rights as are necessary for the reasonable enjoyment and use of the house as owner as well as imposing on the tenant any necessary duties relative to rights so secured. The conditions must include such terms as are necessary to entitle the tenant to receive a good and marketable title to the house. If this cannot be given, for instance because of a pre-emption clause in favour of the landlord's superior, then there can be no right to buy.[54]

If there is a condition which imposes a new charge or an increase of an existing charge for the provision of a service in relation to the house, it must provide for the charge to be in reasonable proportion

---

[48] *Jack's Exrx v. Falkirk D.C.*, 1992 S.L.T. 5.
[49] s. 63.
[50] s. 63(1).
[51] s. 63(2).
[52] s. 66.
[53] s. 64.
[54] *Ross and Cromarty D.C. v. Patience*, 1995 S.L.T. 1292.

to the cost to the landlord of providing the service. No condition is to be imposed which has the effect of requiring the tenant to pay any expenses of the landlord. Option to purchase clauses in favour of the landlord are not permitted unless it is in relation to a house which has facilities which are substantially different from those of an ordinary house and which has been designed or adapted for occupation by a person of pensionable age or a disabled person with a special needs requirement. Where there is such a permitted option to purchase then the price is to be determined by the district valuer on a market value basis taking account of any early-sale recovered discount. The Lands Tribunal has the power to deal with objections about conditions which they may strike out, vary or replace with a new condition.[55] The market value does not constitute a condition which can be challenged.[56]

12.29   Where the landlord disputes the tenant's right to purchase, it must serve a "notice of refusal" within one month of the service of the "application to purchase". A notice of refusal must specify the grounds on which the landlord disputes the tenant's right to purchase or the accuracy of the information upon which the purported right is founded. Where a landlord serves a notice of refusal, the tenant may within one month of receipt of such notice apply to the Lands Tribunal for a finding that there is a right to purchase the house on such terms as it may determine.[57]

There is special provision where an islands council is landlord of property held for the purposes of education and required for accommodation of a person who is or will be employed by the council for educational purposes, and where other suitable accommodation cannot be provided by the council, that the landlord may serve a notice of refusal within one month of service of the application to purchase.[58]

Where an offer to sell has been served on the tenant and a related notice of acceptance has been served on the landlord, a contract of sale of the house shall be constituted between the landlord and the tenant on the terms contained in the offer to sell. The question has arisen as to what happens to this agreement if the tenant dies after the contract has been concluded but before the conveyancing is completed. This has arisen in a Scottish case as well as under similar legislation covering England and Wales. The 1987 legislation provides a series of steps up until the making of a contract but is silent

[55] s. 65.
[56] *MacLeod v. Ross and Cromarty D.C.*, 1983 S.L.T. (Lands Tr.) 5; see also *Pollock v. Dumbarton D.C.*, 1983 S.L.T. (Lands Tr.) 17.
[57] s. 68.
[58] s. 70.

on the conveyance. The view taken by the House of Lords was that the relatives of the deceased tenant were entitled to have the conveyance completed in their favour.[59]

(2) THE RIGHT TO BUY FOR POTENTIAL LANDLORDS

The Housing (Scotland) Act 1988 makes provision for certain   12.30
approved landlords to make an approach to tenants of local authorities.[60] If the tenants are agreeable then a procedure is laid down which the authority must follow.[61] As in the tenant's right to buy, the intention is that the local authority will not be able to resist such a procedure on the grounds of housing policy. This procedure should be distinguished from voluntary transfers in terms of the Housing (Scotland) Act 1987.[62]

4. RIGHTS TO DISPOSSESS CO-OCCUPIERS

Statutory rights of occupancy have been provided since September   12.31
1, 1982 to spouses and certain cohabitees. The notion of occupancy rights for spouses and partners was a novel concept in Scots law when it was introduced in the Matrimonial Homes (Family Protection) (Scotland) Act 1981. It provided that where one spouse had a title to stay in a house, either as owner or tenant, then the other spouse who was neither tenant nor owner was given the right, if in occupation, to continue to occupy the matrimonial home and, if not in occupation, a right to enter and occupy the matrimonial home.[63]

Cohabitees have more limited occupancy rights. They may apply for the right to stay for six months (originally this was limited to three months). There is provision for extensions beyond this original period.[64]

(1) TERMINATION OF OCCUPANCY RIGHTS

Occupancy rights come to an end when the marriage ends, when   12.32
the owner/tenant loses their ownership/tenancy rights, when the matrimonial home ceases to exist or when the rights are renounced in the form prescribed by the 1981 Act.

---

[59] *Cooper's Exrs v. Edinburgh D.C.*, 1991 S.L.T. 518.
[60] Pt III, ss. 56–64.
[61] *Waverley Housing Trust Ltd v. Roxburgh D.C.*, 1995 S.L.T. (Lands Tr.) 2.
[62] ss. 13 and 14.
[63] s. 1(1).
[64] s. 18.

(2) Treatment of Property Owned Jointly or In Common

12.33 In the normal instance, whilst joint owners are not relying on the existence of occupancy rights to remain in property, if they are deserted the 1981 Act is involved. If a joint owner wishes to realise his or her share of a property there is a process open called an action of division and sale. This can be insisted upon by any joint owner. It is important to remember that distinction between joint property and property in common.[65] Where a spouse brings an action for division and sale of the matrimonial home the court has a role in relation to the granting of such a request stemming from the 1981 Act. This will almost always be owned in common. The court may refuse to grant such a request or postpone granting a decree for such period as it considers reasonable in the circumstances or may grant a decree subject to such conditions as it may prescribe.[66]

In deciding on such applications the court must have regard to: all the circumstances of the case along with the conduct of the spouses in relation to each other and otherwise; the respective needs and financial resources of the spouses; the needs of any child of the family; and the extent to which the matrimonial home is used in connection with a trade, business or profession of either spouse and whether there has been an offer by the entitled spouse of suitable alternative accommodation.[67]

(3) Protection of the Non-Owner if there are Plans to Sell the Matrimonial Home

12.34 The non-owner must give their consent to such an action. This consent must be given in a prescribed form in writing before a notary public.[68] There is provision where such consent is not given for the owner to ask the court to dispense with the consent. It must be established either that consent is unreasonably withheld; consent is not possible by reason of physical or mental disability; or the other spouse cannot be found after reasonable steps have been taken to trace them.[69] The criteria for deciding on such a request are the same set of criteria indicated above for declaring and regulation of occupancy rights and for actions of division and sale.[70]

---

[65] See para. 1.09; but see para. 1.10 on "common property" which is often mistakenly referred to as being "joint property".
[66] s. 19.
[67] s. 3(3).
[68] s. 6(3)(a) and S.I. 1982 No. 971.
[69] s. 7.
[70] s. 3(3).

The question of the unreasonable withholding of consent and the dispensation of consent to a sale was dealt with in *Hall v. Hall*.[71] Both the sheriff and sheriff principal refused a motion for division and sale because the husband had failed to establish that it was "fair and reasonably necessary to disturb" his wife's occupation of the five-room bungalow which they had bought with a view to retirement. They quarrelled and led separate lives within the house but shared a common social life. It was up to the party who was seeking to disturb occupancy rights to show that it was fair and reasonably necessary to cause this disturbance. In *O'Neill v. O'Neill*[72] the sheriff was not, however, prepared to allow a wife to withhold her consent to the sale of a second home used by the husband in his job some 85 miles away from the original home. Here the wife had no intention of using the property but was using her right to withhold consent to the sale to obtain a better deal in the couple's divorce settlement.

The circumstances when a spouse can insist on an action of division 12.35 and sale of the matrimonial home and the interpretation of the relevant sections of the Matrimonial Homes (Family Protection) (Scotland) Act 1981 were discussed in *Berry v. Berry*.[73] The Berrys were seeking divorce from each other in separate cross-actions. They were joint owners of the matrimonial home. Mrs Berry wished to have the matrimonial home, which Mr Berry was occupying, sold. Mr Berry refused to agree to the sale of the house and Mrs Berry sought to obtain permission for an action of division and sale which was required from the court. Mr Berry's argument was that the question of the conduct of the spouses and their financial resources were the subject of great dispute and that it would be inappropriate to deal with the division and sale of such an important issue as the matrimonial home as a separate issue. The value of the matrimonial home might well be a very relevant factor in determining what capital payment might be made between the parties. Mrs Berry successfully argued that the whole purpose of the Matrimonial Homes Act was to provide protection of occupancy rights as opposed to decide on the ultimate division of the assets of the parties.

(4) THE NATURE OF "DEALINGS" WHICH REQUIRE CONSENT

The 1981 Act protects non-owners against proposed sales by re- 12.36 quiring various declarations by a seller concerning the existence of any other person who might have occupancy rights in the

---

[71] 1987 S.L.T. (Sh. Ct.) 15.
[72] 1987 S.L.T. (Sh. Ct.) 26.
[73] 1988 S.L.T. 630.

matrimonial home. There is no problem, of course, where there is a joint ownership since the joint owner would not only need to consent to the sale but also to sign the relevant legal documents before witnesses.

Questions have arisen, however, as to what stage must be reached before it can be said that there is a proposed sale ("dealing" is the phrase used in the 1981 Act) to which the non-owner or joint owner can consider giving consent. In *Dunsmore v. Dunsmore*[74] the husband and wife reached an impasse over the sale of the house. They agreed that the husband would buy the wife's half share but disagreed about the amount. The wife raised an action for division and sale and asked the court to dispense with the husband's consent to the proposed dealing. The court did not allow these difficulties to be overcome through dispensing with the consent of the husband to a proposed sale. There was no dealing here. That would require a third party to be involved. What was appropriate was an action of division and sale.

12.37   On a related theme, the Sheriff Principal for South Strathclyde was unwilling to regard a plan to put the matrimonial home on the market at between £80,000 and £100,000 as a proposed sale or dealing in *Fyfe v. Fyfe*.[75] The husband here was trying to get the court to dispense with the consent of the wife where he wished to sell the matrimonial home. He sought sanction of the court to what he termed a "proposed dealing". The sheriff principal did not agree. If a spouse was considering the question of granting or withholding consent they were entitled to notice of what price and conditions of sale were proposed. A broad figure was not something one could apply one's mind to. Until the terms of such a dealing or proposed sale were known it was not possible to see whether the non-entitled spouse was withholding her consent unreasonably. In *Berry v. Berry (No. 2)*[76] Lord Cowie in the Outer House rejected the suggestion by Mr Berry that he should be able to buy out his wife's half-share at half the market price to be fixed by a reporter. He also rejected the alternative suggestion that the old method of public roup (auction) be used. His view was that the modern approach, following *Campbells v. Murray*,[77] was to prefer sale by private treaty, *i.e.* offers over a certain price as is current in Scotland with the accepted written offer binding on the parties.

---

[74] 1986 S.L.T. (Sh. Ct.) 9.
[75] 1987 S.L.T. (Sh. Ct.) 38.
[76] 1989 S.L.T. 292.
[77] 1972 S.L.T. 249.

(5) EXCLUSION ORDERS AND THE SUSPENSION OF OCCUPANCY RIGHTS

In certain circumstances it is possible that a spouse or cohabitee 12.38 can, in effect, lose their occupancy rights by having them suspended. The courts, if they are suspending occupancy rights, are required under the 1981 Act to grant a court order prohibiting the other party from entering the matrimonial home without the express permission of the applicant. To make this exclusion effective the court must also grant two other related orders—unless the other spouse can show the court that it is unnecessary to do so. These involve the granting of an order for summary ejection of the other party from the matrimonial home and an order prohibiting the removal by the other party of any furniture from the matrimonial home. The court may add such terms and conditions as it chooses to such orders.[78]

In addition, the court may make an order prohibiting the other party from entering or remaining in the vicinity of the matrimonial home, adding such terms and conditions as it considers appropriate. There is also a discretion to give directions about the preservation of the other party's goods and effects remaining in the matrimonial home where an order has been granted for the summary ejection in the absence of the other party.[79]

Most of the legal controversy to date in this area centres around 12.39 the swift procedure introduced in section 4(6) of the 1981 Act which provides for interim suspension of occupancy rights. Provision is made for a very early hearing on the question of exclusion, usually within a week of starting court proceedings. In legal terms this is extremely swift since it is only a little longer than the time it takes to serve the legal documents on the other party. Any decision to grant an exclusion order at this time has the same effect as a full hearing after all the legal procedures of a normal ordinary civil action have been completed. The area of interim exclusion orders is the one most often dealt with in applications under the 1981 Act as these are usually part of an action for divorce. Since such orders as exclusion orders end on divorce, there is little incentive to obtain a final order prior to the dissolution of the relationship. The legal tests are the same in any event for interim and final orders.

---

[78] s. 4(4).
[79] s. 4(5).

(a) General Principles for Suspension of Occupancy Rights

12.40   (i) Exclusion cannot result from an order regulating occupancy rights.[80]

      (ii) The general test for exclusion orders is whether or not the order is necessary.[81]

      (iii) The court must not make an exclusion order if it appears that the making of the order would be unjustified or unreasonable.[82]

      (iv) There can be no interim order suspending occupancy rights until the other party has had the opportunity of being heard by or represented before the court.[83]

The courts have indicated what sorts of issues are relevant in deciding whether or not it is necessary for an individual to lose their occupancy rights and in what circumstances it would be unjustified or unreasonable to grant an exclusion order. The statute provides for two stages in the process of deciding about exclusion orders.

(i) Is the Exclusion Order Necessary?

12.41   The 1981 Act indicates that if the necessity test is satisfied the court must make an order (subject to the specific terms of section 4(3) on the question of whether such an order is unjustified or unreasonable):

> "[T]he court shall make an exclusion order if it appears to the court that the making of the order is necessary for the protection of the applicant or any child of the family from any conduct or threatened or reasonably apprehended conduct of the non-applicant spouse which is or would be injurious to the physical or mental health of the applicant or child."[84]

This formulation is more limited than the law in England and Wales which talks simply in terms of whether or not an exclusion order is justified or reasonable. It is rather closer to the law in the Irish Republic which provides for equivalent "barring orders" where the court considers the "safety and welfare of the applicant spouse or of any child" if the family so requires.[85] The Law Reform (Miscellaneous Provisions) (Scotland) Act 1985 made it clear that an exclusion order is available to an applicant whether or not the spouse is in occupation at the time of the application.[86]

---

[80] s. 3(5).
[81] s. 4(2) and *Bell v. Bell*, 1982 S.L.T. 224.
[82] s. 4(3).
[83] s. 4(6).
[84] s. 4(2).
[85] Family Law (Protection of Spouses and Children) Act 1981.
[86] s. 13(5).

There was some evidence that in the early days of the operation of 12.42
the 1981 Act some sheriffs were making decisions at the interim
stage on the basis of how *ex parte* interdicts were decided. They were
using the test of the "balance of convenience". This was explicitly
rejected in *Smith v. Smith*.[87] The reason for this was simply that the
provisions of section 4(6) require the test to be whether the interim
order is necessary rather than any question of balancing convenience. Essentially what some sheriffs' judgments indicated was that
they seemed to be balancing the competing needs of the applicant
and the other party rather than addressing the direct question of
whether there was a necessity for the granting of the order. This was
in practice a matter often more of the phraseology used by judges
than a mistaken test. The most recent comprehensive test was put
forward by Lord Dunpark in *McCafferty v. McCafferty*[88]:

(i) What is the nature and quality of the alleged conduct?
(ii) Is the court satisfied that the conduct is likely to be repeated
    if cohabitation continues?
(iii) Has the conduct been or, if repeated, would it be injurious to
    the physical or mental health of the applicant spouse or to
    any child of the family?
(iv) If so, is the order sought necessary for the future protection
    of the physical or mental health of the applicant or child?

Establishing the need for the protection of an exclusion order was a
practical problem which was also looked at in the *Bell* and *Smith*
cases. Whilst it might be reasonably simple to obtain evidence in an
ordinary action, the speed with which interim hearings reached
court meant that problems could arise in getting satisfactory
evidence to back up claims of harm or threats. The Court of
Session made it clear that they were unhappy about sheriffs simply
accepting the *ex parte* statements of the applicant as opposed to
their denial by the other party. Where possible, some external
evidence was to be provided—convictions; medical certificates; or
an independent report.

In addition, subsequently, affidavits have been approved as a 12.43
more reliable source than mere statements by the parties since, as
Lord Wheatley pointed out hearing the *Brown* appeal, they are
made under oath. They are now frequently used and accepted as
satisfactory evidence in applications at interim exclusion order
hearings.

---

[87] 1983 S.L.T. 275.
[88] 1986 S.L.T. 650.

(ii) Would the Making of the Order be Unjustified or Unreasonable?

12.44 In terms of the 1981 Act the court must also consider a second question in their deliberations about making an exclusion order.[89] However, there are no reported cases where this aspect of the test has been fully discussed. The Scottish Law Commission, in explaining its inclusion in the test for making an exclusion order, had in mind that "exclusion of a husband may have serious economic consequences for the whole family unit which would render an exclusion order a quite inappropriate remedy".[90]

In *Cowie v. Cowie*[91] Lord Grieve referred to "the peculiar exercise required by section 4(3)". In this particular case the matter which the husband had suggested should retain him in the house was his need to give mathematics tutorials from the home. Since this involved no specific apparatus it was no more than an inconvenience that he should be deprived of this possibility in the future. Beyond approving the sheriff's decision, the Inner House provided no clue to the enigma of section 4(3). Perhaps it might be thought appropriate for a patient who has a dialysis machine or something similar installed in the matrimonial home but whose behaviour warrants the protection of an exclusion order. In addition, where a house has been specially adapted for a disabled person it could be argued that it would be a better use of housing stock to keep the disabled person in that house and require the able-bodied but abused spouse to move out. It has been suggested that the test would be required where both parties were able to establish necessity.[92]

(b) Exclusion Orders and Cohabitees

12.45 Cohabitees' occupancy rights include the use of the exclusion order.[93] However, a problem has emerged which calls for attention. In *Clarke v. Hatten*[94] it was established that a cohabitee who was the tenant could not apply for an exclusion order where the other party did not seem to have his occupancy rights declared. The partner was not the tenant and assaulted the tenant causing her to have to leave the house. For married couples the ceremony of marriage brings occupancy rights into existence. Cohabitation has no clear equivalent starting point. For cohabitees, the court may, on the application

---

[89] s. 4(3).
[90] Scot. Law Com., No. 60, para. 4.7.
[91] Inner House, November 4, 1986.
[92] Scot. Law Com., *Family Law—Pre-Consolidation Reforms*, D.P. 85 (March 1990), at 6.34.
[93] s. 18.
[94] 1987 S.C.L.R. 521.

of the non-entitled partner, if it appears that the man and the woman are a cohabiting couple in that house, grant occupancy rights therein to the applicant. Until such an application a cohabitee has what could be called the "potential for a right". The tenant who seeks protection under the 1981 Act cannot, of their own volition, bring this section into force. The sheriff principal reviewed the question of whether an exclusion order could be properly granted if the non-tenant failed to make an application on his own behalf and decided that the pursuer might have a remedy in a common law action of ejection or interdict. The disadvantage with this is that this remedy would not carry with it a power of arrest.[95] The cohabitee therefore can be ejected and interdicted from returning but with no powers of arrest attached.

---

[95] s. 15.

INDEX

Security, rights in, *cont.*
statutory form, 10.01
symbols of, 10.01
Service occupancy
lease distinguished, 11.15
nature of, 11.15
Servitudes
creation of,
express grant, by, 8.43
express or implied reservation, by, 8.45
implied grant, by, 8.44
prescription, by, 8.46
definition, 8.40
enjoyment of, 8.57
essentials of, 8.41
extinction of,
acquiescence, by, 8.63
change of circumstances, by, 8.64
confusio, by, 8.61
express discharge or renunciation, by, 8.60
negative prescription, by, 8.62
statute, by, 8.65
light, air and prospect, for, 8.56
negative, 8.56
positive,
rural,
bleaching, 8.55
fuel, feal and divot, 8.50
passage, 8.54
pasturage, 8.51
pipelines, running, 8.55
quarrying, 8.55
sand and gravel, taking, 8.55
water, 8.52, 8.53
urban,
stillicide, 8.49
support, 8.48
public rights of way, and, 8.66
Roman law, derivation of law from, 8.40
transmission of, 8.58
Shetland
udal land, 5.14
Ships
British, transfer of ownership, 3.12
security over, 10.02
Shops
tenancy of, 9.78
Stillicide
right of, 8.49
Succession
heritable property, to, 2.07
moveable property, to, 2.07

Support
rights of, 7.03, 7.04
servitudes of, 8.48
withdrawal, right of action against, 7.04

Tenement, law of
common property, form of, 1.11, 1.15–1.21
division, no right to insist on, 1.13
floors and ceilings, division of, 1.20
gables, property in, 1.19
passages and stairs, property in, 1.21
roof, maintenance of, 1.16
solum area, ownership of, 1.17
walls, property in, 1.18
Timber
moveable property, as, 2.03
Trade marks
assignation, 4.18
common law, 4.17
register, 4.17
Treasure
Crown, ownership by, 1.05
Trespass
criminal proceedings, 7.18
emergency, during, 7.18
meaning, 7.17
right to prevent, 7.17, 7.18
Trustees
property, ownership of, 1.07

Udal land
tenure, 5.14

Water, rights in
Crown, of, 7.05
definite channel, not in, 7.10
lochs, 7.11
rivers and streams,
navigable, 7.07, 7.08
non-navigable, 7.09
primary and domestic purposes, taking water for, 7.09
riparian proprietors, 7.06
surface, 7.10
aquaehaustus, 8.52
aqueduct, 8.53
servitudes, 8.52, 8.53
Writ registration
details entered, 6.26
General Register of Sasines, 6.26
recording, 6.27
reform, need for, 6.28